With love to Joy, Helen, —

You are my shelter.

CONTENTS

Acknowledgments ix

Introduction: Rhetorical Vistas   1

   Chapter 1. Rhetoric's Development Crisis   23

   Chapter 2. The Public Subject of Feeling (with Exceptions)   44

   Chapter 3. Vultures and Kooks: The Rhetoric of Injury Claims   70

   Chapter 4. Lost Places and Memory Claims   99

   Chapter 5. The Good and the Bad:
               Gentrification and Equivalence Claims   129

   Chapter 6. Inquiry as Social Action   163

   Epilogue: Working in the *Epi-logos*   197

Notes   201
Works Cited   207
Index   229

Austinites protest development. Copyright Alan Pogue, 1990.

ACKNOWLEDGMENTS

Nobody writes alone, thank goodness. Over the years, many people have shared with me their insights, questions, comments, and encouragement. I especially want to thank Collin Brooke, Ralph Cintron, Sharon Crowley, Diane Davis, Sid Dobrin, Rosa Eberly, Cara Finnegan, Byron Hawk, Cheryl Glenn, Josh Gunn, Roxanne Mountford, John Murphy, Christa Olson, Kristan Poirot, Catherine Prendergast, Thomas Rickert, Trish Roberts-Miller, Geoff Sirc, Daniel Smith, Kathleen Stewart, Victor Vitanza, Jen Wingard, Xiaoye You, and the excellent faculty and graduate students at University of Illinois, University of Kansas, and University of Houston who responded to my 2009–10 colloquium talks. Debbie Hawhee deserves a special thank you for sharing such generous feedback, suggestions, and cheer. Jeff Rice not only read everything I sent his way, he also gave me daily encouragement. Thanks also to the audience members who listened to various incarnations of these chapters at the Rhetoric Society of America conference and the Conference on College Composition and Communication. Though I no longer share physical space with my former colleagues at The Pennsylvania State University, I am grateful to them for giving me a running start at this gig. And while I have since joined the program in Writing, Rhetoric, and Digital Media at the University of Kentucky, I want to thank the University of Missouri for allowing me a research leave in order to finish this book ahead of my son's arrival. Big thanks also to Joshua Shanholtzer for being such a friendly and helpful editor. My family has also been very supportive to me over the years, and I'm grateful for them.

Most of all, thank you to my teachers who taught me about rhetorics and publics: Victor, Hans, Katie, Lester, Rosa. And to Diane Davis, my kindest teacher of all, thank you for your warm friendship and for encouraging me past exceptionality.

Introduction

RHETORICAL VISTAS

> How one chooses to read one's self into the rhetorical act thus is of great consequence.
> —Edward Armstrong,
>   *A Ciceronian Sunburn*

If you meander through the University of Texas campus, you will eventually stumble upon the remnants of an old creek hiding among the concrete streets and massive buildings. The campus was built alongside Waller Creek, and it has long served as an urban oasis for nature-loving residents. Its water runs through beautiful limestone banks, which are surrounded by juniper and oak trees. In some places, large trees tower over the cool creek bed. It is easy to forget that you are actually standing in the middle of a busy downtown area and a campus swarming with thousands of students. One retired University of Texas English professor, Joseph Jones, wrote a lengthy book that meditated on Waller Creek's history and the life lessons that could be gleaned from its gentle beauty. Jones tells the story of the creek's beginnings and those early creek lovers who planted trees and cared for them. His poetic meditation reflects how deeply Waller Creek grows in the hearts of many Austinites.

Although the trees in Waller Creek once towered above buildings, many of the oldest trees were destroyed by a particularly harsh kind of development in 1969. Threats to Waller Creek began in the 1960s, when student numbers at the University of Texas rose dramatically. Construction likewise increased in order to keep pace with the growing population. Space was at a premium, yet the university leadership was undaunted in its grand plans for a large and first-rate campus. Board of regents chairman Frank Erwin was at the center of this vision, and it was under Erwin's watch that the university expanded into its current mammoth state. One of Erwin's most dramatic and controversial decisions was for a massive enlargement of the football stadium. The stadium sat next to Waller Creek, and its enlargement required the destruction of many old oak trees that towered over the creek. Erwin and the board of regents negotiated plans for the stadium in complete secrecy, without any input from students or citizens. When it was finally learned that the oak trees would be removed in order to make room for the expanded stadium, reaction from Austin's population was nothing short of outrage. Students proposed a plan to save the oak trees by building an arch in a corner of the stadium. The board of regents refused to consider their proposal, and Erwin called for construction and tree removal to begin immediately.

Early Monday morning, October 20, 1969, workers arrived at Waller Creek with bulldozers and chainsaws, ready to remove the trees in preparation for the new stadium. But they were met with crowds of protesters who were waving signs reading, "Don't Rape Mother Nature" and "Save Our Trees." Protesters physically blocked the workers from using any equipment, and no trees were removed that day. On Tuesday, workers and protesters again met in the creek. This time, workers managed to cut some branches and limbs from the trees, though the bulldozers were still physically blocked by protesters' bodies. By this time, Erwin was growing angry at the mini-revolt that seemed to be holding up progress on his stadium.

On Wednesday morning, Erwin himself marched down to the creek. He saw the protesters sitting in trees, and the workers afraid to do any work for fear of injuring the protesters. He demanded that construction crews remove the trees immediately. Scores of police vehicles arrived with a seventy-five-foot ladder that was clearly meant to remove protesters from trees. "Arrest all the people you have to," said Erwin. "Once the trees are down, they won't have anything to protest" (Jones 218). Police dragged away protesters, arresting twenty-seven for disorderly conduct. The trees were quickly cut down once the protesters were arrested. Thousands of angry students registered their unhappiness by dragging tree limbs to the university's Old Main administration building. They left the limbs and leaves all over the steps. As the protesters were being dragged away, one elderly man told police that they should "arrest the men responsible for vandalism in tearing down these

Protesters drag tree limbs to the steps of Old Main at the University of Texas. Copyright Dolph Briscoe Center for American History, the University of Texas at Austin, 1969–70.

trees" ("Police Nab" A1). A girl in the crowd told reporters, "I hope a tree falls on them. Not the police—the people responsible for this. I'd laugh. I'd really laugh" ("Police Nab" A1).

For months after the October saga, Austin residents painted Erwin almost as a murderer whose weapon of choice was a bloody axe. During an alumni dinner just two days after the protester arrests, Erwin was presented with the "Distinguished Axe Award." He was also regaled with a tongue-in-cheek poem written in his honor:

> I think that I shall never see
> Construction lovely as a tree.
> A tree whose hungry mouth is pressed
> Because the street must angle west.
> A tree that lifted its leafy arms to pray
> That Chairman Erwin would go away.
> A tree that did in Autumn wear
> A nest of students in her hair.
> Upon whose bosom axes are lain

> While pickets utter words profane.
> Poems are made by fools like me
> But only Frank can kill a tree.   (Jones 225)

More serious protests called for Erwin's dismissal, and the bumper sticker slogan "Axe Erwin" became quite popular. The protest was memorialized only a few months later in the *Cactus,* a student publication, with this headline: "The Issue Was Environment vs. Expansion." If you walk through Waller Creek today, it is hard not to conclude that expansion won the day.

This is an early scene of development discourse in Austin. Since then, Austin's growing urban development has become a major flashpoint for many residents. As geographer Joshua Long puts it, Austin "has long served as an ideological battleground between 'developers' and 'anti-growth' advocates" (*Weird City* 3). But development is not just an issue in Austin. It is an issue of growing concern across the United States. In fact, development has become such a familiar issue that it has even made its way into popular culture, including the television drama *The Wire*. One subplot of *The Wire* follows an elusive drug boss, Stringer Bell, who is responsible for some of Baltimore's worst drug and gang crime. As the detectives in the Major Crimes Unit collect mounting evidence against Bell, they uncover his investments in real estate that is part of Baltimore's push for inner-city renovation. In a scene where detectives Lester Freemon and Roland "Prez" Pryzbylewski first make this discovery, they give each other a dumfounded look. "From the looks of things, Stringer Bell's worse than a drug dealer," says Freemon. "Yeah," mutters Prez in agreement, "He's a developer." It is hard to tell whether this statement is meant as a joke or a real evaluation of the depths to which Bell is sinking. In *The Wire,* development plays like a drug, one that spreads misery across the city for the workers and residents displaced by new lofts and flipped neighborhoods.

It is no surprise that *The Wire*'s creator David Simon tackles issues of gentrification and development in his highly praised television series. Urban development is an unavoidable fact of life in most U.S. cities. But Simon also reveals another important detail about development in our cities: it's a hard thing to embrace. In *The Wire,* development chips away at people's lives in small ways. Dockworkers and unions watch their jobs dry up as a granary is turned into upscale lofts for the wealthy. In one episode, Nick Sobotka, a young stevedore, tours an open house for a place he can't afford. Nick tells the real estate agent that this used to be his aunt's house, a one-time affordable place in the working-class Locust Point neighborhood. The real estate agent informs him that the neighborhood has been reborn as Federal Hill, where houses go for close to a half-million dollars. People like Nick, those who once lived in Locust Point, are being displaced from a neighborhood they used to call home. Meanwhile, in later episodes, we follow the twists and turns of developers who grow rich from turning public housing into semiprivatized spaces. Even Stringer Bell gets played by the ruthless developers looking to flip Baltimore's urban spaces into upscale rents.

The changes happening in *The Wire*'s Baltimore mirror changes happening in the very spaces where we live, work, shop, and travel. Even if you have not watched a field of beloved trees bulldozed to make way for urban expansion nor had your neighborhood gentrify to unaffordable prices, you have still likely experienced development as it is currently unfolding in your own urban, suburban, or rural space. Unfortunately, as both fictionalized and very real examples of development suggest, the effects of contemporary development are not always positive. As a person who lives and works in these kinds of changing spaces, I am interested in how to intervene in the negative effects of development. Like many others, I find myself wondering how to promote a culture of sustainability and care for our everyday spaces. As a rhetorician, I also seek a better understanding of how discourse about development operates. How do people argue, debate, and deliberate about the spaces where we live, work, shop, and travel? I also want to understand why development continues to proliferate, even though its negative effects are familiar enough to serve as plot points in popular TV dramas.

In *Distant Publics*, I find an answer to these questions in the guise of one figure, whom I call the *exceptional public subject*. The exceptional subject is one who occupies a precarious position between publicness and a withdrawal from publicness. It is a subjectivity thoroughly grounded in *feeling*, which makes this rhetorical position so difficult to change. The exceptional subject can often seem apathetic, distant, uninterested, and even lazy. This subject is exasperating to those of us who wish to promote active participation in the public sphere. But unlike apathetic or lazy citizens, this subject position does not necessarily consider itself outside the realm of public life.[1]

Perhaps one of the most paradoxical features of the exceptional subject is that it is produced by the very discourse that rhetorical theorists take such pains to promote: deliberation, argument, counterdiscourse, or just plain exchange of talk. In *Distant Publics*, I suggest that perhaps the best answer to the exceptional subject is not *more* investment in the ongoing public scene of debate. Instead, if we want to encourage development talk that creates sustainable futures, then we will need to cultivate a different kind of public subjectivity altogether. We must create a new rhetorical vista from which we may stand and view ourselves in relation to the current landscape.

One of the primary arguments in this book contends that our current habits of public discourse and debate themselves are cultivating public subjects who are not oriented toward making sustainable interventions in rhetorical crises. Instead, exceptional subjects imagine themselves to be part of a wider public simply by feeling (whether the feeling is one of injury, nostalgia, ambivalence, or any other kind of feeling). The problem is not that public subjects feel. Rather, the problem is that feeling too often serves as the primary connective tissue to our public spaces. The fallout from such feelingful relationality is what this book is all about. In the chapters that follow, I frame citizen nonparticipation as an effect of certain rhetorical patterns within current public discourse rather than a symptom of disengagement or misinformation. In other words, our habits of public discourse can paradoxically contribute to the demise of healthy public discourse. Although public opposition to development is vocal and rhetorically engaged, the case studies presented in this book reveal that many common responses also cultivate an attitude of exception among some subjects who feel that they are unaffected by the scene of deliberation. Ironically, instead of democratic engagement, the common patterns of response to development can actually lead to some measure of disengagement.

Although *Distant Publics* discusses exceptional subjects in light of urban development, this exploration could have been accomplished through analysis of other public debates. I have chosen to focus on development, however, because this issue affects almost everyone. I must admit that I am not a disinterested researcher on the issue of development. I am an advocate. As I argue in chapter 1, too many years of careless development in urban landscapes have led to a crisis. Now is the time to rethink how we can respond to the changes happening in our everyday spaces. I want to change how ordinary citizens approach the topic of development. Of course, I can always get involved in my local community in various ways. But, as a teacher of rhetoric and writing, I also have another unique advantage. I can encourage students to be different kinds of subjects—not ones who disconnect from their local spaces, but ones who relate differently to the world around them.

My goal is not to call for a universal state of intervention. It is unrealistic to expect everyone to become an activist about development issues; nor is such a goal even desirable. Instead, I am more interested in questioning and changing the modes of production where public subjects are concerned. My goal is to find strategies for reorienting a publicness that is not based in feeling as a starting point. I hope to interrogate the techniques and technologies used to help people see themselves as beings-in-the-world. This interrogation is a rhetorician's way of intervening firsthand in the public crises around us.

By transforming how people think of themselves as public subjects, we can perhaps begin to encourage more people to see themselves as subjects who can and should intervene in the many different crises we currently face.

Rhetoric and Place

I am certainly not the first in rhetorical studies to sound an alarm about place and its problems. Rhetorical theorists are increasingly concerned with the many crises of place. Not only are there are a number of collections in composition studies devoted to rhetorics and place, but some scholars have turned their attention specifically to the intersection of rhetoric and development. In the past few years alone, we have seen growing interest in a new urbanist influence on community identity (St. Antoine), urban renewal and its influence on public life (Fleming, Makagon), the changing character of neighborhoods experiencing redevelopment (Simpson), and local debates over issues of zoning and land use (Olson and Goodnight). Every year, several panels on space and place appear in the major rhetorical studies conferences, including the Rhetoric Society of America biannual conference, the Conference on College Composition and Communication, and the National Communication Association's annual conference.

It makes sense that rhetoricians are interested in place and its crises. Issues of development, community planning, and gentrification are not only the concern of disciplines like urban planning or cultural geography. In his introduction to the collection *Landmark Essays on Rhetoric and the Environment,* Craig Waddell explains why a topic like the environment is relevant to a discipline like rhetoric. "Classical rhetoric was fundamentally concerned with public deliberation about matters of policy," writes Waddell. "Prominent today among those things about which we make decisions and into which we therefore inquire are matters of environmental policy" (xi). Likewise, Elenore Long argues that rhetoricians are called to serve as activists, insofar as they are primarily concerned with what they can do to improve the quality of public deliberations about our world under pressure (15). Many rhetorical scholars want to improve the quality of public deliberations about our local and global spaces that are increasingly under pressure from thoughtless, harmful, or simply excessive development.

However, I want to suggest an approach to place that differs slightly from popular approaches in rhetorical studies. My approach, which I call a "publics approach," understands publics and their discourse as the best site for making interventions into material spaces. In other words, rhetorical theory and rhetorical pedagogy can make a difference to the current development crisis not by interrogating "place" but by helping to shape different kinds of subjects who can undertake different kinds of work. In order to describe exactly what a publics approach entails, I will briefly contrast its methodology from several popular approaches to place in rhetorical studies. It may help to consider what kinds of questions these various approaches would pose. Different rhetorical approaches to place are not mutually exclusive or even conflicting, but they do pull the analyst's attention in multiple directions. While I believe that all of these approaches are important and correct, I simply want to suggest one additional path that may open up new possibilities for those of us who teach and work in the realm of rhetoric, writing, and communication. In order to begin sketching the kinds of questions posed by these rhetorical approaches to place, I will turn yet again to the trees.

Reading the Trees

Twenty years after Frank Erwin told police to arrest the protesters sitting in Waller Creek's oak trees, another oak was almost destroyed in Austin. This was Treaty Oak, a five-hundred-year-old live oak tree that was the only remaining tree in what was once a group of fourteen trees called the Council Oaks. Legend has it that Stephen F. Austin signed the first treaty with Native Americans under the oaks. Even though some historians now say this legend is a hoax, the huge tree has remained a dramatic and much loved part of Austin's history. Treaty Oak stands 50 feet tall, with a massive spread of 127 feet. It is no understatement to say that generations of families have played beneath the oak. In May 1989, city officials began to worry that the tree was suffering from oak wilt. Its branches and leaves looked sickly and lifeless. A test of the soil beneath the tree revealed something even more disturbing: the tree had been poisoned. More tests showed that someone had intentionally doused the tree's soil with huge amounts of Velpar, a highly toxic herbicide that is typically used by farmers to clear large swaths of land. After a criminal investigation, a mentally unstable man named Paul Cullen was arrested for the tree's poisoning. Cullen admitted that he poisoned Treaty Oak as part of an occult ritual meant to capture the tree's spirit so that he could win a woman's affection. Cullen fully intended to kill the tree by dumping enough poison to kill twenty-five large oaks (Harrigan).

Although Treaty Oak was poisoned by a mentally ill man, some people articulated its destruction alongside other tree removal cases due to development. Days following the poisoning's discovery, a leading story in the *Austin Chronicle* encouraged readers to resist seeing the event in isolation. "Groves of oak trees are presently being destroyed" to complete an access road for a new housing development, announced the story, and Austinites continue to see "ploughing [of] trees to make room for new roads and houses" (Forrest 11).

In a handwritten poem left at the base of Treaty Oak, one anonymous writer mourns the many deaths of trees caused by human development: "Hundreds of you / Fall everyday / The Lungs of the World / by our hands, taken down / Forgive us, Ancient One."[2] A local poet, Robin Cravey, tells a similar narrative in his poem "Treaty Oak," which laments, "The treaty signed within your shade could not / retard the progress of the axe and saw / Your grove-mates fell, your hills were paved and bared / but you we set aside in a little plot. And while the ancient forests daily fall / we cast proud words in bronze: This one we spared." Austin singer Bill Oliver also articulated this connection with his song "Hard Time for Oaks," written shortly after the Treaty Oak poisoning. Oliver sings, "In Austin, it's been a hard time for oaks / Hit by wilt, hit by the dozers / If it's disease, or if it's machine, the oaks around here / Will tell you the times have been mean."

In the months following the terrible incident, people left thousands of letters, cards, notes, pictures, and other personal mementos at the base of Treaty Oak. A small portion of these artifacts has been archived at the Austin History Center. When I asked to see the holdings, the archivist brought up hundreds of papers for me to inspect. "If you want to see more," she smiled, "just let me know. This is only a little bit of what we have downstairs." I browsed through children's drawings and letters that all seemed to be addressing an actual person. They were personal and intimate. Some even referenced inside memories between the writers and the tree. One card read, "Get well soon. You and Austin mean the world to me. T. G." Another note simply said, "Hang in there, kiddo." Children drew pictures of the tree and wrote words like "Get well soon" and "I love you" alongside their images. After arborists pruned limbs of the tree, the city began to sell relics carved from its wood. Residents bought pencils, furniture, bowls, vases, and small coins all made from the dead branches of their beloved oak.

Although no literal connection existed between the oak's poisoning and other instances of tree removal due to development, some public discourses articulated an implicit relationship between them. The common thread in Austin's many tree deaths seems to be the intentional harm caused by human greed or evilness. At least, this is one narrative that has circulated throughout the city's public sphere. "Austin's modern history of crimes against trees wends its way through the Treaty Oak arborcide of the late Eighties back to the mass murder of the late Sixties," writes *Austin Chronicle* contributor Louis Dubose, "when UT Regent Chair Frank Erwin routed a group of students out of a grove of oaks and cypresses he wanted bulldozed to make room for the expansion of Memorial Stadium."

These exchanges are a rich starting point for analysis, what Gerard

Hauser calls "vernacular rhetoric," or networks of nonofficial spaces in which discourse on public matters emerge (*Vernacular* 14). Consider what questions different approaches would encourage us to ask. For instance, one of the most common approaches to place in rhetoric and composition scholarship investigates how spaces are textualized (as well as how texts themselves are spatialized). This approach is rooted in an analogy between "composing" texts and "composing" spaces. Because spaces are constructed, or written, an intellectual bridge often connects the two inquiries. The collection *City Comp: Identities, Spaces, Practices* is an example of how this analogy is used in rhetoric and composition studies. The various essays emphasize how, in the words of editors Bruce McComiskey and Cynthia Ryan, "Urban spaces . . . are texts" (13). Or, as Richard Marback writes in his contribution to *City Comp,* "We can never walk into a cityscape that has not already been inscribed by others and that is not always already inscribed on us" ("Speaking of the City" 143). Urban spaces are thus regarded as primarily representational. This approach sees spaces and places as texts that signify a range of histories and debates. Just as a text is composed and rewritten, a city is also composed through the discourses and debates of its contemporary and historical residents.

The composing link does bridge together the work of cultural theorists like Michel de Certeau, Henri Lefebvre, and Roland Barthes, all of whom study signification and the realm of place and space. If places are "empires of signs," to use Barthes's phrase, then does this not make place a rhetorical matter? "To make a sign in place is to give signification," writes Sid Dobrin. "To signify is to assign meaning, to produce a place, to occupy that place. To occupy that place is to produce that place; to produce that place is to occupy it, to write it in the script of hegemony" ("Occupation" 27). Here Dobrin echoes the work of de Certeau, who has helped to make space and place viable subjects for writing studies. In *The Practice of Everyday Life,* de Certeau imagines standing high above the city from the World Trade Center, where he watches the pedestrians moving on the sidewalks below. These are the "practitioners" of the city, writes de Certeau; the ones who "follow the thicks and thins of an urban 'text' they write without being able to read it" (93). These walking bodies are in the process of writing culture through their trajectories, paths, habits, and avoidances. The stories composed through walking will become inscribed upon the city in any number of ways, constructing cultural maps and texts. Much like the city street scene, culture is comprised of manifold stories and shaping fragments. This is the textualizing of place, which is convenient for people who make a living by studying texts.[3]

If we examine the scene of Waller Creek and Treaty Oak as signifying compositions, or as textualized spaces, we might be led to ask how these places are assigned meanings, as well as what kinds of meanings those places help to create. How are their significations composed through public discourse? We cannot ignore the much larger social meanings that trees have had for millennia. By removing trees, Erwin was not simply getting rid of a beloved landmark. Trees have long been inscribed with meanings of life and vitality. Tree removal, by comparison, is weighted down with the heavy signification of death, murder, and decay. Public accounts of the incident framed Erwin as a kind of murderer ("only Frank can kill a tree"). Death was a recurring theme in many of the protests that happened before and after the trees' removal. An articulation was thus easily formed between development and death, thereby rhetorically placing antidevelopment protesters on the side of life.

Similarly, the fact that Treaty Oak was poisoned led to another articulation between development "poisoning" in Austin, beginning with the Waller Creek removal, and the workings of an insane man. In this way, familiar binaries between (good) nature and (bad) culture are reified. Development itself is posed as a direct challenge to the natural world and those who love it. The transhistorical character of local articulations between development and death are aided by the fact that trees have such significations. By comparison, this same articulation may have been more difficult if Erwin had removed a beloved statue, or if Paul Cullen had decided to toss paint onto a favorite community mural. Popular sentiment against ruthless development was aided by this articulation, which depends upon the circulation of prior significations concerning trees and life.

Another recent approach to place in rhetorical studies is the theory of textual-spatial ecologies. This approach is especially popular in composition studies, and it is partly born out of a frustration with the discipline's historical misunderstanding of writing's physical and spatial embodiment. On one hand, it might seem like space and place have been part of writing studies' agenda for a long time. As Nedra Reynolds points out in *Geographies of Writing*, we draw liberally on spatial metaphors in order to construct an image of ourselves (27–35). We are a "field" that is obsessed with its own "location" in the academy. We talk about "sites of struggle," "scenes of writing," and "working in the margins." Yet, such metaphors do not accurately reflect a disciplinary embrace of spatial thinking. Dobrin rightly points out that the discipline is much more devoted to temporal inquiry: composition's history, development, and its historical figures ("Occupation" 28). The focus on writing in place is often merely a backdrop to the larger obsession with composition's own temporal narrative.

As a corrective to the lack of investigation into spatial theory, some composition theorists have turned to a study of ecocomposition. According to Dobrin and Christian Weisser, two figures who helped to familiarize the concept of ecocomposition, this approach studies "written discourse and its relationships to the places in which it is situated and situates. Ecocomposition locates writing in place and environment; it looks toward the ecology of language" (*Ecocomposition* 10). As Dobrin and Weisser frame it, ecocomposition is about the relationships between discourse and all kinds of ecologies. Ecocomposition encourages us to examine "composition studies through an ecological lens to bring to the classroom, to scholarship, and to larger public audiences a critical position through which to engage the world" (1). Ecocomposition explores how composition itself is ecological, insofar as the act of writing is a relational act (12). In *Natural Discourse,* Dobrin and Weisser explain that an ecological focus in rhetoric and composition is not an attempt to encroach upon others' disciplinary turf. Rather, ecocompositionists want to "improve our understanding of the connections between these related disciplines, discourses, and epistemologies" (*Natural Discourse* 4). Discourse and environments are inseparable from each other. We always write from a place, and our writing itself creates spaces.

The notion of writing as ecological was perhaps best articulated in Marilyn Cooper's "The Ecology of Writing." Cooper fights the commonplace of a solitary author who works from a single idea that emerges from his or her own thoughts. Rather than this solitary version, Cooper proposes "an ecological model of writing, whose fundamental tenent is that writing is an activity through which a person is continually engaged with a variety of socially constituted systems" (367). According to Cooper, writing ecologies are thus akin to webs, where "anything that affects one strand of the web vibrates throughout the whole" (370). The solitary (genius) writer, whose thoughts emerge from his or her inner wellspring, simply does not exist. Instead, this writer works within an active exchange of texts, conversations, responses, and memories. Writing happens within this ecology of language.

Scholars practicing ecocomposition tend to examine a number of questions, but one common theme is the relationships between places and writers. Ecocompositionists do not necessarily spend all their time talking about nature, since environments and ecologies are complex systems that appear everywhere. For example, Julie Drew describes how her ecocomposition classroom focuses primarily on the "politics of place," and the "ways in which place plays a role in producing texts, and how such relationships affect the discursive work that writers attempt from within the university" (57). For Drew, there is important work to be done by critically examining the classroom space itself as a productive force. The classroom space that students enter and exit as travelers shapes the kinds of writing that is produced or withheld. Ecocomposition has the advantage of seeing all ecologies as fair game for analysis. And insofar as everything has a relational quality that places it into larger networks of relations, ecocomposition is as likely to analyze the ecology of a student project as it is a controversial river dam. Thanks to studies in ecocomposition, writing teachers have no excuse for treating texts as solitary pages that have no relation to place, history, time, or social context.[4]

An ecocomposition approach to the Waller Creek and Treaty Oak examples may encourage us to examine how the networks of discourse and environment made possible certain rhetorical gestures, including the outpouring of personal letters, cards, and homemade signs. Although there is no physical link between Erwin's removal of the Waller Creek trees and the Treaty Oak poisoning, their comparisons in public texts (newspaper letters and editorials) helped to make a strong argument against the negative effects of careless development. Unlike Waller Creek, Treaty Oak is located in the middle of a neighborhood rather than in a secluded creek area, which may also help to explain why the form of public expression took such a personal turn. Treaty Oak was not removed from everyday life, as the Waller Creek trees were. Families walked by the tree each day on their way to school and work. The fact that it had a name also helped to personalize the massive Treaty Oak in ways that other natural sources are not. Not surprisingly, letters, cards, and poems were directly addressed to the tree, often in the form of laments and memorializations. The personalization thus helped to frame the rhetorical situation as a somewhat nonpolitical moment, even though activist sentiment emerged from the poisoning. It may have been impossible to engage schoolchildren in letter-writing campaigns regarding the Waller Creek incident. The Erwin tree fiasco was clearly marked as a political moment, no doubt aided by the fact that the trees sat on a campus that was increasingly radicalized by politically conscious college students. Another mode of writing was made possible by this different ecology.

Taking a Publics Approach to Place

The questions raised through these analyses are important to ask, since they serve as starting points for reading various rhetorical relationships of places and public discourse. But there is another possible starting point. Beyond an examination of the relationships between discourse and place, we can also look at the way the discourse helps to create particular kinds of *public subjectivities*. How is the discourse underwritten by specific subject positions, and how does that discourse simultaneously help to cultivate and sustain those subject positions? This is what I call a publics approach to place, which reads discourses of place both as symptoms and as catalysts of public subjectivities. Such an approach investigates the discourse itself in order to understand how people imagine themselves in relation to the publics that populate, change, and undergo this physical space.

This focus on publics is where I begin my own method for rethinking rhetorical interventions into place. Rather than seeing place merely as a composition (which, of course, it is), and rather than seeing place in terms of its ecological character (which, of course, it has), I prefer to examine the habits and practices of the publics who can and do affect that location. This is precisely why I call my gesture a *publics approach to place*. Instead of investigating place itself, either in its material forms or as a space of embodied composition, I prefer to examine how people imagine themselves in relation to (and as part of) those publics that populate, change, and undergo the effects of material places. It is in publics, not places, that rhetoricians can make the strongest intervention into imperiled places.

If our current challenge is the crisis of (over)development and the threat to sustainable living, and if one answer is to encourage healthier public discourse, then rhetorical activists must consider how to intervene in the causes of unhealthy and unsustainable public discourse. In short, this intervention goes beyond questioning how spaces and places are composed through discourse (although they certainly are), or how material spaces affect publics (although they certainly do). The difference between a publics approach and other common approaches to place in rhetorical studies has to do with the critical goals in each case. My goal in this book is to imagine how we can improve discourse in order to repair damaged places and promote long-term, sustainable futures. More specifically, I examine how public discourse cultivates subjectivities that tend to encourage or discourage intervention in the crises of place.

In the cases of Waller Creek and Treaty Oak, a publics approach might begin by asking how the discourses of personalization with trees helped people to imagine themselves in a collective affinity with the trees. We might ask how the discourse encouraged participants to position themselves as personal allies of the trees, even to the point (to borrow a term from Kenneth Burke) of identifying their ways with the trees' ways. When the trees were "attacked" by Erwin and Cullen, many people felt themselves to have been symbolically attacked as well. Consequently, an agent of destruction was also imagined through this public discourse. In the Waller Creek incident, that agent is located in the guise of developers. A publics approach would then consider the implications of this discourse in terms of how people read themselves into the public scene. We would keep in mind how public discourse allows us to see ourselves within a public scene of crisis. Or, as E. Armstrong writes, we would keep in mind that "how one chooses to read one's self into the rhetorical act thus is of great consequence" (66). A publics approach looks to common patterns of everyday talk in order to uncover the ways people read themselves into these rhetorical acts.

The way that Austin residents read themselves into the two crises was indeed of great consequence, especially from the viewpoint of sustainability. On the one hand, some participants read themselves out of a more complex scene of agency. Destruction of trees was posed as acts of (domestic) violence, rather than as a structural problem caused by a variety of sources, including everyday acts of movement and living. By discursively framing tree removal as a murder scene, therefore, participants position themselves outside of an agentive position. They become victims, much like the trees are victims, rather than responsible agents who participate in development. Linking Erwin and Cullen helps to calcify this narrative, making developers a manifestation of "bad" and development opponents a manifestation of "good."

On the other hand, other participants used the occasion of Treaty Oak's poisoning to make larger connections with ordinary activities that damage our natural spaces. We all travel on roads and live in spaces that were once populated by trees. While we do not purposefully dump gallons of poison into those spaces, we do own some degree of responsibility for the trees' destruction. The letters, poems, and songs written about Treaty Oak relay this responsibility in a number of ways. This type of discourse writes rhetors into an agentive position where development and destruction are concerned.

Participants in these rhetorical scenes used public discourse to orient themselves to the scene of public crisis. That is, they inhabited a certain kind of public subjectivity. A critical reflection suggests that some participants imagined themselves in a role that encouraged sustainable thinking, while others may not have. In fact, by somewhat removing themselves from a scene of agency, many participants obscured the ways their own lives contributed to the negative impacts of urban development. As this brief analysis shows, a publics approach does not challenge other forms of rhetorical analysis where place is concerned. Instead, it simply interrogates place-based exchanges for the kinds of public subjectivities that are being cultivated and drawn upon. Although a publics approach is certainly not the only means of reading rhetorics of place, interrogating the underlying discourses of public subjectivities is the best way rhetoricians can intervene in actual crises. Getting people to see the relationship between discourse and place/ecology will do little good if the same troubled public subjectivity remains intact. As environmental educator David Orr remarks, the crises of place cannot be solved by the same educational practices that created those problems (83). To Orr's sentiments, I add that the crises of place cannot be solved by the same subjectivities that allow those problems to continue.

Talking Place

By separating out place and discourse, I also hope to re-emphasize that our strength as rhetorical theorists and activists is primarily in discourse. This recognition may seem like a step away from the interdisciplinarity that has become a virtue among rhetoricians. Scholars of place have enriched their own analyses by turning to urban theorists and geographers as a way to expand composition studies into more material realms. Although there is much to be learned from engaging the questions and theories of other disciplines, it is important to remember that we are not geographers, urban planners, environmental scientists, or designers by discipline. We are rhetoricians. I say this not in order to police disciplinary borders, but rather because I want to celebrate our strength as critics of public discourse. A publics approach intervenes in crisis in an appropriate way for a rhetorician: at the level of public talk. As I will argue throughout this book, it is public talk that most needs our critical intervention.

For example, one of the hindrances toward sustainability in local communities is that vernacular publics often feel they do not have a strong say in development decisions. Ideally, write Tarla Rai Peterson and C. C. Horton, discourse about place-based policies "should throb with the sometimes contentious sounds of public debate" (140). However, Peterson and Horton continue, discourse about environmental policies, such as land preservation, sometimes systematically ignores community voices. Peterson and Horton report their study of controversies between local property owners and preservationists who wish to place restrictions on private land in order to protect endangered species. Although the issue was certainly important to local ranchers, Peterson and Horton find that many ranchers did not actively speak out in public about the controversy. When asked why they did not engage in public deliberations about this local controversy, ranchers commonly expressed a belief that "the broader culture no longer accommodates their interests" (167). Peterson and Horton see this silence as part of a larger perception among U.S. citizens that "the public sphere is, at best, irrelevant to their lives" (167).

This same problem is also reflected in other sites of development. Even though development issues do raise noisy and contentious debates, a number of voices are conspicuously absent from public deliberations. One obvious reason may be the institutional opacity, or the fact that decisions are often made in processes that are far removed from the public sphere. But another reason is buried in the rhetorical habits of public discourse itself. That is, our most common public discourse habits actually contribute to a troubled sense of public subjectivity, rather than the other way around. Even where development discourse seems to be throbbing with the sounds of public debate, these exchanges are not as rhetorically powerful as they should be. If we genuinely wish to encourage sustainable thinking and intervention into place crisis, therefore, we must make public discourse as productive as possible. My goal in *Distant Publics* is to call attention to how discourse patterns help to cultivate both productive and unproductive public subjects.

My method draws upon Robert Asen's discourse theory of citizenship, which imagines that everyday talk is precisely where real activist work can be accomplished. Asen writes, "In both scholarly and popular assessments discourse is too often regarded as prefatory to genuine action. According to this view, talk is . . . a bargain only insofar as it leads to activities such as voting and volunteering. Citizenship should not be reserved for special occasions, however. Discourse practices present potentially accessible and powerful everyday enactments of citizenship" (207). Asen's discourse theory of citizenship suggests that ordinary exchanges of talk are an important mode of citizenship's enactment. The above examples of Waller Creek and Treaty Oak take ordinary exchanges of talk as the stuff from which publics are made. It was in the acts of protest slogans, comments to reporters, poetry, letters, and the like that citizenship was enacted and embodied. The less sunny flip side of Asen's discourse theory is that everyday talk is also where poor citizenship habits are cultivated. Either way, discourse is where rhetorical theory can actively intervene into the crisis of place.

Furthermore, a focus on public talk is where rhetoricians can make the most difference to those disciplines that can, in turn, make more material interventions in place. In fact, urban studies specialists are becoming quite vocal about the need for discourse analysis and rhetorical critique in urban studies. Robert Beauregard's 1993 study, *Voices of Decline: The Postwar Fate of U.S. Cities,* was one of the first works in urban planning to examine how public discourse affects urban space. Since the publication of *Voices of Decline,* questions about how to analyze discourse (and what to make of the analyses) are still being debated in fields like urban planning and cultural geography. In 1999, *Urban Studies* devoted a special issue to the topic of "Discourse and Urban Change." Geographer Loretta Lees likewise considers the importance of discourse analysis and urban research in a 2004 article, where she admits that the field has a profound misunderstanding of how discourse should be read and interpreted within urban studies. One problem, Lees writes, is that the urban theorist is a "novice" where discourse is concerned (101). Unfortunately, while rhetoricians can and should address this area with expertise, Lees and her fellow geographers do not turn to our field for any insight.

How specifically does a focus on public discourse lead to an intervention into the crisis of place? How can it help to cultivate a public subject that is sustainability-minded? A focus on discourses about place can prompt us to rethink public subjectivity, or the way people are encouraged (through exchanges of everyday talk) to imagine themselves in the public sphere. By examining the discursive makeup of public subjectivity, we can see how people are encouraged to read themselves into the rhetorical act, to borrow Armstrong's words. How do people "read themselves" in relation to publics that change, undergo, and populate material realms? More specifically, how do people imagine themselves as actors (or not) through common patterns of public talk?

Publics, Empirical and Otherwise

In order to transform our physical spaces, we need to start by transforming our publics. My use of the term "publics" is the result of a long line of rhetorical scholarship on the public sphere, much of which is usually traced back to Jürgen Habermas and his critics. It is probably an understatement to say that Habermas's model of debate in the public sphere is still one of the most compelling and provocative models of deliberation. In his own terms, the public sphere comprises private individuals engaging in a public discussion: "Citizens behave as a public body when they confer in an unrestricted fashion . . . about matters of a general interest" ("The Public Sphere" 49). Of course, critiques of Habermas are many. Nancy Fraser adroitly points out the problem with Habermas's notion of universal accessibility and the suspension of status necessary to enter the public sphere. She emphasizes the impossibility of ever suspending one's materiality in order to become part of the bourgeois public sphere. As Fraser sees it, the problem with a single, unified public sphere is in the silencing effects on groups without "participatory parity." Fraser ends up proposing a model of subaltern counterpublics, or "parallel discursive arenas where members of subordinated social groups invent and circulate counterdiscourses to formulate oppositional interpretation of their identities, interests, and needs" (123). If there were only a single sphere, as Habermas imagines, these groups would be "less able than otherwise to articulate and defend their interests in the comprehensive public sphere" (123). Subaltern counterpublics allow subordinated groups to articulate their own needs within a framework that unbrackets their particular historical and material situation.

While I am interested in the question of how publics engage in the various spheres that comprise our social scenes, I tend to think about publics in a slightly different way. Rather than thinking of publics (or counterpublics) as bodies that join together in deliberation in a discursive arena, I prefer to think about publics as active manifestations of talk. Gerard Hauser aptly describes publics as "emergences manifested through their vernacular rhetoric" (*Vernacular* 14). Vernacular discourse, or what Asen simply calls "talk," is more than a medium for previously existing publics. Talk is the very substance through which publics come to be formed. Hauser further defines vernacular rhetoric as a "network of associations from which and in which a communally sustained consciousness of common meanings are developed and enriched" (34). He insists that a rhetorical public sphere is based in polyphonous discourse, and its conversations might not be contemporary. Publics materialize as clusters of conversations happening at various times, across different places. This is what Hauser calls "vernacular voices," or the networks of nonofficial spaces from which discourse on public matters emerges.[5]

In the case of Waller Creek and Treaty Oak, public talk emerged in a number of nonofficial spaces. People wrote letters to both popular and underground newspapers, created cards and letters for the ailing Treaty Oak, debated the cases in bars and classrooms, and so forth. Others drew pictures and wrote songs or poems to memorialize the trees. Many people connected the two events together in their ordinary conversations. The "publics" of Austin's trees are not locatable in any fixed sphere or subaltern counterpublics. Rather, they emerge across ordinary instances of talk that coalesce through texts.

When I use the term "publics," therefore, I am referencing the active exchanges of discourse that are happening in ordinary spaces of encounter. Listening to publics demands that we pay attention to the nonofficial spaces where such communally sustained consciousness is developed: letters to newspapers, blogs, informal conversations that happen in public spaces, talk radio calls, online message boards, bumper stickers, flyers, community newsletters, rallies, and neighborhood meetings. These are not simply spaces in which publics meet together, but the discursive exchanges that happen here are actually (re)creating publics with every moment. As Michael Warner explains, a public is "an ongoing space of encounter for discourse. It is not texts themselves that create publics, but the concatenation of texts through time" ("Publics" 62). A publics approach takes seriously what Cicero calls the purview of a rhetorician: "the language of everyday life, and the usage approved by the sense of the community" (*De Oratore* 1.3.12). Publics are not reducible to individual speakers or writers; the exchange of talk cultivates communal meanings and public subjectivities.

When I look at examples of public talk surrounding development issues, I ask what role these discursive patterns of talk help to produce. But how can I be so sure of a causal relationship between public discourse and subjectivities (or the public roles that we imagine for ourselves)? It is certainly true that in order to see this causal relationship, you must be willing to accept that subjectivities are created through prior and ongoing talk. You also must be willing to accept that vernacular public discourse is generative. It goes without saying that some of what I am about to argue is speculative. I am making an argument about something we can't see: subjectivities. And I am also making causal claims: that certain talk cultivates subjectivities, and these subjectivities can sometimes lead toward ineffective ways of acting in the world. Readers who seek quantitative evidence of my claims about public subjectivities and unsustainable discourse may be disappointed. I have no positivist evidence to prove once and for all that this kind of talk leads to a certain kind of public subject. However, I do my best to slowly read empirical publics and their discourse. I follow Rosa Eberly's empirical method of "reasoning based on records [and] also on the judgment of the teller: empirical as opposed to positivist and as opposed to theoretical" (*Citizen* 33). By following the patterns of actual public talk, I develop my argument through reason based on the records and the tellers themselves.

In this book I have limited my reading of empirical publics in order to focus on three common patterns emerging around conversations about urban development. These three patterns can also be described as commonplaces, or topoi, since they serve an inventional role in public discourse. That is, these commonplaces generate arguments by focusing the range of references and claims. Eberly defines topoi as "bioregions of discourse" that "disclose argument from the common ground up" (*Citizen* 6). My own understanding of topoi or commonplaces includes the sense that commonplaces generate and delimit the range of discourse. In the case of urban development controversies, much of the public talk is generated around three commonplaces that I call *injury claims, memory claims,* and *equivalence claims*. Injury claims, which I discuss in chapter 3, help rhetors to frame themselves as victims when interlocutors challenge their position. Memory claims, which I examine in chapter 4, allow rhetors to anchor themselves in a different deliberative scene than the one taking place in new spaces. And in chapter 5 I discuss equivalence claims, which help to create exceptional public subjects by substituting undecidability for rhetorical judgment (*krisis*). In the following chapters I will be closely reading these commonplaces and the kinds of subjectivities they help to cultivate.

I focus on injury claims, memory claims, and equivalence claims because they are common in vernacular discourse surrounding development. Where issues of development emerge (whether in the case of a new downtown high-rise or the removal of old growth trees for stadium expansion), these three patterns of response are some of the most common. Of course, they are not universal in their deployment. All three kinds of claims emerge in a number of ways in actual everyday contexts. I can only examine a handful of instances, which may not adequately reflect the different ways these claims get made and restated. However, I will pay close attention to them as general patterns without losing sight of their case-by-case particularity. After examining the general patterns of these claims (as illustrated by certain cases and contexts), I will then consider how these claims generate a particular role or public subjectivity. If public talk is the soil, then public subjects are the fruit that grows from it.

Unfolding the Sites

Two specific rhetorical vistas are visible throughout *Distant Publics*; the first is disciplinary in nature. Although I frequently use the term "rhetorical studies" in this book, my disciplinary home has traditionally been in English departments and rhetoric-composition. I draw equally from scholarship in both communication studies and rhetoric-composition, however, and I make little distinction between the two (sub)fields of a much larger discipline called rhetorical studies. The fact that we share a single vibrant organization like the Rhetoric Society of America, as well as several journals featuring rhetoricians from both (sub)fields, means that we can move past the differences that exist within our individual disciplinary homes. Moreover, our pedagogical goals have more in common than we might think. Although my courses often focus on writing and textual matters, my larger aim is to teach students how to become rhetorically engaged within civic and public spaces. My colleagues who teach public speaking courses often tell me that they have the same goal. To use a phrase by network theorist David Weinberger, our disciplinary homes are small pieces, loosely joined.

Another rhetorical vista that can be seen within these chapters is a more fixed space. Although I draw upon examples of development rhetoric from across the country, many of the case studies I examine in *Distant Publics* draw from events in Austin, Texas. My decision to draw from Austin is partly due to my own experience with the city. I lived in Austin for over a decade, walked its streets every day, and even generated the beginning of this project while in Austin. My inclusion of the cityscape is more than nostalgia, however. Austin is also a perfect example of urban development and place-change. When I first moved to Austin in 1993, it was a far cry from the city it is today. Since the mid-1990s, Austin has experienced a remarkable explosion of capital investment, new development, and increased population. Austin repeatedly tops the charts of cool cities. So cool is Austin, in fact, that it has been cited as a model for other cities that are experiencing economic and developmental slumps. Richard Florida repeatedly cites Austin as a successful example of the "creative class" at work. Florida's books are filled with praise for Austin's creativity index, a measure that is meant to teach other cities how to be more creative (and, in Florida's logic, more economically successful). Almost no space in Austin has been untouched by the development happening in record time. It is a city in the midst of change.

Furthermore, Austin serves as a good site for case studies because few cities have simultaneously celebrated and despised development as passionately as Austin. It is a city that people love, and a city that seems to love its people in return. Unlike other cities that generate such widespread feelings of affection, however, Austin has been relatively small for most of its life. Its population has historically paled in comparison to New York, San Francisco, Chicago, and other cities with devoted fans. This has made issues of development even more significant to Austinites: should the city expand into something bigger, or should its character be preserved by fighting development? So dramatic is this question in Austin that other scholars have begun to study the city's development rhetoric in some detail. As I was finishing *Distant Publics*, geographer Joshua Long published *Weird City: Sense of Place and Creative Resistance in Austin, Texas*. Long's book documents the "Keep Austin Weird" movement that actively resists overdevelopment and homogenization in the city. The publication of *Weird City* suggests to me that something is indeed in the air where Austin's development is concerned. Its unique character has helped to produce many memorable instances of discourse rhetoric. Long and I both seem to believe that there is value in studying Austin's rhetoric (both its development aspirations and its "creative resistance") as an individual case study and an example of much larger patterns happening in the United States. While your town may not be experiencing the dramatic changes seen in Austin, the conversations are likely to be familiar.

Rhetoric's Development Crisis

> Sprawl. Overdevelopment. Conurbation (Mumford's term). Megapolis. . . . To me, it is a landscape of scary places, the geography of nowhere, that has simply ceased to be a credible human habitat.
> —James Howard Kunstler, *The Geography of Nowhere*

It's ten o'clock in the morning and the humidity is already making it feel like a summer afternoon. I reluctantly pull into the strip mall that I have driven by almost every day for three years. The huge parking lot is always empty, maybe because half the storefronts are empty and abandoned. One big box electronics store anchors the mall, and only a few smaller chain stores dot the row on either side. A real estate sign advertising space for lease seems to be permanently affixed to the building. I park my car in front of the electronics store as I silently pray to quickly find the special battery I need so that I can make a fast escape. The size of the massive parking lot suggests that great hopes once existed for this strip mall. Maybe it had seen better days, or maybe those great hopes just never panned out. Whatever the story once had been, right now this place is little more than an ocean of concrete along the town's main road. It seems to be a living lesson in development gone wrong.

Less than a mile away from this half-abandoned strip mall are two other abandoned buildings that had once been someone's idea of positive development. Overgrown weeds and a large For Sale sign loom in front of a vacant

Ethan Allan store that sits prominently along our largest shopping artery. Only a little further down the road is an abandoned Circuit City, which closed in the wake of the company's financial collapse. These two failed businesses abandoned their buildings across the country, and I cannot help but imagine that other Circuit City empty shells —567 hulking properties in all —look eerily similar to ours. While many strip malls in my town are slowly decaying from years of neglect and abandonment, new mall developments spring up in the very same neighborhoods. Properties are rarely rehabilitated; they are deserted. Several Web sites are devoted to documenting the country's numerous sprawling indoor malls that now sit with ultra-low vacancy rates.[1] Social networking and image-based sites like Flickr even feature online groups dedicated to visually tracking and photographing vacant retail spaces. Development in many cities and suburbs has gradually morphed into a problem of overdevelopment. For economically booming cities, the development is sustained by a steady flow of traffic and parking lots full of eager shoppers. Other cities have not fared so well. Strip malls sit half-empty and large storefronts slowly decay without much hope of revitalization.

This scene is hardly unique to my midsize town. In 2001, the Department of Agriculture published the National Resources Inventory, which found that between 1982 and 2001, around thirty-four million acres were converted to developed uses for office parks, malls, apartments, subdivisions, and the like. While much of this developed area was formerly cropland, a significant amount of developed land was originally forest and rangeland. It is not too difficult to see how this land is being developed. Shopping areas alone have soared in number. Consider the largest retail chains in the country. Their numbers offer a window onto recent development trends. Currently there are 4,100 Walmart facilities in the United States, and 3,100 in other countries. Target stores lag behind Walmart, though there are nearly 1,700 Targets across the country. As of January 2008, Starbucks boasted over 11,000 stores in fifty states. In my current city of less than 100,000 people, there are five Starbucks stores and three Walmart locations. And these are just three major retailers. There are many more major retail chains that populate most towns: Best Buy, Toys"R"Us, Home Depot, Barnes & Noble, Costco, and so forth. Then there are the chain restaurants that usually appear close to these retail stores: Applebee's, Starbucks, Chili's, Olive Garden, T.G.I. Friday's, Macaroni Grill, Cracker Barrel. If we started to account for every new subdivision, apartment complex, loft development, or office park, the list would grow even longer.

Of course, the story of urban development is not a perfect tale of corporate success. The overconstruction of the past few decades, combined with a major recession, has resulted in some extremely high commercial vacancy rates in major cities. In 2010, office vacancy rates across the country were at their highest in almost sixteen years ("Office Vacancy Rate Hits 16-year High"). Between 20 and 25 percent of downtown office buildings in Louisville, Detroit, and Austin are sitting empty ("Office Vacancy Rates Vary Widely"). An independent study of vacant commercial space in one large city found that "big box" retail stores (25,000 square feet or more) accounted for almost 57 percent of vacant commercial space (R. H. Johnson Company). If the statistics don't tell a complete story, however, you would only need to drive around your hometown to find evidence of vacant buildings, decaying strip malls, and brand-new commercial developments that seem to be lacking potential tenants. Not only are commercial developments experiencing a glut of empty space, but neighborhoods are also marked by a record number of empty houses and apartments. In 2009, one study showed that at least one in nine housing units was vacant across the country ("No One Home"). And sprawl, which geographer Dolores Hayden defines as "unregulated growth" marked by "careless new use of land and other resources as well as abandonment of older built areas" (*A Field Guide* 7), is a problem in almost every metropolitan area.

Development is a nearly ubiquitous condition. It is something most of us share. There are many ways to define development, but I define it in terms of the built environments that increasingly take up space in our cities, suburbs, and rural areas. The built environment includes shopping complexes, apartments, new neighborhood developments, parking structures, civic buildings, and corporate office parks. Built environments are constructed by humans, and they are often structured to accommodate commercial and social activity.[2] Urban development is nothing new, of course. Greek and Roman cityscapes were also carefully planned along an urban development trajectory (see Fleming, "The Space of Argumentation"). Yet geographers and urban theorists have pointed out the different characteristics of modern development. Our current practices of development are rooted in standardization and efficiency. Not surprisingly, some have called development a by-product of modernity (Arefi 185). Modern development is designed to maximize efficiency. Contemporary designs have all but eradicated the chaos and randomness that characterized nineteenth-century street life.

While big box stores and wide highways running throughout cities make for greater convenience, both urban theorists and ordinary citizens often express concern about the social deadness of such development trends (see Berman; Jacobs). As Joshua Long writes, "To many citizens, the term 'growth' no longer carries positive connotations. Instead, *growth* is a word increasingly associated with the negative images of sprawl, traffic congestion, big box store dominance, and homogenizing development" (*Weird* 9). The sometimes oppressive and depressive character of unchecked development has become a common trope in popular culture. Consider classic songs like Joni Mitchell's "Big Yellow Taxi" or The Pretenders' "Ohio," which lament suburban parking lot cultures and missing downtown areas that have given way to shopping malls. The band Modest Mouse revisits this theme in its song "Novocain Stain," layered with depressing images of impersonal developments that have destroyed a natural landscape, and the observation that "more housing developments go up / named after the things they replace."

My own memory of a similar revelation came when I was in junior high. My parents had moved into a new subdivision called Lexington Woods. The street names were bucolic and lush sounding: Oak Hollow, Meadow Glen, River Bend. But any remaining oaks, meadows, or river bends were nowhere to be found in our neighborhood. What must have once been forest and green space had given way to brand-new tract homes and the strip malls that had sprung up for our convenience. I attended Twin Creeks Junior High, but I never remember seeing any creeks along the route to school. Instead, we were surrounded by a four-lane major road and a slew of new homes in yet another subdivision. Even in my current neighborhood, whenever I see undeveloped green space, it usually has a sign announcing its acreage and development possibilities.

A generation after Jane Jacobs introduced many of these problems in her classic work, *The Death and Life of Great American Cities,* best-selling books like James Howard Kunstler's *The Geography of Nowhere* and Andres Duany, Elizabeth Plater-Zyberk, and Jeff Speck's *Suburban Nation* help to articulate the troubled condition of development for a wider audience. Subtle critiques of the "McDonaldization" of American spaces are not confined to esoteric cultural theory. Most people are at least familiar with arguments for and against urban development, even if they have no deeper knowledge of how decisions about development actually take place. Even though some reviews of *Geography of Nowhere* were critical of Kunstler's reductive arguments about modern architecture and the effects of automobile culture, many popular reviews saw the book as an approachable explanation for why our current environments look and act the way they do.[3] Reader comments on Amazon.com frequently call *Geography of Nowhere* "life-changing" and "eye opening." Similarly, the *Believer* magazine remarks, "Kunstler created a vocabulary for suburban dissent, and made a lot of people realize they were neither crazy nor alone in their unarticulated aversion to sprawl development" (Polycarpou). One review in *Entertainment Weekly,* a magazine known mostly for celebrity gossip and glossy images of Hollywood stars, gives *Suburban Nation* a perfect A+. The popularity of these books suggests that people notice the changing landscapes, and they want to know why they seem so unsatisfying. In short, people recognize that we are in the midst of crisis.

In popular entertainment, issues of development are beginning to creep into even the most popular movies and books. John Sayles's 2002 film *Sunshine State* deals with complex issues involved in gentrification and development. Sayles focuses on the role played by greedy corporate developers, as well as the complexity of residential life in the midst of gentrifying areas. Similarly, Nathan McCall's 2007 novel, *Them,* explores the lives of African-American residents in Atlanta's Old Fourth Ward neighborhood, which is experiencing the early stages of gentrification. This same topic was again the focus of *Everyday People,* a 2004 film that tells the story of a beloved diner in Brooklyn that could not ultimately survive development and gentrification. In 2003, directors Linda Goode Bryant and Laura Poitras won a number of awards for their documentary *Flag Wars,* which follows the lives of residents in a historically black, working-class neighborhood in Columbus, Ohio. When white, gay, upper-class residents begin to move into the neighborhood, the complexities of gentrification and development become a commonplace discussion for all residents.

For me, however, one particular film still lingers in my mind as the most horrific image of development. *Poltergeist* has become almost schlocky with age, yet it is my first memory of "development" as a concept. The families in *Poltergeist* live in a new suburban development, Cuesta Verde, which was designed by a shady developer. Unfortunately, the developer built the neighborhood directly on top of a cemetery without properly relocating the bodies. Evil spirits arrive to take their revenge on the families living in Cuesta Verde. By the film's end, the developer's secret is exposed as the culprit of Cuesta Verde's evil. This horror film still seems to be an oddly apt reflection of many people's social imaginary where developers are concerned. Development can be scary; what I did not know as a kid was that it is scary for a whole other set of reasons. Real development does not bring ghosts and evil spirits, but it does bring sprawl, homogenization, unequal tax policies, lost local businesses, gentrification, and a host of other haunting effects. The day that I pulled into the parking lot of our town's half-empty strip mall, I sadly realized the irony of development's real poltergeists. Evil spirits can be cast out by the prayers of a good priest, but the lasting effects of overdevelopment are not so easy to banish.

Development as Crisis

Rhetoricians certainly do not have to worry about evil spirits haunting shifty developments built on sacred spaces, but there are good reasons to see modern development practices as a crisis. In the next few pages, I will explain how development has become a problem for rhetoricians and why I have chosen to call it a crisis. I use the term "crisis" in three different senses, all of which have an impact upon our rhetorical lives. First, I borrow the term from early Chicago School urban studies literature. In the earliest days of the Chicago School, researchers theorized urban spaces as ecologies, a concept that continues to gain favor in a number of fields. Robert Park's classic essay "Human Behavior in theb Urban Environment" suggests that the city is particularly marked and affected by crisis, by which he means "a disturbance of habit" (20, 27). Cities are marked by many exigencies brought about because of close proximity and social divisions. The lasting contribution of the Chicago School's ecological theory is a recognition that places are constantly experiencing shifts in response to new linkages and adjustment to those linkages. New linkages may include structural elements, changes in transportation technologies, obsolescence of formerly useful resources, changes in demands and needs among the population, and so forth (McKenzie 75). Because of this ecological model, the Chicago School theorists did not see social disorganization as pathological (see Burgess). In fact, Park argues that disorganization is normal since it is "preliminary to reorganization of attitudes and conduct" ("Human Behavior" 54). To call urban development a crisis is to recognize that changes are happening to the ecology. Those changes have effects and demand adjustments from everyone who is part of that ecology, whether or not people realize those effects.

In some sense, urban development is a crisis of disorganization and reorganization. The ecology shifts, and we must adjust. Sometimes these new linkages seem to weaken other linkages, as in the demise of downtown areas in the wake of strip malls and shopping centers with large parking lots that are inaccessible by pedestrians. Individual contact on the street is thus lessened as we stay in our cars more regularly. However, the linkages can also strengthen weak links, as in the work/live philosophy of new urbanists (see Katz). The new urbanist movement is guided by such principles as increased density, stronger connectivity between pedestrian walkways and everyday destinations, mixed-use housing, and central public space. Just as suburbanization caused a dramatic shift in the national consciousness beginning in the mid-twentieth century, new urbanist principles are beginning to affect the way "good design" is promoted in cities and suburbs. When Chicago's Cabrini-Green public housing projects were dismantled in the mid- to late-

1990s, the city turned to new urbanist principles in order to create mixed-income housing that would feel more like a "real" neighborhood with green space, pedestrian walkways, and aesthetically pleasing designs (see Fleming, *City of Rhetoric*). Of course, new urbanist goals do not always result in a better urban ecology. Some gated, suburban communities have adopted principles of increased density, central green space, and connectivity without actually addressing the larger issues of suburban sprawl. Whether the links create positive or negative new relations, the Chicago School theory of urban ecology helps us to see development as a process of ongoing change.

Long-term changes to our habits can be quite dramatic. For example, development changes how we relate to space. It changes our personal geographies. On a summer road trip several years ago, my spouse and I found ourselves stuffed into a car packed full of suitcases, gifts for friends, and every possible toy I could find to keep our young daughter entertained. Both coolers were full of sandwiches, milk, water, and snacks. We were proud to be self-sufficient travelers. There would be no roadside stops at those fast food chains sitting right off the highway. After driving a few hours, we decided it was time for a rest stop. My daughter would need a diaper change and maybe a bottle. I climbed into the backseat to look for the box of supplies I had carefully packed the night before. Looking around the backseat, I didn't see the box in the mix of bags and coolers. "Where's her box?" I asked my husband. He paused for a moment, "What box?" I could picture the box sitting by the garage door right before we pulled out of the driveway. Had I forgotten to mention it to him? "The box with all her stuff. Her diapers, her wipes, her bottles . . ." We both let out a sigh. We were in the middle of nowhere, in a whole different state that neither of us knew. Outside the car windows were endless rows of corn and wheat fields. "Oh well," I casually said. "It's not a problem."

In fact, we both knew that the missing box was not really a serious problem. All we had to do was keep our eyes open for what we inevitably knew we would encounter. Before too long there would be a Walmart, a Target, a Walgreens, a Costco, or some other big box chain store. Its signage would almost certainly be visible from the highway, and we trusted that we would be able to exit from the highway and easily make our way into the parking lot. The store would likely be an anchor in a strip of other stores. Before we even spotted any stores, I began thinking about other possibilities. "As long as we're going to stop, let's see if there's a Starbucks or a Panera so we can get some coffee." We drove about twenty miles before spotting a familiar sign in the distance. It was a Walmart, sitting conveniently off a highway exit. We pulled off the highway and made a quick trip into the store. There was even a Starbucks' drive-thru in the same shopping center. It had all happened just as we had thought, even though we had never been to this area before. We did not owe this good fortune to any knowledge of the local physical landscape, but to a contemporary geography of ubiquitous development. We navigated commercial space, not geographical space.

That incident helped me to think about how our geographies are reorienting us to the land, thanks to current development trends. Even before the ubiquity of GPS systems, many of us had already learned how to navigate the commercial spaces of new or unfamiliar cities. We know that an off-highway shopping area will often have a big box general store next to a fast food place, and maybe even a home supply store. If you travel with animals, you can even depend on midsize cities having a large pet chain in the shopping plazas. For my mother, who does not trust local food spots, eating in a chain restaurant like Chili's or Cracker Barrel is a source of comfort. No matter where she goes, her taste buds never leave "home."

Cultural geographers and urban planners have been wrestling with the homogenized conditions of development for a long time. Urban planners such as James H. Carr and Lisa J. Servon have conducted studies showing how many cities have pursued policies that have stressed homogeneity (often in the guise of big box stores) over local, vernacular culture. Carr and Servon argue that preserving local assets, such as ethnic heritage sites and local businesses, can actually be a more economically successful strategy for urban centers. Avoiding homogeneity and suburban sameness also preserves the unique character of regional and local spaces, which is not an insignificant detail. Yet cities do not always take this route. Many geographers and urban planners are devoted to studying the human effects of development in neighborhoods and urban centers. Not only is displacement and inequality a primary concern for many cultural geographers, but the effects of personal well-being are also repeated topics in this literature. Carr and Servon state that they are investigating how local culture can be preserved in the pursuit of development because they want to advance the argument that "the people who create the culture and the businesses must own the culture and be rooted in place" (29). Part of their exigence is that contemporary development has largely created spaces not rooted in place.

Because development creates change in our ecologies and habits, and because contemporary development so often leads toward homogeneity, humanist geographers have found serious consequences for what they call our "sense of place."[4] Urban theorists and geographers have spent much time considering what constitutes a "sense of place," an elusive concept that has obvious impact on people's lives. There are many different explanations of what place is and how its affective experience is created. Thomas Gieryn defines place according to three primary characteristics: (1) "a unique spot in the universe" (464), (2) a material collection of actual things and people (465), and (3) a place with meaning and value that has been attributed to it over time by people (465). If development is displacing the local uniqueness of place through homogeneous built environments, then these three characteristics are thrown into some question. Big box stores and sprawling megamarts disrupt the ability of places to signify their identities as unique spots in the universe.

Finding our way in the world increasingly means that we must navigate homogeneous patterns. (This was certainly the case with my Walmart emergency trip.) Yet, humanist geographers and urban theorists want to know how these changes affect not only our sense of place, but also our sense of self. Geographer Yi-Fu Tuan famously outlined his concept "topophilia" to describe the "affective bond between people and place" (4). Meaning is made in the activity of this bond. Tuan's phenomenological take suggests that our selves are constructed through place. Other phenomenological perspectives (authored by theorists like Tuan, Edward Casey, Gaston Bachelard, Christian Norberg-Schulz, and Edward Relph) teach that place is what enables us to be human. Places are "profound centers of human existence," according to Relph (43). To be conscious, we must have some kind of orientation to each other and to the world. Only place provides this kind of orientation, although place may orient us in many different ways. To describe changes in place as a crisis, therefore, makes sense. A change in place's ecology disturbs the centers of our existence.

Nowhere is the anxiety of ecological disturbance felt more than in nonplaces. Although newly developed spaces are sometimes rooted in their specific material locale, many familiar spaces of development, such as retail stores, chain restaurants, apartment complexes, office parks, and even new housing developments, have the character of what Marc Augé has called a "non-place." They lack the specificity of history, and they intentionally elide fixed relations among people. What is important in a nonplace is simply the present moment (Augé 104). It is easy to understand why these developments require such elision, of course. Walmart or Chili's must not depend upon the specificity of their locations in order to operate smoothly. The prefabricated designs can be placed anywhere, which is precisely what allows them to work. Moreover, anyone can fill in as customer, employer, or employee. Office parks or strip malls have much the same logic. They are designed in order to allow anyone anywhere to fill in for the last occupant. The historyless character of these spaces minimizes the friction felt by interruption in turnover.

Smooth and steady flows also demand that users of a nonplace minimize personal interactions. Nonplaces are temporary gathering sites, and only for the people you have previously agreed to meet in that space. They are simultaneously free of anything like politically oriented public discourse. Mahyar Arefi writes that the rise of nonplaces and placelessness has sparked a crisis of place identity. Communities of interest have superseded communities based on place (Arefi 181). Our relations to other people based on proximity have weakened significantly. What have replaced places are attempts at constructing instant experiences of being in-place. New loft sites are built to look like they have a long-standing history and character, just as new restaurants are constructed to look old and authentically *something*.[5]

While early Chicago School theorists did not necessarily see change and development as a pathological crisis, many contemporary scholars seem to agree that development is not always in our best interest. As I recount these different takes on development, I am reminded of Marshall Berman's poetic look at what he calls "the tragedy of development." Berman recalls Faust's nasty deal with the devil that is fueled by an overriding interest in development (albeit self-development), which becomes a simultaneous transformation of his entire social world (Berman 40). It may seem overly dramatic to speak about contemporary urban development in Faustian terms, yet the allegory is not without significance. In the reach toward economic and social development, entire social networks are transformed. The built environment affects all of us economically, intersubjectively, psychologically, physically, and politically.

Urban Development as Crisis of Judgment

In rhetorical terms, urban development is also a *krisis* situation. Aristotle uses the term *krisis* to denote the kind of practical judgment that must be made in contingent situations that have no clear solution. William Grimaldi remarks that Aristotle's *Rhetoric* repeatedly maintains that "all rhetoric is directed toward *krisis*, or judgment, as its final goal" (37). In the *Nicomachean Ethics,* Aristotle writes that "justice is a discrimination [*krisis*] between what is just and what is unjust" (1134a31–32). Some commentators interpret Aristotle's *krisis* to be more in line with perception and cognitive discrimination, as he seems to use the term in *De anima* (see Charles 112). Yet, it seems worth noting that judgment and *phronesis* are closely linked for Aristotle. In book 6 of *Nicomachean Ethics,* Aristotle tells us that the person of practical wisdom has the ability to deliberate well. Aristotle claims that things deliberated about must be concerned with human affairs, and not interesting topics that are "not human." In other words, the deliberation characteristic of *phronesis* is concerned with matters that need some kind of response or decision, since a clear answer is impossible to deduce.

Consequently, Aristotle continues, practical wisdom does not deal only with universals. "It must also be familiar with particulars, since it is concerned with action and action has to do with particulars" (*Nicomachean Ethics* 1141b). This is why someone who lacks scientific knowledge can be more adept at practical matters than the scientist, according to Aristotle. Why is it that young people trained as mathematicians and geometricians do not have practical wisdom? According to Aristotle, it is because "practical wisdom is concerned with particulars . . . and knowledge of particulars comes from experience" (1142a). The lack of engagement with everyday experiences removes certain people from being truly prudent. *Phronesis,* or practical wisdom, can be called rhetorical insofar as *phronesis* always ends in rhetorical production or action (see *Nicomachean Ethics* 6.6).

The changes to our material spaces call for us to make different judgments, sometimes in the most mundane ways. We can either shop at the new strip mall or not. We can move to a bigger house in the suburbs, or we can stay in smaller houses within city limits. We can buy local, or we can pay slightly cheaper prices at a big box chain store. Each of these decisions is created from the omnipresent rise of urban development. The moment of *krisis* is thus an effect of the ecological disorganization theorized by Park. Changes in our local ecologies call for new judgments and decisions. While choosing to shop at a local store versus Walmart may not seem like a crisis to most people, this decision does require a certain amount of judgment. It also demands that we think (or not) about our material spaces and the effects that they have on us. The fact that we must make new judgments is also what makes ordinary response to development a rhetorical issue.

However, contemporary development is often made opaque, which throws a wrench into our ability to practice sound *krisis.* I started thinking about crisis and urban change sometime around 2004, when I took a long look at the half-finished building right in the middle of downtown Austin. On my daily bike rides through the city, I passed this structure more times than I can count. The huge steel beams looked like they were in the process of construction, on the verge of becoming a giant office building in downtown's central space. If you had just arrived in Austin, you might think that this building was ready to become something great. It looked like a new downtown high-rise that held the promise of future corporate moving and shaking. But it had actually been sitting in its unfinished state for several years. The hulking steel structure was originally celebrated as the future home of Intel's Austin location. Intel was wooed not only by the fast-growing Silicon

Hills culture that was springing up in Austin during the late 1990s, but also by the promise of huge subsidies and over fifteen million dollars in waived fees. When the dot-com collapse hit Austin, however, Intel backed out of its deal. The building sat like a skeleton for the better half of a decade, until it was finally imploded on a gray February day in 2007. Hundreds of people huddled around a chain-link fence in order to cheer on the demolition of a hulking shell.

Selling the original Intel deal to residents was no easy task, but city officials were rhetorically savvy. While they promised Intel a fifteen-million-dollar incentive package, city leaders promised residents that the deal would add at least two thousand new jobs to Austin. It would also revitalize a somewhat sagging downtown area (Rivera B10). Additionally, officials promoted the Intel deal as part of its new Smart Growth initiative in what they called Austin's "Desired Development Zone."[6] City council argued that the incentives would not only attract Intel downtown, but the money was also an assurance that Intel would not build in the environmentally sensitive Barton Springs aquifer area. In the council's own language, the Smart Growth initiative promised to "modernize Austin's long-range plan for growth, managing and directing growth that minimized damage to the environment and helped build a more livable city" ("Smart Growth"). Mayor Kirk Watson touted Intel's campus construction as a first step in creating a first-rate downtown area, as well as an environmentally wise choice. Intel's new building would be built inside a compact downtown area that is serviced by public transportation and newly developing living areas. The alternative would be to build in Austin's outskirts, where land is certainly plenty and cheap, but would necessarily increase highway congestion and traffic pollution ("Creating a Great Downtown"). Thanks to Austin's Smart Growth initiative, residents would have the benefit of greater economic opportunity and a protected environment.

Watson's vision of Smart Growth was persuasive to many residents. Smart Growth's birth was launched in the 1998 vote on Proposition 2, which allowed the city to purchase as much as fifteen thousand acres of undeveloped land in order to direct development in ways that the city desired. The undeveloped land would be off-limits to developers, steering them instead to the downtown area for future growth. The vote for Smart Growth was framed as an endorsement of Watson's plans to use a combination of directed development and monetary incentives to attract new companies. Watson touted his plan as a win-win opportunity for everyone concerned. He explained, "If we destroy our environment, we destroy our economy. The two are closely linked. . . . By protecting our environment we are ultimately going to enhance and sustain our tax-base" (Watson A15). The language of Smart Growth was steeped in an appeal to the value of maximizing benefits. In this case, Smart Growth almost seemed like a chain reaction of benefits. Protecting the environment meant enhancing the local economy, and enhancing the local economy means a more livable city for all residents. Many citizens echoed these same sentiments, linking Intel to both current and future growth. As one resident wrote in a letter to the *Austin American-Statesman*, "Smart Growth or not, if we don't help big employers come downtown, we'll never have more retail, residential and other tenants that contribute to a lively downtown" (Beniash). The Intel deal was sold on a wave of multiple promises about mass benefits for all.

The complexity of Austin's Smart Growth initiative and its deal with Intel (and an almost identical deal at the same time with another digital corporation called Vignette) led some to accuse the companies of greenwashing their motives in order to gain massive incentives from the city. Even environmentalists who supported Intel's downtown construction, as opposed to construction in more sensitive environmental areas, saw the company as using the aquifer as a bargaining chip in exchange for subsidies (A. Smith). The *Austin Chronicle* featured an editorial cartoon drawn to look like a ransom note from Intel, with cutout letters reading, "If you want to keep your aquifer healthy, give us your $." City council and pro-development supporters recuperated the discourse by assuring the public that their own ethical goals trumped Intel's corporate greed. During one city council hearing about the Intel deal, council member Daryl Slusher remarked that companies like Intel had to be given incentives in order for the good work to be accomplished. "In an ideal world, [businesses would locate downtown] because they want to support the city's goals, but that's just not the way it works" (Fullerton). In other words, Slusher seemed to say, the city council has laudable goals (protecting the environment, economy, and every citizen's livability), even if they must deploy some less than savory means of doing it (like paying incentives). True, Intel and Vignette were being offered huge incentives. But the payoff was in the realization of pro-environmental goals for a livable city. According to this rhetorical structure, the real benefits do not accrue to the company, but to the citizens as a whole.

The Intel situation is quite complex. Initial plans were steeped in technocratic language about bonds, tax bases, and local propositions. Beyond the economic issues and environmental concerns, the plans also had to be contextualized within a public memory of development and progress discourse. To understand why Austin officials saw Intel as integral to their twenty-first-century downtown, one must understand the city's legacy of technology partnerships. In the 1940s, Austin made its first major push into corporate technology when an aggressive businessman named C. B. Smith launched the Austin Area Economic Development Foundation in order to attract technology business to Austin. Smith's campaign was so popular that newspaper editorials endorsing Smith's plan ended with a reader pledge card that asked readers to join the Development Foundation (Orum 231). Aggressive marketing to the city's residents encouraged them to consider their own well-being as dependent upon Austin's future as a technology center. Such status was secured in 1949 when Austin won a contract for the Balcones Research Center. The costly research center promised to do work that benefited the public, all while generating major source of revenue through military and private funds.

In 1982, Microelectronics and Computer Technology Corporation (MCC) chose Austin from among fifty-seven other cities to locate. The importance of MCC's move to Austin cannot be overstated, since it helped to jump-start Austin's reputation as a center for technology. In 1988, Austin added to this reputation by landing SEMATECH, a consortium of most of the U.S. semiconductor manufacturers. Companies like Apple, 3M, Freescale, and Dell would also later look to Austin as a destination for operations. The growth of Austin's technology sector led Presidential Medal of Science winner and renowned business thinker George Kozmetsky to label Austin a "technopolis." When Intel seemed interested in building a large chip design location downtown, the plans seemed to be part of the natural arch in Austin's trajectory.

Although the Intel development had an odd ending, this story is not unusual in terms of its process. It is also not unusual in terms of the complexity involved in each step, from proposal to final approval. Citizen input was limited to an earlier vote for Smart Growth. By the time the deal with Intel was actually negotiated, citizens were mostly limited to making complaints and protesting verbally. When citizens complained about the tax breaks and other problems with the plans, their arguments were met with an intense public relations campaign from the mayor's office.

This scene reflects what urban planners Jacobs and Appleyard identify as "giantism," where decisions about what is built and how changes are made do not happen at the grassroots level of ordinary citizens. In "Toward an Urban Design Manifesto," Jacobs and Appleyard write, "The urban environment is increasingly in the hands of the large-scale developers and public agencies. The elements of the city grow inexorably in size, massive transportation systems are segregated for single travel modes, and vast districts and complexes are created that make people feel irrelevant. People, therefore, have less sense of control over their homes, neighborhoods, and cities than when they lived in slower-growing locally based communities" (114). Giantism, which Jacobs and Appleyard call one of the greatest problems of modern urban design, is more than a problem of scale. With giantism, decisions are privatized and placed beyond the scope of daily life. Jacobs and Appleyard's design manifesto looks toward a better ideal: "People should feel that some part of the environment belongs to them, individually and collectively, some part for which they care and are responsible, whether they own it or not. The urban environment should be an environment that encourages people to express themselves, to become involved, to decide what they want and act on it. Like a seminar where everybody has something to contribute to communal discussion, the urban environment should encourage participation" (115). Those of us who teach rhetorical theory may recognize this call to action as a familiar rhetorical goal for public discourse. Yet, it is telling that Jacobs and Appleyard express this as a radical goal, worthy of turning into a manifesto, which means that we are far from that state just yet.

Giantism affects our ability to use judgment just at the time that we need it most. Getting involved in development issues is not impossible for ordinary citizens, of course. We can attend hearings and city council meetings, join civic groups that represent public interests, or even write our local political figures. However, these activities are not realistically available to many people. Ordinary daily activities involve errands, multitasking, and badly needed downtime. Some of us have illnesses that leave us tired at the end of the day. Others of us have children and older parents to care for. Many citizens have been diagnosed with depression, anxiety, and other maladies related to stress. We sit in work meetings, we write memos, and we take work home in the evenings. Thanks to e-mail and social networking sites, our communication expectations have grown. Before bed, perhaps we check in with our friends on Facebook, blogs, message boards, or listservs. There is so much to do in so little time.

All of these demands explain why Michael Schudson argues that we have morphed into "monitorial citizens."[7] Schudson argues that the classic model of the informed individual as citizen is not adequate to describe what is happening in public life today. Citizenship is not defined by voting booths and civic town hall meetings. While this may be an ideal, it is far from practical. We have lives, jobs, families. We have increasing numbers of stresses and exigencies that pull us into many directions at once. For this reason, Schudson advocates thinking of responsible citizenship as embodied by the "monitorial citizen," one who surveys the scene of public life for crises and urgent demands. According to Schudson, "A monitorial citizen scans (rather than reads) the informational environment in a way so that he or she may be alerted on a very wide variety of issues for a very wide variety of ends and may be mobilized around those issues in a large variety of ways." The monitorial citizen is not the traditional image of an ideal civic activist. But she instead watches for moments of break that pull her into action.

The monitorial citizen is interesting for rhetoricians. For one thing, Schudson broaches a fundamental reality for many of us, but one that is strangely absent in our most revered theoretical models. We know that people are too busy for taking on any additional responsibilities, even for civic participation. When crisis does call to the monitorial citizen, life does not get simpler. Unfortunately, by the time Intel's crisis registered for many Austin citizens, the structure had already been abandoned in the middle of the city. Added to this complexity is the fact that, as the Intel building example suggests, a crisis demands some degree of expert knowledge (about bonds, city strategic missions, tax abatements, and environmentally sensitive areas). It is unrealistic to think that the ordinary citizen will delve deeply into expert knowledge in order to respond.[8] Although she is no expert, the monitorial citizen is not clueless, however. I agree with Johanna Hartelius's distinction between knowledge and expertise: "Being highly knowledgeable is not necessarily the same as being received as an expert, which requires a rhetorical effort" (20). At the same time, ordinary citizens may not have time or resources to join the ranks of citizen-activists who research the issues and attend meetings where these matters are discussed. Contemporary development has benefited from this lack of citizen input, since fewer voices potentially means less opposition. From a rhetorical perspective, however, the problem of giantism provokes a crisis of *krisis*.

Urban Development as Crisis of Public Discourse

Some of the most damning critiques of urban development trends come from scholarly inquiry into development's capacity to erode public engagement. "The American city is being systematically turned inward," writes Mike Davis. "The 'public' spaces of the new megastructures and supermalls have supplanted traditional streets and disciplined their spontaneity" (155). As private communities emerge, formerly public spaces become privatized and restricted in terms of who can enter and speak. Setha Low shows how the growing trend of gated communities emerges from middle-class anxieties over social differences. Living behind gates serves to diffuse and mask conflict about otherness, yet these suburban developments also intensify very real problems of racism and social segregation. Instead of building spaces that encourage public engagement, our spaces are actually displacing engagement altogether.

Rhetorical theorists have likewise considered how (sub)urban spaces can both enable and disable the potential for public discourse. In *City of Rhetoric: Revitalizing the Public Sphere in Metropolitan America,* David Fleming offers one analysis of a Chicago neighborhood's loss and recovery of public discourses about that space's development. Fleming's unique argument is that physical spaces themselves can enable or disable shared deliberation about mutual issues. When Chicago politicians tried to "fix" the Cabrini-Green housing projects by dispersing former residents into new suburban (and thus more remote) Illinois towns, the former Cabrini-Green residents had less opportunity to debate and deliberate about how Chicago's urban redevelopment should look. Fleming writes, "The suburbs may be, by their very form, unfavorable to public life. . . . Their scale is too awkward (things are too far away from one another), their land use too rigid (too much segregation of functions), their density is socially unsatisfactory (too little unplanned contact among individuals, and what public spaces they have are few and far between)" (119). Fleming's conclusion turns back to the city neighborhood as an optimum space for democratic encounter and deliberation. If we lived in democratically scaled spaces that were conducive to ongoing debate, we might be better able (and willing) to participate in deliberations about zoning laws, gentrification trends, and housing patterns. Yet, he offers little hope for suburban spaces as democratic or rhetorical sites. Unfortunately, these are the very places where many of us live and work. And if the researches of urban theorists like Davis, Low, and others is correct, then the city itself is becoming equally as unfavorable to public life.[9]

One of the biggest blows to public life is the disappearance of public space. Physical common spaces are rapidly decreasing in both urban and suburban areas because of private corporate development. As Don Mitchell argues, "Corporate and state planners have created environments that are based on a desire for security more than interaction, for entertainment more than (perhaps divisive) politics" (138). Public gatherings usually happen in pseudopublic locations, like bars or restaurants (see Goss). Corporations like Starbucks have capitalized on this lack of public space by fashioning themselves as "third spaces," or a gathering place away from home and work. The lack of common space arguably stunts our ability to imagine ourselves as a public. Johnathon Mauk's study of pedagogy and placelessness, "Location, Location, Location: The 'Real' (E)states of Being, Writing, and Thinking in Composition," offers a vivid description of how the lack of physical common space affects students at his local community college. Mauk captures the almost painful isolation that the "commuter campus" can sometimes spawn:

> Rather than groups of students walking or sitting casually, I saw students waiting alone in cars for their classes. They were cut off from one an-

other, sealed up in their own mornings, staring ahead, sipping coffee or Mountain Dew, and listening to their radios. . . . Students had no place to settle—no place to define. They had no dorm rooms, no student lounge (other than vending areas or the main cafeteria), no spirit rock, no mall, no communal lawn or park. . . . In short, students did not have a place at Gordon, other than classrooms. And because class attendance tended to be erratic, according to instructors, the classes constantly shifted character and so rarely took on a sense of place. (370–71)

For those of us who have taught (and have been taught) at similar commuter schools, where students are usually in a temporary relation to the school, Mauk's words ring true. Some students explain that they hope to transfer to a "better" school after a period of proving academic worthiness. Others are returning to school in order to gain the resources for their "real" destination, such as a better job or a new career. Whatever the case happens to be, though, few students linger around the commuter campus after the class meeting ends. Part of this is due to commuter students' heavy work schedules. Yet, the commuter campus is often not designed for lingering or communing. It is not surprising, Mauk concludes, that students lacked the desire to engage politically or socially on campus. Sadly, the same might also be said about our cities, suburbs, and workplaces that increasingly lack a "sense of place" in which communal life happens.

The Need for Rhetorical Intervention

I offer this lengthy account of development's crisis in order to show how this crisis is relevant to rhetorical studies. Perhaps more than ever, we need to help cultivate and support public subjects who can make ethical interventions into our endangered places. Not only do we need rhetors who can make changes at the level of individual crises, but we need rhetorical agents who can work toward sustainability in a larger sense. The meaning of sustainability has been variously described by a number of ecological scholars, environmental scientists, urban planners, biological scientists, anthropologists, and many others working across disciplines. In *Sharing the Earth*, Tarla Rai Peterson points out that a general concept of sustainability transcends a purely ecocentric view (whereby the needs of the natural world are placed above already existing human processes) or a purely anthropocentric view (whereby ecologies are merely valued for their instrumental use in human processes). Peterson defines sustainability as "a conceptualization of ecological integrity which includes humanity" (1). Or, as Gabriel Moser writes, sustainable development is a way of "ensuring the long-term integrity of bio-cultural systems" (1). These definitions indicate that sustainable thinking is concerned with how we can conduct our lives in some way that preserves ecological health and endurance. Going "off the grid" or denying the importance of our built environments does not seem to reflect true sustainable thinking, therefore. Many of us do not have the capacity to live without shopping centers, cars, apartment complexes, or any other forms of development that have become the spaces of home life and work life. At the same time, our home/work process of everyday life should not unnecessarily damage the ecological integrity of our natural world. This balance marks the challenge of sustainable thinking.

Sustainability has been an interdisciplinary concern for several years, although rhetoric and writing studies are only now beginning to take on sustainability as a serious topic for scholarly and pedagogical work. Derek Owens has issued a call to "sustainability" in English studies by arguing that "sustainability—as a metaphor, a design problem, a cultural imperative, and a social and ecological necessity—will become one of the new paradigms shaping much of our work as teachers and scholars. If it doesn't, so much the worse for us" (*Composition and Sustainability* 1). Owens argues that compositionists especially have a unique opportunity due to their position within the university curriculum. Not only do composition classes reach a majority of students, unlike more specialized courses in environmental studies, but they also have the ability to address local contexts and rhetorical exigencies through writing pedagogy ("Sustainable" 29). We can teach sustainable pedagogies, not because we are authorities in environmental subjects, "but because we supposedly know something about designing pedagogical environments where information from a variety of sources might be choreographed with student writing in ways that are . . . supremely relevant to students' lives" ("Sustainable" 35). Composition classes, as well as courses in rhetorical theory and public speaking, can take biocultural systems as their focus because this nexus is precisely the scene of our everyday lives. Nothing is more ordinary than the places where we live, work, travel, and visit. And it is in the ordinary (complete with its many exigencies) that rhetorical work begins.

Rhetorical scholars are beginning to make unique contributions to the question of sustainability. For example, Peter Goggin notes that humanist scholars can use their strengths in order to "look critically and skeptically at who is doing the defining and to what ends" where the concept of sustainability is used to serve special interests (1). Similarly, Tarla Rai Peterson sees rhetorical criticism as a means of discovering "how to utilize the human capacity for language to understand better and reflect upon technologized conditions of our own making but not necessarily to our liking" (*Sharing* 2–3). Rhetoricians, as those who teach how to produce and understand communication, are uniquely capable of analyzing how language operates in the balance between human processes and the ecological sphere. It is not that sustainability is a purely rhetorical concept. But sustainability is embedded in language and texts that circulate to actually existing historical publics. Problems are framed and solutions are posed all through language. This makes sustainability very relevant to the work we do as rhetorical critics, textual critics, and teachers of writing.

True sustainability demands more than scholarly input, however. Sustainable living demands public subjects are who capable of considering how to balance the home-life and work-life nexus with the environmental integrity of our natural world. These public subjects are also willing to use the communicative moment in order to change "technologized conditions of our own making but not necessarily to our liking," as Peterson puts it. These sustainability-oriented public subjects are thus able to imagine themselves as situated within many complex networks. Not only are they located within a specific home-work nexus, but they are also located within regional, national, and global networks. Furthermore, each of us is situated within transhistorical and transspatial networks of place. The choices we make for ourselves have effects on future times and places that do not only parallel our own lives. Thinking through these networks demands an ability to imagine the incongruent and asymmetrical networks within which our agency is lodged. For example, it is not simply my own "future generations" that inherit the decisions I make about where and how I live, shop, and work. These decisions also impact immediate lives in spaces of which I am personally not aware. Similarly, the decisions of my regional network (currently located in the U.S. Midwest) will affect individuals in the distant future. Issues like water policies, recycling, and land management in the Midwest may impact the health of individual people. The kinds of public subjects necessary for true sustainable thinking are ones who can think in terms of these incongruent and asymmetrical networks, where our agency is located in multiple and complex ways.

The challenge of sustainable thinking was put to the test when the BP Deepwater Horizon drilling rig exploded in 2010, causing crude oil to gush into the Gulf Coast's open waters. Tens of thousands of barrels poured into the Gulf of Mexico every day. Birds and sea turtles were daily shown on the news, covered in oil. Workers in the fishing industry suddenly found themselves out of work, since people were understandably nervous about eating seafood from waters contaminated with chemical dispersants used to help control the spill. Nobody quite knows the environmental impact that the BP oil spill will ultimately leave, but everyone seems to agree that it will not be good.

In the weeks and months following the initial explosion and spill, many people called for a boycott on BP gas. Floods of e-mails and Facebook messages urged drivers to pass BP filling stations the next time they needed gas. Such action does indeed feel good: hit them where it hurts. Yet, if we consider the crisis across incongruent and asymmetrical networks, we are likely to find that this action does not carry the true mark of sustainability. The product sold by BP gas stations actually has very little to do with the work of BP drilling. Gas is likely to be extracted and refined by a number of other companies, with only a small amount of BP additives added toward the end process (Lieber). Additionally, driving past a BP station and into another gas station does not solve the problem of petroleum mining that led to the Deepwater Horizon tragedy in the first place. Choosing Exxon or Mobil to fill up my car still retains the system that causes problems over time (Vidal).

Furthermore, boycotting BP as a sign of protest does not consider how drilling is spread asymmetrically across many networks. The Deepwater Horizon spill gained much attention because it happened "close to home." Yet, even greater oil spills in the Niger Delta have been happening for decades. Few people in the United States are aware of Nigeria's own spill crisis caused by companies like ExxonMobil and Shell (Begley). The popular call for us to boycott BP gas stations failed to place the event within multiple networks, which ultimately calls for us to consider much more dramatic changes than where we fill our tanks. Sustainable futures demand a strong ability to think about ourselves as beings who exist in such multiple and asymmetrical networks. Intervention must also happen within networks. Public subjects are never single.

One response to the crisis of development and sustainability is to encourage *more* public discourse, *more* debate, *more* deliberation. Yet, I do not see this call as the most productive way to address this particular rhetorical crisis. Instead, we need to address the ways in which our key public subjectivities are somewhat debilitated when it comes to doing this kind of work. In fact our current habits of public discourse and debate are cultivating public subjects who are not oriented toward making sustainable interventions in such rhetorical crises. Our most common public discourse habits actually contribute to poor public deliberation. In order to address the exigencies that we currently face, we will first need to address this somewhat debilitated public subject.

2

The Public Subject of Feeling (with Exceptions)

> An equal fate to the one who stays behind as to the one who struggles well.
> —Achilles, *The Iliad*

Public subjectivity increasingly occupies what I call a space of exception. Because our key modes of public orientation are rooted in feeling, we are faced with certain limitations where rhetorical interventions are concerned. Paradoxically, distance does not always deter stronger public subjects, but can in fact serve as the condition of their existence. Subjectivity is one of those topics that has a long, complex history in critical theory. We generally recognize that subjectivity is not a state of self-presence or consciousness, nor is subjectivity something solidified over time. It is an articulation of multiple narratives, practices, and apparatuses that coalesce at any given moment. Michael Warner cautions against theorizing a single universal subject at the expense of all others who are denied entrance into the single public sphere ("Mass Public"). We do not only exist in one role or speak as only one kind of public subject. Among other things, I am simultaneously a college professor at a state school, a homeowner, a registered Democrat, and a Jew. I enact multiple subjectivities when speaking in/as any of these roles. Moreover, the meanings and readings of a Jewish public subject or a state employee (or any other role I may temporarily inhabit) exist through discourses and apparatuses (like institutions and cultural practices) that precede and exceed me as an individual.

By "public subjectivity," then, I mean to suggest the role(s) we inhabit when we speak and act about matters that put us into relation with others. Examining public subjectivities is not a process of listing characteristics. The critic must instead ask how these subjectivities "invite certain modes of encountering and interacting with others," as Robert Asen puts it (193). Public subjectivity is a process of interfacing with others, a kind of being-in-the-world. We act as public subjects when we are in a relation to claims made by others about public situations. For example, I am both a pro-choice advocate and a parent. Whenever I compose advocacy letters and blog writings on the subject, I am acting in relation to various claims made by others who speak and write on this same subject. Every time I blog about being a pro-choice parent, I am in a relation to multiple other claims, including claims that one cannot be both a caring parent and pro-choice. The subject role of "pro-choice parent" does not emerge from within my own inner self, therefore. It emerges whenever I act in relation to these multiple claims that are circulating in public.

Each time I make an argument as a mother, I am drawing from a collection of prior assumptions, ideologies, and beliefs. According to Foucault, the subject does not preexist the discourse that creates it, since the subject is generated from cultural patterns and habits. The practices by which a subject crafts the sense of self are "not something that the individual invents by himself. They are patterns that he finds in his culture and which are proposed, suggested and imposed on him by his culture, his society and his social group" (11). The subject position is thus created through the resources of a social imaginary. As Warner puts it, publics are a poetic world-making: "Public discourse says not only 'Let a public exist' but 'Let it have this character, speak this way, see the world this way'" (*Publics and Counterpublics* 114). Historical discourses have framed mothers as caring, nurturing, and natural protectors of children. Mothers are good, and being a mother is often rewarded as a pinnacle of womanhood. The discourse of motherhood is indeed a poetic world-making, as Warner suggests. Therefore, when I speak in the role of "pro-choice mother," I am stepping into webs of discourses, images, affects, and histories that have been circulating for ages. When speaking as a pro-choice mother, I am in a discursive relation with the warm images associated with motherhood, as well as the cold images sometimes associated with pro-choice women. Furthermore, my blog writings put me in another set of relations to circulating discourses and claims about abortion, choice, and parenting.

The notion that subjects are constituted in discourse has already been well rehearsed in rhetorical scholarship. Maurice Charland's essay "Constitutive Rhetoric: The Case of the *Peuple Québécois*" shows an example of how publics create subject positions from which people are invited to speak. Charland explores how, in the debate over Quebec's sovereignty, pro-separatist discourses generated images of Québécois, a *peuple* who were distinct from Canadians. These discourses reached back into a distant history in order to prove the Québécois' status as a separate people. Current citizens of Quebec were encouraged to think and speak as "a people." That is, they were encouraged to speak of themselves in relation to the history of Québécois. As a distinct *peuple*, the move for secession was infused with political and legal justification. Therefore, the discourse of pro-separatist publics generated subject positions that Quebec citizens were encouraged to inhabit.

Furthermore, some of our earliest examples of how public subjectivities are crafted come from the oratories of Greek leaders, who construct a shared image of the city and her citizens while performing funeral orations for fallen soldiers. Pericles' well-known funeral oration circles around the development of Athens more than the actual greatness of the dead men he claims to celebrate. His speech cultivates the image of a people, a role his audience is invited to inhabit: "What was the road by which we reached our position, what was the form of government under which our greatness grew, what were the national habits out of which it sprang—these are the questions which I may try to solve before my panegyric upon these men" (in Finley 267). Pericles answers his questions by looking at Athens' cultural habits as contributing factors to the city's greatness. Not only does Athens bar class considerations from advancement in public life, Pericles proclaims, but the city's many celebrations and festivals refresh the mind and draw visitors from all over the world. The city is not a mere place, he says, but she is more like a lover who must be honored and cared for (271). Pericles and other Athenian rhetors poetically create the Athenian citizen as a prideful subject who should imagine himself as open to the world. He is also a loving citizen of Athens, though Athens herself transcends the existence of its citizenry. Pericles invites his listeners to inhabit this subject position, much like an actor might step into a stage costume.

The example of Pericles demonstrates what would later be described by Louis Althusser and others as a process of interpellation. Through interpellation, an individual "recognizes" himself or herself within the previously circulating discourses that define a subject within particular ideological parameters. Pericles was arguably drawing on a process of ideological interpellation that hailed his audience as particular kinds of citizens: loyal, brave, and sacrificial. However, Ronald Walter Greene points out that the subject is more than an effect of language. Subjectification is a process embedded in material forms of production. Greene argues that rhetorical critics should interrogate the "technological dimensions of rhetoric—that is, how the rhetorical techniques and technologies manufacture a rhetorical subject" (51). Greene is specifically interested in rhetorical subjectivity, which is a role that is oriented toward communicating with others (whether it emerges in the form of debaters, salespeople, political activists, or some other form of communication). Critical examinations of rhetorical subjectivity thus require us to investigate the ways in which individuals come to think of themselves as communicating subjects. What apparatuses, narratives, and social practices help to materially produce this subject?

We can follow Greene's lead in our examination of public subjectivity, or the roles that are oriented to encountering and interacting with others. This examination calls for investigation into the ways people come to think of themselves as subjects who exist in relation to others and to the world. The methodology for such an investigation might begin by reading the techniques and technologies of such production. Furthermore, this method might also examine the institutions and material apparatuses that house these technologies. Although Greene is right to point out that subjectivity is more than an effect of language (whereby the subject "recognizes" himself or herself in well-worn ideological narratives), I am interested in how familiar patterns of public discourse serve as a productive technology for crafting public subjects. These patterns of discourse are housed in vernacular apparatus of response. They are lodged in the form of cultural commonplaces, and they are given shelter (so to speak) in material places like newspaper stories, letters to the editor, flyers, neighborhood newsletters, and ordinary conversations.

To some extent, I am circling around the classical Greek distinction between *koinos* and *idios*. Whereas *koinos* implies a kind of common orientation toward public life, *idios* conjures up a solitary figure who is stowed away deep inside his house. Though *idios* has parallels with the idiot, this figure is not one who lacks intellect. Rather, the *idios* is one who lacks engagement with public matters. As Rosa Eberly summarizes from Isocrates, the idiot "is one who cannot imagine what might be in the common or public interest, one who cannot practice with a common purpose" ("Plato's Shibboleth" 48). Jürgen Habermas similarly makes a contrast between a *koine* or common character of a public, as opposed to the *oikos* (or individualistic) realm of separate lives. In Habermas's own terms, the public sphere comprises private individuals engaging in a public discussion: "Citizens behave as a public [*koine*] body when they confer in an unrestricted fashion . . . about matters of a general interest" (49). The ability to address the consequences of mutual impact might seem to be the very definition of *koine*. The *idios*, meanwhile, seems outside the *koine* realm—outside the common, the public—with no ability or desire to confer about matters of general interest beyond the idios's own *oikos*.

The argument I make throughout this book is that the same kinds of rhetorical technologies are responsible for producing these two "different" kinds of subjects. Moreover, as the scare quotes in the previous sentence indicate, I am skeptical whether these subjects are different at all. My peculiar thesis is that certain rhetorical technologies of production (lodged in commonplace patterns of vernacular discourse) simultaneously produce people who are eager to participate publicly and people who are eager to remain politically and publicly quiet. In other words, these seemingly "different" kinds of subjects exist in a similar relation to others and to the world. Both are produced through rhetorical technologies of subjectification, and both are what we can properly call public subjects. Today's key mode of publicness produces subjects that inhabit a kind of public-private limbo.

But how could a private subject and a public subject be cut from the same cloth? Kenneth Burke describes this dual production in terms of identification. In his classic illustration of the shepherd and the butcher, Burke shows how two different roles can emerge from the same technological apparatus. Although the shepherd caring for his sheep may be most visible in his role of caretaker, Burke tells us that he is also "implicitly identified with their slaughter" (*Rhetoric* 302). The shepherd may never be persuaded to slaughter the animals in his care. Yet, at the same time, he communes at the same "spot" as the butcher. Both the shepherd and the butcher are identified with the act of killing sheep, even though the shepherd is devoted to keeping his sheep healthy and living. In Burke's reading, identification involves one's proximity to common acts, discourses, images, and so forth. Both the shepherd and the butcher can be mapped in close proximity to the act of slaughter. The shepherd raises sheep to the point of slaughtering, and the butcher performs the act for which the sheep were carefully raised. Though the shepherd and the butcher have very different goals, they identify with a common act.

The obvious difference is that the shepherd and the butcher do not feel the same way about their relations. The shepherd and the butcher may be similarly identified with the same scene of sheep slaughter, but they certainly do not feel the same way about this enterprise. A good shepherd may feel sorrow at the prospect of giving up his sheep to the slaughterhouse. The butcher, however, is happy to see the sheep coming into his arena, since he is about to enact his craft. Burke's example of the shepherd and the butcher suggests that the feelings we experience about our relations to public claims help to explain a qualitative difference in subject positions. Public subjects are not only defined by the fact that they act in relation to a constellation of discourses, but they are often shaped by the particular feelings they have about that relation. The role of feeling is crucial for understanding a key form of public subjectivity today. Furthermore, if we wish to understand why development discourse currently unfolds the way that it does, we must understand that this public subject is a *feeling* public subject.

In order to illustrate this point in more concrete terms, I turn to a scene of development that sparked a national debate. Susette Kelo's landmark battle against the New England town that annexed her home through eminent domain gained attention when it reached the Supreme Court and ended with a dramatic legal decision. I read the Kelo case as an example of how multiple and conflicting public subjectivities are created through a relation to claims, as well as through the experience of *feeling something* about that relation. The Kelo case demonstrates how public subjects are cultivated through discourses of feeling that circulate across deliberative scenes.

The (Public) Subject of True Feeling

In 1996 the federal government closed the Naval Undersea Warfare Center in New London, Connecticut. As a result of this closing, many people in and around New London lost their jobs, and the economy took quite a hit. Almost 1,400 jobs disappeared overnight, which meant that the city's unemployment suddenly doubled that of any other city in Connecticut (I. Peterson). The downturn in New London's economy created extraordinarily cheap property, which helped some people purchase good houses for low prices. When Susette Kelo, a nurse who was recently divorced, saw an old house for sale in the Fort Trumbull section in New London, she decided to take advantage of the low price. Kelo's house was a bright pink cottage in the middle of an older neighborhood that had been devastated by economic hardship. The house itself was unremarkable in nearly every way, yet it would soon be at the center of a national controversy.

Soon after Kelo moved into her house, the city council decided to turn abandoned and crumbling parts of the city into economically viable spaces. The city created the New London Development Corporation (NLDC) in order to purchase nine acres of land that would hopefully become a profitable "urban village" for shoppers and tourists. The new space was imagined as a booming collection of shops, restaurants, and other entertainment venues. And then there was the promise of a major corporate player: Pfizer announced that it would build a research and development center in the middle of Fort Trumbull's neighborhood as a way to stimulate job growth by attracting upscale employees and new residents. In order to proceed with these plans, however, New London found itself relying on the heavy-handed tactics of eminent domain. While some residents agreed to sell their homes to the city, other holdout residents were legally forced to sell their land under the auspices of public good. When Kelo was told that she would have to sell her house, she decided to launch a lawsuit against the city. Kelo's suit against NLDC was carried all the way to the Supreme Court, and the nation watched the struggle over her little pink house with great interest. In 2009, the Supreme Court delivered its controversial decision in favor of New London's use of eminent domain.

Public discourse in the Kelo case involved competing claims about homeowners' rights and urban economic development. This tension was established as a fundamental issue by both local and national media reports, including profiles in *Ladies Home Journal, Time, Newsweek,* and *People.* Kelo's story in *Ladies Home Journal* began with a hard luck narrative similar to most profiles of the story: "After a difficult divorce in the summer of 1997, Susette Kelo was intent on just one thing: realizing her lifelong goal to live near the ocean. But within months of moving into her dream home . . . [the] Pfizer pharmaceutical company announced plans to build a research facility next to her neighborhood, and the city of New London, desperate to bolster its faltering economy, decided to demolish homes there to make way for the development ("This Old House"). The profile highlights the clash between beleaguered homeowners and a city that wants to boost economic development for its residents. Similarly, a *People* magazine story painted Kelo in heartbreaking terms while simultaneously acknowledging New London's serious economic troubles. The *People* profile begins by describing Kelo's personal sadness at losing "her place in the world" (P. Lambert). Yet, further into the article, we read about the "distress" and potential "collapse" of New London's economic infrastructure. Stories and profiles like these helped to frame eminent domain's underlying tensions for a national audience. On one side is the homeowner and her beloved home, while on the other side is a struggling city that is desperate to expand economic opportunity for its residents.

In the years following Kelo's original lawsuit against New London, people from across the nation contributed to public debate about eminent domain—as well as the specifics of Kelo's case. Participants identified with claims about the fundamental clash between homeowners and cities, although they registered different feelings about this identification. For example, supporters wrote and spoke about tensions between homeownership and government intervention. As one Kansas resident explained in a letter to *Money* magazine, "It makes me livid that the eminent-domain law can be abused for private purposes. . . . I'd like to encourage Susette Kelo in her fight. She is waging a battle for my rights and those of all Americans who own property" (Wilson 22). Another letter in the *Wall Street Journal* remarks that the Supreme Court's decision against Kelo is "an affront to those who cherish the Constitution and our citizens' private property rights" (Preston). George Will also strongly criticized Connecticut's decision against Kelo, calling it a form of "despotism." Kelo's story does not only mean that a woman lost her beloved home, writes Will, but her story also forces us to ask whether our own homes or businesses "will be safe from grasping governments pursuing their own convenience." The conservative group Concerned Women for America even took the matter directly to their supporters, asking readers to imagine themselves in Kelo's position. "Imagine getting a letter in the mail from the City Council that reads, 'We think your home and property would be put to better use as a hotel and health club, so start making plans to move out'" (Cranston). They asked readers to consider how they would feel if it had been their little pink house, instead of Susette Kelo's. By posing such a hypothetical scenario, Concerned Women for America was activating real feelings of outrage and fear on the part of their readers.

The city's supporters also found themselves in proximity to this fundamental tension between homeowners and governmental economies, yet they registered different feelings about the tension. Wesley Horton, an attorney who represented New London, defended the city's actions in a television interview by Tucker Carlson by explaining why corporate development was necessary for the public welfare of all citizens. When grilled by Carlson to justify the use of eminent domain, Horton paints New London as a terminal patient who is slowly fading away. "If a city is dying," he tells Carlson, "it seems to me that it's certainly in the public interest to do something about an economically depressed city to bring it back and put it on the map" (*Ed Show*). Another NLDC member, Claire Gaudiani, argued that the eminent domain option was driven by a compassionate desire to help people in need. "The city needed an economic shot in the arm," she explained, and the NLDC was a last-ditch effort to "mobilize the city's assets on behalf of its own future" (99). Other supporters similarly framed the city's development plans as a relief from poverty, unemployment, and widespread despair among local families.

The pro-development discourses revolved around the same fundamental clash that Kelo's supporters identified—homeowners versus economic development—yet the affective linkages to those issues registered differently. Many NLDC supporters saw economic development as a kind of healing process. George Milne Jr., a Pfizer vice president who sat on the NLDC and spearheaded the land grab in New London was vocal about Pfizer's desire to do good. In a lengthy *Wall Street Journal* profile, Milne insisted that "idealism and social conscience motivated Pfizer. . . . It was an opportunity to do something really transforming" (Lagnado A1). From this perspective, stubborn homeowners like Kelo were blocking the kind of relief that New London desperately needed. Tom Londregan, director of law for the city of New London, told *People* that the fundamental clash was between one stubborn homeowner and the well-being of all New London citizens: "Is one person supposed to hold hostage a plan that is going to benefit 30,000 people?" (P. Lambert).

Throughout the debates about Kelo's case, the display of feelings was frequently discussed as a measurement of public orientation and validity. The question of feelings—genuine and artificial—became a commonplace in the debates over Kelo and her little pink house. For example, NLDC supporters openly questioned the authenticity of Kelo's care. Did she truly love her house as much as she claimed? Members of the NLDC circulated evidence that Kelo had purchased a second home in New Lyme during the time of her court case. According to the reports, Kelo had signed a mortgage showing her home in New Lyme as her primary residence, which suggested that Kelo was not truly attached to her little pink house in New London. One pro-NLDC opinion piece in *The Day*, New London's local paper, sought to "dispel the myth" that Kelo loved New London as much as she claimed: "Susette . . . first registered to vote in New London only within the last several weeks. During this litigation, she has been registered to vote in one of the other towns in which she has owned properties" (Costas). Her detractors suggested that she may have only been using the house as an investment property to fix up and sell, which "very much throws a different light on the [plaintiff's] tugging at our emotional heartstrings that someone is losing her home," according to Michael Joplin, president of the NLDC (Moran). Other NLDC supporters argued that Kelo's feelings were artificial when compared to the genuine feelings of New Londoners. "If anyone has a right to be bitter," writes one Kelo critic, "it is the citizens of New London who, during a five-year period when the economy was strong and stable, watched the possibility of improvement and development at Fort Trumbull stymied because of Ms. Kelo's, et al., obduracy and selfishness" (Allen). These claims sought to establish Kelo as someone who was (not so) secretly indifferent to New London and even to her little pink house.

Perhaps as a response to this attack on her feelings, Kelo carefully managed her own public performances to demonstrate evidence of caring. Her public statements in interviews and speeches repeatedly emphasized the labor and love she put into her home: "I spent every spare minute fixing it up, and making it the kind of home I had always dreamed of," she declared in a speech to the Cato Institute (Kelo). Another profile in *Money* magazine told of the "time, sweat and money" Kelo put into her cottage: "For Kelo, the issue is more basic than dollars and cents: She loves her home and wants to stay in it" (D'Agostino). Images of Kelo circulated widely, many of them posing her next to the pink house while she is frowning or looking pensively into the distance. One of the most widely circulated images of Kelo shows her leaving a meeting in the Connecticut legislature. She is biting her lips in an effort to hold back tears, looking as if she might burst into tears any minute.

The display and consideration of feeling was even more dramatic in the release of a strange 2006 Christmas greeting Kelo sent to members of the NLDC and the city council. Her holiday card showed a snowy image of her little pink house, along with a poem that wished a curse upon its recipients:

> Here is my house that you did take
> From me to you, this spell I make
> Your houses, your homes
> Your family, your friends
> May they live in misery
> That never ends
> I curse you all
> May you rot in hell
> To each of you
> I send this spell
> For the rest of your lives
> I wish you ill
> I send this now
> By the power of will.   (Slosberg)

The card was mailed after the Supreme Court's decision that NLDC's seizure of her home was legal. In online blogs and both national and local news media, Kelo's Christmas greeting and her lingering anger were zealously debated. One *Hartford Courant* reader responded to another letter that publicly doubted whether Kelo was actually bitter, or whether she was milking the attention for monetary reward (beyond the $440,000 she received as payment for her property). Maybe the writer who doubted Kelo's feelings "should be forced to move from her home so that she knows what it is like" ("Bah Humbug"). Another *Hartford Courant* reader was also moved to defend the authenticity and validity of Kelo's anger: "For these lawyers and what not to say that they cannot understand why she is so upset because she got all that money is disgusting" ("Bah Humbug"). When asked by a local New London newspaper, the *Day*, if the card was truly her work, Kelo affirmed that it was entirely her idea. "I'm very upset with what these people did to me," she explained (Slosberg).

But at least one NLDC member questioned the authenticity of Kelo's rage. After receiving her own card, Gail Schwenker-Mayer told reporters, "It's amazing anyone could be so vindictive when they've made so much money" (Slosberg). Kelo made an incredible profit from the sale of her house, according to Schwenker-Mayer. Could anyone in their right mind actually be angry or bitter after receiving such a payout? Reid Burdick, another NLDC member, came to the conclusion that Kelo's anger did not reflect genuine bitterness. Though she may seem angry, Burdick told reporters, "the poor woman has gone around the bend" (Slosberg). Therefore, what might appear to be anger is simply a case of mental instability. As the Christmas card curse makes plain, Susette Kelo's feelings continued to be performed and evaluated for years after she lost her fight.

The management of feeling-display in the Kelo case reveals something about how feelings can legitimate public subjects. Feeling has long been used as evidence of one's public orientation (or lack thereof). Recall Kanye West's infamous proclamation on live television that "George Bush doesn't care about black people" in the wake of Hurricane Katrina. In some sense, West's words encapsulated what people had been saying about Bush for years: he is an idiot. But this time, the idiocy related not to his intellect, but to his inability or unwillingness to orient himself as a public subject.[1] Edward Soja writes that the idiot/*idios* is "'one's own, a private person,' unlearned in the ways of the polis" (235). The Greek philosopher Heraclitus makes a similar distinction between the *idios kosmos*, which is literally a private world, and the *koinos kosmos*, or a world that touches a shared reality. Heraclitus contrasts these two worlds as one inhabited by a sleeping dreamer who interacts only with his own thoughts, and one inhabited by a waking body who interacts with others (*DK* 22 B89). For many people, Bush's lack of care, his seeming lack of feeling about the crisis in New Orleans, was evidence that his public subjectivity was also lacking. West's declaration exposes the ways that feeling has become a sign of public orientation. More specifically, feeling about public issues is what legitimates subjects as public subjects.

Nowhere is this condition better summarized than in the popular bumper sticker: "If you're not outraged, then you're not paying attention." The pithy statement speaks volumes about how we measure whether others are acting publicly (*koine*) or privately (like an idiot). The experience of outrage becomes a warrant that proves I am indeed "paying attention" to whatever public crises need to be addressed. However, my seeming lack of outrage may be evidence that I am not properly acting as a public subject. But outrage is only one example of how feeling serves as a legitimating device. If feeling outrage can legitimate my status as a public subject, then feelings like joy, boldness, sadness, and fear are no less likely to legitimate my status. Lauren Berlant suggests that this feeling-full legitimation marks a new kind of citizenship that is characterized by what she calls the "true subject of feeling." This feeling subject is one whose very humanity is registered through an experience of affect: "Feeling politics . . . claims a hard-wired truth, a core of common sense. It is beyond ideology, beyond mediation, beyond contestation. . . . [Feeling] seems the inevitable or desperately only core material of community" ("The Subject" 58). The subject of true feeling renders all emotions and affective experiences as primary orientation devices between self and the world. In the Kelo case, both sides made claims that were rooted in the appearance of authentic feelings. The political games in New London were most certainly a feeling politics, which looks to emotion as the ground of subjectivity. Extending Berlant, I would suggest that the true public subject is also a subject of feeling. That is, public orientation is measured and warranted by the experience of feeling about public crises and debates.

But what about feelings of remoteness, distance, or even indifference? Can these feelings also serve as the grounds for a public subjectivity? Sara Ahmed critiques the notion that emotions are something we either have or don't have, like a possession. Emotions are more like affective orientation devices, according to Ahmed: "Emotions are relational: they involve (re)actions or relations of 'towardness' or 'awayness' in relation to such objects" (8). Even the experience of feeling no impact—neither sadness nor joy—is still an orienting device toward (or perhaps away from) public action. Just as feeling pity may orient me in certain ways to public life, or just as the feeling of happiness may orient me in other ways, so the feeling of no feeling is a way of relating myself toward others. David Hume posits differences in what he calls the "calm" and "violent" passions as a difference in the experiences of emotion as felt by an individual (*Treatise* 2.4). Whereas violent emotions cause one to feel uneasy or are identified as a kind of disorder, calm emotions are felt as a nondisturbance. Hume's point here is that a feeling of no disturbance is not a lack of emotion, but is instead a particular kind of emotion. Furthermore, Hume tells us that a calm emotion is not less intense or strong than a violent emotion. In fact, calm emotions can overtake strong emotions in the right circumstances.[2] According to Hume, calm emotions sometimes have "absolute Command over the Mind. The more absolute they are, we find them to be commonly the calmer" (*Letters* 1). The feeling of no feeling can be quite passionate, according to Hume.

At first glance, defining public subjects through the lens of relations and feelings would seem to render apathetic or distanced persons as nonpublic subjects. These people appear to fail in any kind of public identification. They are disconnected, out of the loop. In fact, this very definition has led to our favorite remedy for the nonparticipation problem: we should attempt to help this type of person connect. After all, regardless of nonparticipants' indifference, lots of problems do indeed affect them. So the problem must be that they fail to recognize or register feelings about their proximity to those matters. When Herbert Gans examined the root causes of American apathy in his 1952 article "Political Participation and Apathy," he identified two primary reasons why Americans often failed to participate actively in political deliberation. One reason is that voting and civic action are not mandatory. No legal entity compels us to vote. Another reason, according to Gans, is that the average American "is not emotionally involved in any aspect of the political process which would motivate him in any way to be actively interested in it" (277). Gans's response to this problem is a familiar one: show people why they should be emotionally involved. Fight apathy by exploiting those points of personal impact. Show where and how political questions affect you on a personal level. Make politics "hit home."

However, I argue that this version of the public versus nonpublic subject involves a misunderstanding. Even though this figure does not actively participate in the debates and deliberations that have emerged about public crises, it is not helpful to think about the nonparticipant as separate from the polis. Instead, we are better off thinking about multiple forms of public subjectivity, one of which includes the "apathetic" public subject. Although boredom almost registers as a lack of feeling, the experience of boredom can be redescribed as an actively produced emotion. Boredom, like the more passionate feelings of joy and excitement, are all part of what Kathleen Stewart calls "ordinary affects." Stewart states that emotions are "public feelings that begin and end in broad circulation, but they're also the stuff that seemingly intimate lives are made of. They can be experienced as a pleasure and a shock, as an empty pause or a dragging undertow, as a sensibility that snaps into place or a profound disorientation" (*Ordinary* 2). Boredom is a mode of being-in-the-world that actually does a great deal of work as an interface between subject and world. Boredom, even when experienced as an empty pause, is no different than any emotion that helps us to orient to our immediate surroundings.

Even our feelings about place are incredibly powerful means of orienting to that place. Phenomenologists of place and space have shown us how feelings shape our understanding or knowledge of certain places. "Space that has been seized upon by the imagination cannot remain indifferent space subject to the measures and estimates of the surveyor," writes Gaston Bachelard in *The Poetics of Space*. "It has been lived in, not in its positivity, but with all the partiality of the imagination" (xxxvi). Or, as urban studies scholar Helen Liggett mentions in relation to place and space, "Learning how to feel about urban space is to make urban space" (24). That is, affective states—the prick of anxiety, the drag of boredom, or an intense feeling of apathy—puts us in a mood and attitude in relation to places. These attitudinal lenses become another mediating apparatus about how we come to "know" the world around us.[3]

But why does this affective feeling become the grounds of publicness? Why is it that one's own measurement of public subjectivity is grounded in the experience of feeling? There are two good answers to this question. The first answer is simply that all thinking and rhetorical orientation is grounded in pathos. Ernesto Grassi argues that rational, or primary, speech is itself derivative from an affective realm. Rational discourse depends upon tracing back various claims to their prior principles, a process we have come to call the demonstrative process of rational discourse. Yet the demonstration of prior principles within logical/rational discourse does not itself rest on ultimate principles. "It is clear that the first *archai* of any proof and hence of knowledge cannot be proved themselves because they cannot be the object of . . . demonstrative, logical speech; otherwise they would not be first assertions," Grassi argues (19). Primary principles cannot be proven via the same process of demonstration that they ground.

This leaves philosophical and rational speech in a bit of a bind. "If the original assertions are not demonstrable," asks Grassi, "what is the character of speech in which we express them? Obviously this type of speech cannot have a rational-theoretical character" (19). In response, Grassi argues that the first principles, or *archai*, are instead indicative or allusive, not rational. That is, the first principles cannot be proven, but they can be evoked, revealed, and conjured by a nonrational sense. As Grassi continues, "we are forced to admit that the primal clarity of the principles is not rational and recognize that the corresponding language in its indicative structure has an 'evangelic' character, in the original Greek sense of this word, i.e., 'noticing'" (20). If the most originary of principles cannot be proven (for if it could, it would no longer be an originary principle), then it can only be disclosed in a kind of revelation. Grassi explains that it is only through a kind of pathetic framework that (quasi-)rational choice is able to take hold in the first place.

Following this logic, we might conclude that "feeling" as a measurement of public orientation is not avoidable. Insofar as all thinking is grounded in feeling, then the very idea that I have no rational stake in a crisis must begin with the feeling of remoteness and detachment. In a different version of this argument, Martha Nussbaum suggests that emotions are cognitive, insofar as they contain a thought about their objects (*Upheavals* 26–28). Even emotional states like diffidence or apathy would be directed toward certain thoughts and evaluations about the object, scene, or crisis at hand. While Nussbaum is far from Grassi, her argument also makes it reasonable to conclude that the experience of feeling is intimately tied to one's own role as a public subject, even if that subject appears to be MIA from the scene of deliberation.

Another explanation for why one's measurement of publicness is tied to feeling is that the rise of postindustrial capitalism has created an affective subject. Although Fredric Jameson argues that a postmodern depthlessness, or "the waning of affect," has replaced self-present feeling and emotional expression, many cultural theorists have recently taken issue with Jameson's assertions. Brian Massumi, for example, argues that we are experiencing not a waning of affect but a surfeit: "Affect has been deterritorialized, uprooted from spatiotemporal coordinates in which it naturally occurs and allowed to circulate" (*Users Guide* 135). Furthermore, writes Massumi, "affect is central to an understanding of our information- and image-based late capitalist culture" (*Parables* 27). In fact, Massumi identifies one key emotion—fear—as an organizing force in everyday life under capitalism. There is nothing to fear but fear itself: the pressure is always beyond reach, beyond target range. Massumi explains, "The enemy is not simply indefinite (masked, or at a hidden location). In the infinity of its here-and-to-come, it is elsewhere, by nature. It is humanly ungraspable" ("Everywhere" 11). The "general threats" of late capital fear do not identify "predicates expressing a property of the substantive to which they apply," Massumi continues. "What they express is a mode. . . . Fear is not fundamentally an emotion. It is the objectivity of the subjective under late capitalism" ("Everywhere" 12). In short, to be a subject under late capitalism is to live out this generalized anxiety. To lack fear would be a sign of ultimate naïveté that is only possible for preemergent subjects: children, sociopaths, and the delusional.

These are just two possible explanations for why public subjectivity is grounded in the experience of feeling, and I find both of them compelling. Regardless of the explanation, I am persuaded that feeling has become a measurement of our publicness. Or, to put it a bit differently, feeling has become a primary means of orienting oneself to the world. By making this point, I am not attempting to revisit the old binary between feeling/rationality. To say that one of today's key public subjectivities is grounded in feeling is not to deny that we have ever been anything but feeling beings. However, I am less interested in ontological questions of subjectivity than I am in the question of how we come to think of ourselves as beings that exist in relation to others. That is, I am interested in certain modes of encountering and interacting with others.

If the first question can be called ontological, then the other question might be called a matter of rhetorical engagement. We can affirm the ways that, ontologically speaking, we are thinking-feeling beings all the way down.[4] We can simultaneously affirm that feeling is one way we encounter and interact with others. This certainly seems to be the case in public discourse surrounding Susette Kelo's little pink house. Kelo, her detractors, and her supporters encountered each other through the medium of feeling. Kelo's own measure of publicness was judged according to the kinds of feelings she produced and how authentic those feelings seemed to be. As a rhetorical critic, I am interested in questioning whether or not this mode of encounter and interaction is the only one possible. My *telos* in this book is to suggest that it is not. Although we cannot change the fact that human consciousness is as much emotional as it is rational, we can transform the ways we encounter and interact with others.

Just 'Cause You Feel It, Doesn't Mean It's There?

Two problematic self-understandings of publicness emerge. First, and perhaps most obvious, are the reified links between feeling and action that are justified in a powerful way. Bad feelings have long served as a pretext for action and intervention. Starving children, landmine victims who are missing legs, displaced hurricane victims, homeless families struggling to survive, abused dogs with chain marks permanently embedded in their skin. Hearing their stories is like a call to arms. Emotions like sadness, sympathy, and compassion wash over us and perhaps even move us to donate money to whatever cause is sending these images in the first place. However, Ahmed points out that the relationships created by this situation are complicated. We do not simply feel sadness alongside these figures, as if in some kind of real solidarity or attunement with their emotional life. "Rather," writes Ahmed, "we feel sad about their suffering, an 'aboutness' that ensures that they remain the object of 'our feeling'" (21). When that object no longer makes us feel that particular aboutness, the relationship is also likely to change. Stories of communities' healing, joy, happiness become a new object of our feeling: we feel content about what seems to be their own happiness. We are not called to action because the aboutness does not seem to urge us into action. I feel good about their feeling; everything is fine. This is the most obvious explanation for why donations to desperate causes drop off once "good news" begins spreading about relief efforts.

The links between feeling about someone's feeling and a legitimate call to action were certainly in play during the Kelo case. Detractors openly questioned whether Susette Kelo truly cared about her house—was her sadness real?—as a way to also question whether or not her acts were legitimate. If she did not truly care for her little pink house, then she had no real exigence (beyond personal greed) for her public campaign against the New London plans. The critics were drawing on what Ahmed calls "aboutness" where others' feelings are concerned. Not only is Kelo "tugging at our emotional heartstrings," but she has no right to be bitter. Critics linked Kelo's "false" feelings to a particularly odious rhetorical exigence: greed. She did not want to save her house from eminent domain out of true love, but out of selfishness or even an opportunity to make some fast money. What seems to yoke this articulation together is a deeply ingrained relationship between one body's capacity to generate feelings of aboutness, and the legitimation of a public's call to action. If Kelo's feelings were false, thereby "tugging at our emotional heartstrings," then the public was falsely called into action against a citywide plan for economic recovery. The aboutness her story created among sympathetic readers was not authentic, or so goes the anti-Kelo criticism.

One serious problem with this articulation is that feeling easily becomes a substitute for action. That is, feeling becomes both the evidence of and the actual activity of public relationality. Feeling angry is not a prelude to action; it is the action itself. Consider the recent political revival of compassion. While the phrase "compassionate conservatives" sparked innumerable jokes, critiques, and analyses, two things can reasonably be argued: (1) the concept is paradoxical on its face, and (2) the concept resonated for many people. The concept is paradoxical insofar as compassion for poverty and social inequalities would seem to call for massive structural changes in the system that created such conditions in the first place. Conservatism, however, seeks to uphold many of these structures in a status quo that would only extend how inequalities are produced. At the same time, the concept of compassionate conservatism does ask its adherents to do one thing: feel something about those who are suffering.

In George W. Bush's own White House "fact sheet" defining compassionate conservatism, the former president announces that this new "approach of hope and optimism will make a real difference in people's lives" ("Fact Sheet"). At the same time, no significant government intervention accompanies this philosophy. "The policies of our government must heed the universal call of all faiths to love our neighbors as we would want to be loved ourselves. We are using an active government to promote self-government," explains Bush enigmatically. The new philosophy of compassionate conservatism resonates so well with conservatives because it substitutes material, structural changes to American society (more "big government") with the experience of loving, hoping, and feeling good about the lives of others. Furthermore, as Kathleen Woodward writes, the compassion of "compassionate conservatism" may not actually reflect any emotional depth. Rather, Woodward argues that the compassion called upon by Bush and other conservatives is more like a burst of "short-term intensity," like the thrills and chills you might feel when watching a good action movie (62). The intensity itself thus becomes the substitution for any real structural change.

Secondly, insofar as the true public subject of feeling is grounded primarily in the experience of feeling, then feelings of distance (or disinterest, apathy, boredom) about public issues also serve as a means of public orientation. We must remember that emotions are all relational. Feeling towardness and awayness both contain the affective relationality that counts as what we call feeling. Apathy or withdrawal is not an empty cipher. Feeling a relation is the very beginning of public orientation. To connect publicness with a feeling about one's relation to crisis leaves open the possibility that feeling nothing is how one kind of public subject comes into being. Feeling subjects always already are public subjects.

Even ostensibly unengaged citizens do not suffer from a lack of public orientation any more than they suffer from a lack of feeling. Their role as public subject is not simply an empty cipher. Earlier I argued that public subjectivity is characterized by a relation to claims about public crises, and attendant feelings about that relation. More specifically, technologies and techniques help to produce this imagined relationship and our feelings about it. In national conversations about eminent domain, perhaps people feel distant from the claims and discourses because they are renters in a fairly stable neighborhood. Perhaps eminent domain feels neither helpful nor harmful to them. Or perhaps details about the issue simply feel boring. Instead of marking those feeling of distance as a lack, I suggest that we should instead recognize them as a materially produced form of public subjectivity. That is, feeling distant from conflicts and public scenes of crisis is another mode of public subjectification. By orienting to the public world through feeling, subjects can therefore legitimate withdrawal or distance as a public orientation.[5]

Both the participant and the nonparticipant are in a relation to claims about public crisis. Moreover, both experience some kind of feeling about that relation, even if the nonparticipant experiences a feeling of not being proximate. If the feeling self has become the "true self," as Berlant suggests, then the self who feels distant from public crisis is no less oriented toward the public scene. Simply by feeling (whether compassion, sympathy, outrage, care), I have become part of a wider public. Production of feeling in relation to public claims thus becomes a mode of creating legitimate public subjects. As critics, we may ask who benefits from this production of an exceptional public subject. Is there a governing apparatus that is sustained by such subjectivity? Who benefits from a subjectivity grounded in the "true feeling" that Berlant describes? One obvious answer is that a status quo of power structures benefits, especially where issues of development and place-change is concerned. Another answer is that those who produce feeling (those who can generate and manipulate affect) are obviously served by a grounding of public subjectivity in such feeling.[6] For good reason, therefore, we should find the motivation to investigate the rhetorical technologies and techniques of production where public subjectivity is concerned.

Spaces of Exception

In chapter 1, I argued that we need to encourage public subjects who are able to address the changes happening within our everyday spaces, make ethical judgments about those changes, and work toward rebuilding public spaces for discourse. Yet, I also stated that we are cultivating subjects who are not oriented toward sustainable intervention. That is, the public subject of feeling is not the most productive role to take up such work. But why not? What prevents this mode of public orientation, grounded as it is in feeling, from being capable of making strong rhetorical interventions? The short answer is that today's key public subjectivity creates a space of exclusion that allows subjects to remain "publicly oriented" while also being distanced from the kind of rhetorical gestures necessary for sustainable interventions. For example, consider the gaps between citizens' actual participatory engagement and the still popular ideals of participation. Although voter registration is shockingly low (and actual voter participation even lower), an overwhelming majority of nonvoters tell pollsters that voting is an important civic and community act.[7]

This disjunction was vividly illustrated in my Rhetorical Theory course last semester when I asked students if they regularly read any news media or listen to any kind of news program. Only three students out of nineteen raised their hands. Later in this same class period, during a conversation about the public sphere and participation, students turned critical toward "apathetic" and "indifferent" citizens. One student voiced her disgust with people who do not follow current events, yet none of the students stopped to consider their own lack of engagement with news media.

What might allow disjunctions like these to be smoothed over? For one thing, many people do not see themselves as outside the polis. Rather than reading scenes like these as examples of paradoxical or even inconsistent positions, I suggest that there is actually a rhetorical apparatus at work that makes these disjunctive positions feel perfectly consistent. The theory of a true public subject of feeling helps to explain this disjunction. As I explain above, the experience of feeling, even if it is the feeling of distance, is one way public subjectivity is produced. Nonparticipating citizens do not lack positions of agency within public discourse, in spite of what they may claim. Their agency is not missing. Though nonparticipating subjects are perhaps playing an unsavory role, one that we should discourage from proliferating, these subject positions read themselves into the rhetorical act no less than antidevelopment activists who are aware of their agency.

The complexities of agency within seemingly apolitical or nonparticipatory discourse are well illustrated by Jennifer Seibel Trainor's research into racism among white college students. Trainor examines typical sentiments among some white students who are confronted by questions of race. One particularly interesting sentiment that Trainor explores is the argument that because "my ancestors didn't own slaves," issues of racism are irrelevant to me. I have heard versions of this same argument from my own students. As Trainor writes, this sentiment can be seen as a way for students to absolve themselves from current debates about racism and the effects of racial injustice in the United States. Perhaps this is the most obvious reading of such sentiments, and it was certainly my interpretation when I first heard a student verbalize it in response to an essay by bell hooks. As we began to discuss hooks's essay in class, one student angrily asked why she should even be expected to comment on such an essay about the legacy of racism. She declared that her family never owned slaves and that she hated the very idea of racism. So, when hooks critiques the toxic legacy of American race relations, "she's definitely not talking about me."

At first, the notion that one's own family had "no part" in the legacy of racism appears to be a withdrawal of agency. When my student explained that her family never owned slaves—and that she herself is not a racist—I heard her as articulating a kind of willful passivity regarding the ongoing crisis of racism. Indeed, she refused to respond to hooks at all, since she was "not responsible" for the cultural conditions hooks identified. However, Trainor suggests that this sentiment does not (merely) reflect a withdrawal of agency. Her research suggests that it is also "a way of connecting with people of color, a way of expressing, ironically, racial solidarity, by suggesting that they are on the 'right' side. . . . The claim that 'my ancestors didn't own slaves' taps a world where differences between oppressor and oppressed groups are eradicated by the claims of family" (146–47). This sentiment is equally problematic, of course. And it is still possible to read these claims as an abdication of responsibility from ongoing debates. However, Trainor's careful analysis reflects something more complicated about agency in this scene: the student is not refusing a position within the crisis, but she is instead actively articulating a position that is othered from the "real" oppressors. Trainor suggests that apolitical subjects may not be as removed from the polis—especially in their own perceptions—as we think.

Another way to complicate the divisions between participants/nonparticipants, political/apolitical, public/private, or agentive/passive is by rethinking the traditional opposition between democratic deliberation and political apathy. Jeffrey E. Green suggests that the opposition between engagement and apathy implies a misunderstanding of democracy's fundamental egalitarianism. Green challenges the popular sentiment that apathy and nonparticipation are largely the result of domination and political oppression. In fact, Green argues that political apathy can actually be seen as "a democratic phenomenon that emerges out of the very egalitarian principles whose full proliferation it simultaneously restricts" (749). He turns to several examples from ancient Greece to uncover this strange affinity between apathy and democracy. Green argues that the ancients did not necessarily hold apathy in stark opposition to political participation. Indeed, for the ancients, "political apathy was understood as a specifically democratic mode of being-in-the-world" (749). This odd claim is grounded in the understanding of democracy as defined through egalitarianism: a democratic subject was one whose self emerged through an array of equal possibilities.

Green points to Achilles' political apathy in Homer's *Iliad* as an example. In book 9, Achilles has pronounced a disdain for battling in order to win glory, honor, and personal distinction. He refuses to return to the battlefield, instead spending his days playing the lyre and making perfunctory plans to return to Phthia. When called upon to explain his apathy toward public and political life, Achilles explains that his chosen fate is no better or worse than the fate of a warrior. "An equal fate to the one who stays behind as to the one who struggles well," explains Achilles. "In a single honor are held both the low and the high" (9.318–20). Both kinds of men will face death in the end; the final fate is exactly the same. Green reads this moment as an example of how the egalitarian ethos flattens all kinds of action into a single expression of personal fate. Achilles muses on the equality of all action; it makes no real difference, then, what form of action one man chooses. The egalitarian self is one who chooses among many possibilities for being-in-the-world, including the possibility of being the one who stays behind. Or, to put it differently, staying behind does not preclude one from living fully within the egalitarian ethos. Green's analysis suggests that the language of democracy actually cultivates the political nonparticipant through a principle of egalitarianism. Within democracy, all actions are (supposedly) equally available to every person. The fact that we are not compelled to choose is a hallmark of democracy, yet this lack of force also flattens our fullest range of possibilities. Green argues that the apathetic subject is an effect of the very discourse it seems to counteract.[8]

Although the anachronism of discussing Homer's Achilles as democratically minded may make this scene a poor example, Green's analysis prompts us to rethink our typical remedies for the nonparticipant. Calling for "more democracy talk" is not enough to transform an Achilles-like figure from apathetic to participant. The cure, in essence, is killing us. Increasing "emotional involvement" is not necessarily the best response to political nonparticipation, since the nonparticipating subject is already cultivated through a kind of involvement. Of course, traditional responses to political apathy have called upon this precise recommendation for more involvement, more investment, more care. Consider such anti-apathy calls like the Generation X "Rock the Vote" campaign or the popular bumper sticker ostensibly quoting Mahatma Gandhi's line that "You must be the change you wish to see in the world." Each of these admonitions teaches the central lesson of public orientation: you can become a public subject by feeling invested and relevant to the scene of public deliberation. However, because any feeling is an orientation device, then any feeling about public issues becomes a means of interfacing with(in) the public sphere. Feeling distant may create an undesirable public subject, of course. Yet, we cannot overlook the important point that this feeling legitimates public subjects. In other words, encouraging the apathetic, distant subject to "be a public subject" is redundant. This complex figure has not failed to answer the call of the polis, but he or she actually inhabits its discourse.

There is good reason, therefore, to conclude that apathy is not a lack of pathos. Daniel M. Gross suggests that apathy is more than ground zero of emotion. Gross traces the history of apathy's vilification as a "condition of moral depravity, a defiant retreat from the world of God and humankind" (51). However, Gross turns to the Stoics in order to reframe apathy as an emotional state that is actively produced through social action, as well as one that actively produces the social. The fear of irrational political passions led the Stoics to advance apathy as a sound approach to political crisis. Stoic views imply that apathy is a kind of response to social conditions. Similarly, other scholars suggest that it is possible to see apathy as a political response to the fragmented and nonrepresentative character of the public sphere. Susan Wells writes, "Cynicism, distrust of politics, even apathy, are neither moral failings nor signs of a romantic (or postmodern) political innocence; they are strategies for addressing a public that no longer supports the illusion of organic integrity" ("Rogue Cops" 333). In other words, apathy is a kind of response to the political possibilities that seem to exist in the public sphere. It is, therefore, its own kind of political position.

What we see developing is a kind of doubled space where public subjectivity is concerned. There is a kind of simultaneous inside and outside that is being inhabited by these subjects. This doubled space recalls what theorists like Carl Schmitt and Giorgio Agamben have dubbed a "state of exception." Schmitt originally outlined the state of exception in his writing on sovereignty, which is a juridical concept for Schmitt and those who extend his work. His infamous statement declares, "Sovereign is he who decides on the exception" (5), which is to say that the sovereign is one who can stand apart from the system that he is part of. As Agamben puts it in *Homo Sacer,* "The paradox of sovereignty consists in the fact the sovereign is, at the same time, outside and inside the juridical order" (15). He is simultaneously a part of and apart from this order. One of my favorite examples of the state of exception came from a picture my friend took of a sign taped to a glass door at DePaul University.[9] The sign simply read: "Please do not post flyers on the glass." But, of course, the sign announcing the rule was already breaking this rule. The irony doesn't amount to much, since everyone would recognize that the handwritten sign exists in a state of exception. It is simultaneously outside and inside the judicial order (against posting signs on the door).

As Agamben makes clear, the exceptional sovereign is not in opposition to the order. Nor does the exception remove the sovereign subject from a relation to that order. Agamben writes:

> The exception is a kind of exclusion. What is excluded from the general rule is an individual case. But the most proper characteristic of the exception is that what is excluded in it is not, on account of being excluded,

> absolutely without relation to the rule. On the contrary, what is excluded in the exception maintains itself in relation to the rule in the form of the rule's suspension. The rule applies to the exception in no longer applying, in withdrawing from it. . . . In this sense, the exception is truly, according to its etymological root, taken outside (*ex-capere*), and not simply excluded. (*Homo Sacer* 17–18)

This is an important point. In the case of the sign, while the paper itself is an exception to the rule, it is not unrelated to the rule. It is not opposed to the rule, but is related to the rule by virtue of being outside of it. In this case, outside is not a binary to anything inside. Just as an easement on the side of a house can be said to be both outside and inside, so too are the exception and the order held in a kind of mutual relation.[10]

Agamben shows that being outside is not the same as being unrelated. In fact, the outside has an immanent relationship with the inside. They mutually define each other. Agamben goes on to describe this state as the "relation of exception," or the "extreme form of relation by which something is included solely through its exclusion" (*Homo Sacer* 18). As I argue above, the link that holds together this mutual relation is the work of feeling-politics. We feel our way toward towardness with others and with world, and we feel our way toward awayness with others and with world. The exceptional subject is one who is related to the public through a feeling of awayness just as much as towardness. Likewise, the nonparticipating subject is not opposed to the obvious public subject, or one who is clearly participating in discursive exchanges over public issues. This kind of exceptional subject maintains a relation to the polis by being withdrawn from it. More specifically, the public subject within an exceptional space (or what I am calling an exceptional subject) maintains this relationship through the act of feeling. The public subject is taken outside (*ex-capere*) the practical realm of the polis, though they still retain an important form of relationality. The exceptional subject is not opposed to public life but is a mode of public life.

Distant Publics and Exceptional Techniques

One of the things that a concept of exceptional subjects challenges is a distinction between private and public subjects. The "private" life of the *idios* is not truly private, but neither is the "public" life of an actively engaged citizen without relation to a space of distance. Ironically, we often set up the problem of rhetorical engagement as one of (re)turning the *idios kosmos* back to the *koine kosmos*. We remain steeped in the distinction, so beautifully imagined by Heraclitus, between the dreamer's world and the waking body's world. Science fiction writer Philip K. Dick likewise makes this distinction in his meditation on the schizophrenic, who is locked deeply within a private world with no ability to reach a *koinos kosmos*. According to Dick, human development is a process of slowly waking to a common world:

> In many species of life forms, such as the grazing animals, a newborn individual is more or less thrust out into the *koinos kosmos* (the shared world) immediately. For a lamb or a pony, the *idios kosmos* (the personal world) ceases when the first light hits his eyes—but a human child, at birth, still has years of a kind of semireal existence ahead of him: semireal in the sense that until he is fifteen or sixteen years old . . . fragments of the *idios kosmos* remain, and not all or even very much of the *koinos kosmos* has been forced onto him as yet. (175)

Dick's observations recall the self-absorption that most children possess until a degree of maturity takes place. Socializing children is a process of teaching them to understand that their actions have consequences in a shared world. When my toddler daughter shoves another child on the playground, the tears of her victim do not register very strongly. She is mostly concerned with her private universe, including her own feelings of frustration and relief. Yet, as a mature adult, I hope that she will inhabit a *koinos kosmos*, where she recognizes that her actions profoundly impact others. In a civic context, the figure of the *idios* is one who also lacks an ability to fully engage a *koinos kosmos*. He is more interested in his own feelings, events, and experiences than in the common purposes of public life.

The idiot haunts civic activists and scholars alike. Robert Putnam's popular book *Bowling Alone* tracks the emergence of an *idios kosmos* and the sad demise of a shared world: "Without at first noticing," writes Putnam, "we have been pulled apart from one another and from our communities over the last third of the [twentieth] century" (27). Whatever the reason, it seems clear to many rhetorical scholars that civic discourse is not what it used to be. In short, writes Lauren Berlant, the public sphere—our arena of citizenship's enactment—has gone up in smoke. There is no more "context of communication and debate that makes ordinary citizens feel that they have a common public culture" (*Queen of America* 3). Instead, Berlant continues, what has replaced a shared world is an intimate public sphere comprising innumerable private lives on display for mass consumption. The intimate public sphere turns citizenship into a collection of simultaneous private worlds. Public discourse has been displaced by idiocy.

Questions about how to remedy the political and rhetorical nonparticipant repeatedly emerge in our field because rhetorical studies has an unusually powerful commitment to repairing and strengthening public discourse.[11]

In both theoretical and pedagogical scholarship, the ends of such research ask the same colossal questions: How do we encourage a revitalization of the public sphere, and how do we encourage individuals to imagine themselves as practicing with a common purpose? How do we help students to think and act as part of a polis? I also want to take up these questions, especially where public crises like the ones presented by urban development are concerned. How do we help to cultivate subjects who imagine themselves in strong roles that seek sustainable interventions into place crises?

However, my own response does not begin from a traditional split between public and private subjects, or between the *idios kosmos* and the *koine kosmos*. Though political nonparticipants do indeed appear to be their own private persons, I do not see these figures primarily defined by a lack of engagement with the polis. The line between private (*idios*) and public (*koine*) is blurrier than we might imagine. Even where public discourse about rhetorical exigencies does exist, where people are acting as participants, we find public subjects whose orientation to the public is primarily mediated through feeling. The feeling-full mediation still creates a simultaneous relation and withdrawal where rhetorical intervention is concerned.

One of our jobs as rhetorical critics and teachers is to help cultivate public subjects who are capable of using the communicative moment in order to change "technologized conditions of our own making but not necessarily to our liking," to use Tarla Rai Peterson's words. My argument is that this job cannot be accomplished well if we fail to rethink what public subjectivity is and how it has been created. If we cling to the belief that our primary problem is getting private people to act more publicly, then we have already missed an opportunity to understand how public orientation today often exists in this complex space of exception.

The exceptional subject and the space of exception can help to explain why unsustainable national trends like big box stores, sprawling suburbs, and overdeveloped housing tracts show no signs of slowing, even though many people object. And, at the same time, this figure offers insight into why more people do not feel compelled to intervene in the changes that are happening in their own neighborhoods and cities. By understanding the exceptional subject, we may be able to understand how today's key public subjectivity allows us to remain actively and productively distanced from intervention, while never being outside of its discourse. In the next three chapters, we will take a close-up look at how such distance is cultivated through common patterns of vernacular talk.

3

Vultures and Kooks
THE RHETORIC OF INJURY CLAIMS

> Ample evidence suggests that current debates regarding injury . . . are far from exceptional.
> —Carl Scott Gutiérrez-Jones, *Critical Race Narrative*

On June 7, 1990, an unusual thing happened in Austin. Hundreds of people crammed into a small place in order to listen to an all-night string of musicians, poets, and regular citizens talk about the beauty and sacredness of Austin's natural swimming hole, Barton Springs. Normally this kind of all-night jam session wouldn't go down in the history books, except for the fact that this one took place in the Austin City Council chambers at a regularly scheduled city council hearing. During the marathon thirteen-hour meeting, hundreds of citizens spoke about the contentious vote council members were about to make. At issue was a four-thousand-acre "planned unit development" (PUD) deep in the hills of Austin. The huge planned development—to be named Circle C Ranch—was designed as an all-inclusive community. Circle C Ranch would not only build neighborhoods but also its own schools, country clubs, and shopping areas. Original plans sketched out approximately 2,500 homes, 1,900 apartments, 3.3 million square feet of commercial space, and three golf courses. The PUD planners were not too concerned about getting past city council, since Circle C Ranch's developers believed that they had all city council votes in their favor.

Yet, the land that would eventually become Circle C Ranch also sits on top of Edwards Aquifer, which supplies Austin's water and its natural springs. The most visible and beloved part of the aquifer is Barton Springs, a natural swimming hole that has been Austin's public gathering place for many generations. Opponents of the Circle C Ranch plans feared that runoff and pollution from the development would irreparably harm the fragile aquifer and destroy the beloved springs. To understand the exigence among Austinites, you must first understand that Barton Springs is no ordinary place. It is a spring-fed pool that has been special to local people for centuries. The pool was constructed in the early 1900s when a free-flowing spring was dammed. The cool, clear water in the one-thousand-foot-long pool is sixty-eight degrees year round. Limestone rocks add incredible beauty, and diehard Barton Springs lovers swim in the cool water throughout the year. Texas writers Frank Dobie, Walter Prescott Webb, and Roy Bedichek famously held daily talks there in the early twentieth century, and Robert Redford even learned to swim in Barton Springs' natural waters when visiting Austin as a child (Dunn).

Over seven hundred people signed up to speak in the council chambers on that hot Texas evening. At one o'clock in the morning, when exhausted city council members announced that they would cut off testimony and call for a vote, the crowd demanded that every speaker have a chance to testify. "Let us speak! Let us speak!" came the shouts. After the crowd refused to disperse, the council allowed the meeting to continue for several more hours. Chants came from the street, and passing cars honked their support (Collier, "Developers" A1). The lobby door's hinges even broke that evening from being opened and closed so many times. Longtime Austin activist Mary Arnold recalls her experience that night: "I can remember going to that all-night public hearing and sitting next to two members of the Austin Symphony Orchestra. So it wasn't just the rag-tag people who didn't get off their job at the bar until two a.m. that came down. But it was also people from very much the mainstream who were concerned about the quality of life in our community" (Arnold). Protesters sang, pleaded, shouted, and performed all through the night until sunrise. The unusual meeting was covered by all local media, and the issues of development were suddenly thrust into the spotlight across Austin.

In the months before and after the initial city council vote, arguments against the Circle C Ranch emerged in a number of ways, ranging from a critique of corporate interests to concerns about environmental damage. Developers responded by claiming their own interest in bringing maximum benefit to a majority of Austinites. They countered protests by showing that Circle C would benefit all Austin residents in multiple ways. These counterclaims, of course, were met with skepticism by protesters. While all kinds of claims and counterclaims circulated in this public debate, one rhetorical commonplace ran throughout many of these exchanges. I call this commonplace a discourse of "injury claims," since it is mostly defined by the way it positions rhetors as injured by anyone who challenges their position.

Injury claims are well-worn patterns of response from both pro- and antidevelopment forces. Although we may see these exchanges as "just talk," it is important to remember that talk is the very substance through which publics come to be formed. As vernacular rhetoric, exchanges like these form a "network of associations from which and in which a communally sustained consciousness of common meanings are developed and enriched" (Hauser, *Vernacular* 34). We may also read these exchanges as a mode of production, or what Ronald Walter Greene calls techniques and technologies of production, for public subjectivities (44). While the bulk of my study traces explicit exchanges between people engaged in injury claims, I want to keep in mind the larger question of how this discourse enables people both to participate and to write themselves out of participation.

In order to explore the rhetorical operation of these claims, I trace their patterns in two different situations. One situation is the local debate over Circle C Ranch's massive planned community in Austin and how competing claims of injury dialectically produce a "site" of public feelings and their management. This site encourages certain modes of public orientation over others. The other situation I explore in this chapter reflects a national debate about a different kind of mass development: the ubiquitous big box store. In this case, I scan national conversations about Walmart's presence in nearly every corner of the country (and beyond). My goal is to uncover how the dialectical work of injury claims and counterclaims help to cultivate a space of exception where public subjects are concerned.

Someday You'll be Sorry: Circle C Ranch

Jim Bob Moffett, the chief executive officer of Circle C's development corporation, is what many people think of when they think of Texans. Moffett is a former University of Texas football star with a thick Texas accent and a penchant for folksy sayings. During the all-night city council hearing, Moffett approached the microphone in a room that was clearly against him. His usual folksy manner turned serious as he addressed city council members: "I came onto this campus at the University of Texas in 1956 as a young boy from Houston," he began. Moffett recalled his days as a football star, but quickly got heckled from audience members. His face turned into an annoyed grimace and he moved back to the issue under question. "I got a bachelor of science degree in geology with honors.... And as a *geologist*," he stressed the word emphatically, "I promise you that I know more about Barton Creek than anybody in this room. We come out of the blocks with zero degradation. It's the other people who have septic tanks and run cows in the creek who are causing the problem."[1] His testimony was peppered with jabs and jeers from an unreceptive audience.

Moffett ended his angry testimony, and a gentler figure took the microphone. This was Robert Dedman, a real estate developer for Circle C Ranch. In contrast to Jim Bob Moffett's irritated tone, Dedman almost seemed conciliatory. He calmly addressed the council members: "You are talking to people who have a lot of heart. But we also have a lot of heart and a lot of emotion in it. And for anybody to suggest that we're not out here to save Barton Creek is a tremendous fallacy. We have more reasons to do it than anybody." The room was overflowing with opponents who openly challenged Dedman's words, yet he continued undeterred. "We're the best thing that could conceivably happen to Barton Creek and Barton Springs." Later, Austin Chamber of Commerce representative Michelle O'Reilly faced the hostile crowd. The chamber of commerce had been a major supporter of the PUD. Her voice was nervous as she spoke. "We do love Barton Creek," she began. As she paused nervously to take a breath, someone in the crowd shouted, "*But?*" The audience broke into mocking laughter and taunted her with shouts of "But?" O'Reilly smiled and continued, "But we urge reason and balance when considering this matter. Barton Creek is important in marketing the city of Austin. It's an important symbol to the city of Austin." Through a chorus of jeers and boos, the pro-development witnesses repeatedly took the microphone to argue that Circle C Ranch would not only protect Barton Springs, but it would also enhance the life of the city as a whole.

Circle C supporters did not sway the hundreds of antidevelopment speakers during the council hearing. One young man took the microphone and pointed at the Circle C representatives. "They're against Barton Springs," he said, "the people who want to do this. If you're free from the influence of developers and lobbyists, this is your chance to show it." Throughout the night, people spoke of the Circle C development as an almost criminal act. Jim Bob Moffett and his crew were clearly cast as the bad guys who were standing toe-to-toe with the proverbial little guys. When Austin activist Bill Bunch stood up to speak, he warned the council members, "Do not be an ac-

Standing room only at the Austin City Council hearing over the Circle C Ranch development. Copyright Alan Pogue, 1990.

complice to the death of Barton Creek. Do not be an accomplice to the death of Barton Springs." Local singer Shannon Sedgwick took the microphone to sing a bluesy protest tune written especially for the meeting. "Someday you'll be sorry when Barton's blue turns brown / It will have cost us a river, lost us a river / Don't let the people of Austin down / Run those developers out of town." The crowd cheered at this last line, simply one more testimony to Jim Bob Moffett's unpopularity. Protesters spilled onto the sidewalks outside. They held protest signs saying, "Go home, Jim Bob" and "Your golf course is killing Barton Creek!" Finally, at six o'clock in the morning, the council unanimously voted against the PUD.

The events of that historic meeting became a main topic of conversation in Austin for many months. Moffett and Dedman criticized the protesters, whom they characterized as a small band of special interest group members. Moffett told the *Austin American-Statesman* that the protesters were "just as bad as any un-American activity that's ever been carried on in this country" (Collier, "Barton Creek" A1). Dedman's assessment was slightly more tempered, but equally as dismissive of the protest's significance. He explained that the crowd did not truly represent the real soul of Austin. "It would be devastating for Austin if it was," he said. The Circle C developers were undaunted by their initial defeat, and they publicly laughed away the actions of what Dedman called "a few kooks" who were led by their emotions. As Moffett bitterly summed up, "These guys were venting their spleen against the system. There are people who just don't like Fortune 500 companies and guys in suits and ties" (Collier, "Developers" A1).

As unapologetic as Jim Bob Moffett was about being a developer in a suit and tie, the protesters were equally as unapologetic about fighting his plans. Some of the most dramatic responses to the Circle C plan were the anticorporate citizen letters to Austin's local newspapers. Many critics suggested that the planned community's only interest was profitability, and the developers were primarily motivated by greed and selfishness. Just days before the city council meeting, resident Gioconda Bellonci wrote a letter that sums up this anticorporate sentiment: "Quite simply, Barton Creek and Barton Springs are the heart and soul of Austin. To consider even risking (more) pollution by developing further on Barton Creek is nothing less than evil. I'd like to challenge the developers to exchange their business suits for swimming suits and their focus on the greedy bottom line to the visions one can only enjoy in the clear, pure water of Barton Springs. I certainly hope that the (old) council will vote no to the 4,000-acre Estates on Barton Creek project at the June 7 council meeting" (Bellonci A6). Responses like Bellonci's reflect a moral reading of the development. Several letters even went as far as casting Jim Bob Moffett and fellow developers as "evil," since their goal seemed to be pure profit. The accusations became so overwhelming in the days following the PUD's defeat that an attorney and representative for Circle C Ranch, David Armbrust, publicly objected to being called an "evil person" by people who did not know him (Collier, "Developers"). But residents like Steven Uteley refused to apologize for their harsh words: "Mr. Armbrust reveals not only that he, too, is 'very disappointed' by the outcome of the PUD hearings, but also that he is hurt when people who don't know him think of him as 'some evil person.' Perhaps we who don't know him would stop thinking of him as some evil person if he would stop being a shill for greedy and arrogant businessmen" (A14). Other citizens threatened to hold Circle C's future residents "as culpable as those who first send in the bulldozers," since they were greedily sacrificing the city's natural resources in exchange for more personal land and a newer home (Landreth C2). Even more dramatic is local writer (and year-round Barton Springs daily swimmer) Susan Bright's poem about the developers, "Crows, Vultures, Blacksuits." Bright's poem begins underwater, where a woman is swimming in the cold world of the springs. Above her, in the distance, she sees hulking figures that lurk like vultures. "They are men in black suits, their beards are diplomas with no courses in literature or ethics, philosophy or art. They are standing on a hill above the cold water, making pronouncements, backs turned to the water, words pouring out" (92).

A closer look at these claims reveals that the "evil" pronouncement relates not so much to the developers themselves as much as to the perception that a small group was acting in its own interests against the larger public. Letter writer Terry Dubose articulates this perception in his letter shortly after the city council meeting: "Round one of the Barton Creek fight goes to the swimmers and environmentalists, thank goodness. But this is far from over, and it is much more important than the right to swim in clean water. This issue strikes at the heart of the concept of private property ownership. Does holding title to a parcel of land give the owner the right to do anything he desires to that land, regardless of the long-term effects after they . . . have gone off to enjoy their profits in some exotic playground?" Dubose poses a difficult question that draws upon older principles of progressivism and utilitarian senses of democracy. Legally speaking, Moffett may own the tract under development, but what is the more fundamental (and ethical) duty of private owners in relation to the community at large? While Dubose's question is subtler than the moralistic accusations of evil, his argument is grounded in the premise that benefits should be maximized for a majority and not for a smaller minority. Change must be seen as giving advantage to the community as a whole. The loss of a social benefit, however, is coded as an injury (or a "death," in activist Bill Bunch's words). Austin residents composed songs, poems, signs, speeches, and letters in order to ward off the looming injury from Jim Bob Moffett's group.

Injury claims typically presume that something precious is being encroached upon. For many Austin citizens who did not support the Circle C Ranch plans, the potential loss of community space, as well as social history, was just such an encroachment. The cause of injury was easy to identify: development and developers themselves were the threats. In the case of Austin's PUD, encroachment and the offending encroachers were manifest in the sites of Barton Springs and the four thousand acres under debate. Encroachment and injury were also part of the discourse surrounding pollution and the loss of water purity. For some opponents, the solution to such injury was simply to halt Circle C Ranch's construction. "Let Moffett and his like go peddle their poisoned wares elsewhere," declared resident Nicolo Festa (A14). If developers are the cause of injury, then banishing the developers is how to remove the threat of injury.

A number of texts framing the problem of encroachment and injury circulated across the city. Not only did opponents write letters and editorials in local newspapers, but more organized efforts helped to produce flyers, pamphlets, and bumper stickers that drew attention to the situation. One group even produced a short animated film for children that explained how we are all being encroached upon by development. The formidable group Save Our Springs produced "Sal Tells a Story," a cartoon narrated by Sal A. Mander, an endearing young salamander who lives in Barton Springs. "Once upon a time in Texas," the narration begins in a child's voice, "there was a sleepy college town, where people swam in clean flowing springs and sunset cast a violet crown. The people were smart and healthy." Images of laughing children and joyful families filled the screen. Ominous music begins to play in the background, and a cartoon man in a suit begins to wave in large construction trucks. "But then one day," continues the child's narrative, "a big company said, 'We want to build in the watershed. . . . We won't pollute. We promise.' The people knew this was a bad idea. They wrote to [the company's] big cheese, 'Please don't poison our water. Please don't do it. The highways, malls, and parking lots will choke the life right out of here'" ("Sending Out"). In this short film, encroachment is literally visualized by the cartoonish images of dump trucks and massive buildings that are placed on top of the joyful families playing in the springs. The voice of a begging child underscores a sense of harm that accompanies the development (highways, malls, and parking lots) imagined as a poison.

One of the most frequently repeated refrains in protesters' injury discourse drew upon images of Barton Springs' sacredness. The fact that Barton Springs served as a key victory for Austin's desegregationists in the 1960s helps to create its fixed status as a socially magical place in the public imaginary. Former *Texas Observer* editor Michael King described the springs as a "magic place for the Austin environmental community very early on, not only for ecological reasons but also for social ones. It was a gathering place. It was a place where there were battles over integration" (King). During the public debates over Circle C's development, people repeatedly claimed that Barton Springs was almost supernatural for its ability to generate unity. Bill Collier, the environmental reporter for the *Austin American-Statesman*, wrote a lengthy front-page exposé on the springs just days after the infamous city council meeting. His language not only outlined the Circle C Ranch situation for a wider audience, but his commentary also helped to make plain the stakes of losing such magical springs. "The crowds swimming at the springs have changed little over the years, other than their attire," writes Collier. "They have always been . . . from every walk of life in Austin. High-tech engineers, university professors, bankers, mechanics, college students and kids from East Austin swim side by side. The springs have a way of stripping people of their accoutrements and demonstrating that they have much in common" (Collier, "Barton Creek" A1). It is as if the springs themselves washed away the ugly trappings of class, race, and gender. Allusions to magic and transcendence helped to make plain the stakes of encroachment. Damage or pollution to the springs would mean an injury to sacredness itself.

Throughout the debate over Circle C's plans, the springs were described as commonly something more than beautiful or enjoyable. They were spiritual, holy, and beyond human creation. During the legendary city council meeting, Brigid Shea, who would eventually become a city council member a decade later, argued that "Barton Springs is the equivalent of a sacred shrine in this city." If other people's testimonies can be believed, her words were no exaggeration. Texas singer Jerry Jeff Walker remarked, "I've heard over the years that the Indians of the Hill Country called it the Sacred Springs and would come there to heal their wounds. So do I" (Walker). Other religious and spiritual leaders likewise testified to the springs' sacredness. In the wake of the debate, local rabbi Monty Eliasov created a short online video in order to testify about his own religious uses of the springs. "There's no question in my mind that Barton Springs has healing properties," says Rabbi Eliasov. "I feel that whenever I'm out of sorts, whenever my energy is low, I spend time meditating there. . . . When I injure or hurt myself, going to the springs has helped my healing process." Likewise, former city councilman George Humphrey, who baptized his son in Barton Springs, told reporters, "There is no question that Barton Springs is the spiritual center of Texas" ("Jim Bob Moffett").

The imagery of a sacred Barton Springs added weight to the argument that development ultimately poses man against a transcendently divine realm. To develop on top of the aquifer would mean, as one letter writer put it in the *Austin American-Statesman,* to destroy "a treasure that all the bulldozers in the world couldn't create, a treasure that only God could make" (Ross). Part of the sacredness of the springs is its transcendent qualities: its ability to transcend material differences, humanmade creation, and even the physical realm. One resident angrily declared to the city council, "Going to Barton Springs is my religion. Don't take my religion away from me." The logic of this discourse argued that if Jim Bob Moffett was allowed to build, and if development caused harm to the springs, then the purity, sacredness, and beauty would be irreparably injured.

Injury claims were made in a number of ways throughout this debate. They ranged from charges of literal injury to the springs, to charges of injured standards of fair community practice. In this way, injury claims resemble a rhetorical *topos*. They might even be read under the heading of what Chaim Perelman and Lucie Olbrechts-Tyteca call the locus of the irreparable. Irreparability executes an action that cannot be undone, which is often "a source of terror for man. . . . It acquires a value by the very fact of being considered under this aspect" (92). Perelman and Olbrechts-Tyteca explain that the locus of the irreparable calls attention to an action by imbuing it with the qualities of urgency, precariousness, and uniqueness. Such rhetorical gestures are not uncommon, as J. Robert Cox points out, "Claims that a decision . . . may cause an irreplaceable loss are invoked in strategic moments in almost every aspect of our personal and public lives" (227). The discourse about Barton Springs certainly seems to invoke these terms, since the decision about whether or not Austin should allow the PUD to continue was heavily framed by talk about uniqueness and precariousness. As one resident put it to city council members during the all-night hearing, "Are you going to stand by and watch these developers pour their own poisons into the limestone and kill Barton Springs?" (Collier, "Council Considers" A1). The terror of permanent and imminent loss is a threat to those who value the object (community, beauty, sacredness, history) about to be irreparably changed or removed. Such loss is a pain and, like the removal of one's own limb, can be framed as irreparable injury.

Injury claims can also be described as a topos insofar as they have the ability to generate multiple, and even conflicting, discourses. Edward Casey defines a topos as something that "bonds the participants, who converge on it even as they disagree about its status or implications" (35). Participants may be so divided on the matter that no conclusion or resolution is possible. Nevertheless, they are linked together by the fact that this topos focuses the bulk of their attention. In the case of the Circle C Ranch debate, the developers responded to critiques by inventing discourse that is strikingly close to the protesters' own claims. Only hours after the unanimous city council vote, representatives for Circle C Ranch made vague warnings that a failed development would inevitably lead to less corporate partnerships in Austin's future. Moffett and Dedman argued that the high-profile actions of a few "kooks" would scare away businesses that might see Austin as unfriendly toward corporate investment. According to Dedman, "It's going to be very difficult to get responsible companies to come into Austin. You would only have kooks attracting kooks."[2] Such threats are scare tactics, yet they originate from a similar topos as antidevelopment rhetoric. In the face of opponents' arguments that Circle C was acting selfishly, developers claimed that development and profits are good for the community because they attract greater economic stimulus. By preventing development in the PUD from continuing, Austin risked losing the possibility of expanding beautiful areas for living and working, and it also meant the encroachment on precious freedoms of business development—all instances of irreparable injury.

Three days before the infamous all-night meeting, a full-sized advertisement for Circle C Ranch appeared in the pages of the *Austin American-Statesman*. The ad featured two letters from local sports heroes Darrell Royal and Ben Crenshaw. Both letters testified to the integrity and professionalism of Jim Bob Moffett, a claim based on Royal and Crenshaw's longtime friendship with Moffett. The letters also boasted that the development's beauty would be unparalleled. "Austin and the surrounding area are very lucky to have two companies with international credibility and financial strength to bring in the best experts so that the planned area will . . . allow 4,000 acres to be developed in an area where people can live in concert with nature," proclaimed Royal's letter. (Crenshaw's letter actually used this same wording.) Below the reprint of both letters appeared numerous facts about the development's plans for natural beautification. Circle C Ranch would include "a national showcase for environmental preservation," as well as "2200 acres of open space—five times the size of Zilker Park." If nature was what the antidevelopment forces wanted, nature was what they would get.[3]

Similarly, a prospective buyers' brochure emphasized the ranch's beauty, nature, and preservation. "Providing a green belt with a 'hike and bike' trail, and doing a little landscaping at the entry, is not enough," reads the brochure. Circle C Ranch does not add outdoor space as an afterthought; Circle C Ranch is a natural space. "In some developments, park land is whatever is left over after development occurs. In Circle C Ranch just the opposite is true." The brochure paints a picture of its 412 acres of park land dedicated to the City of Austin, with plans for an additional 300 acres to be dedicated in the future. Just in case the magnitude of these sizes was possibly missed, the brochure again emphasized that the park space in Circle C Ranch will be "over twice the size of Zilker Park." By repeatedly making a comparison to Zilker Park, the home of the Barton Springs pool, developers connected the future Circle C park space to the public park space already open to all citizens. If you like Zilker Park and Barton Springs, then you will love what Circle C Ranch has in store.

The underside of these claims is that the attempt to stop beneficial development would inevitably bring injury. If Circle C Ranch was not allowed to complete its construction, then more green space would not become available. Environmental preservation would lose out because the "experts" who build "in concert with nature" could not pursue their vision. Moffett warned that even greater harm will befall the springs if his own company was not allowed to pursue its plans for Circle C Ranch. "You can forget Austin having a major real estate developer come in and do it right," he cautioned (Collier, "Point of Contention"). At the same time, future economic benefits may have been lost to the city. Developers and businesses might have been scared away from Austin, meaning that few "responsible companies" would consider relocating to Austin. Could this mean fewer new jobs or less responsible corporate neighbors? Moffett certainly implied as much in his interviews with local and national media. Moffett told reporters that by "torpedoing" the development, protesters were also torpedoing the city's future ("Jim Bob Moffett Takes"). Much like the antidevelopment discourse sparked by the all-night city council meeting, the pro-development discourse was also organized around appeals to the qualities of urgency, precariousness, and uniqueness. Both kinds of public talk thus revolved around claims to injury and irreparable harm.

Furthermore, there is still another way in which injury claims and counterclaims can be described as topoi. This sense draws upon the more literal definition of topos as a place or site. Jim Bob Moffett and his critics seemed to be at odds, yet their discursive exchanges interacted in a way that could only be described as collaboration. Injury claims collaborate together in order to dialectically produce a site of discourse. Understanding the collaborative dialectic as a single site of discourse is important, since this also helps us better understand why and how subjects can be distanced from public discourse without being outside of such discourse. That is, what gets mutually produced by injury claims is the "space of exception," perhaps more appropriately renamed a "site of exception," that cultivates the exceptional subject.

The Site of Injury

Many cultural theorists have expressed concern about how injury discourse shapes us as subjects. Some feminist critics, most notably Wendy Brown, Sara Ahmed, and Lauren Berlant, argue that when injury constructs our identities as subjects, we find ourselves invested in the ongoing maintenance of the wound site as a primary mode of identification. "Subaltern subject become invested in the wound," writes Ahmed, "such that the wound comes to stand for identity itself. The political claims become claims of injury against something or somebody" (32). Likewise, in *States of Injury: Power and Freedom in Late Modernity,* Brown explores how injury claims can actually create disempowering conditions by investing identity politics in their own historical narratives of suffering and exclusion. Injury claims are often lodged in a logic of "ressentiment," writes Brown. Although politicized identities rail against the privilege and power of a masculine, white, middle-class subject, any move away from this response would effectively destroy claims to injury and political significance within a realm of difference. As Brown puts it, "politicized identities generated out of liberal, disciplinary societies, insofar as they are premised on exclusion from a universal ideal, require that ideal, as well as their exclusion from it, for their own continuing existence as identities" (65). Injury claims thus produce and maintain the citizen-victim that transforms the wound into an identity. As Ahmed puts it, the fetishization of the wound "turns the wound into something that simply 'is' rather than something that has happened in time and space" (32). The wound site is a stable displacement for a more complex history of social wrong, yet it is also the site of invention.

In other words, the wound is both stable and generative. It keeps in place the same old structures, even as it rages against this system. Brown considers the fantasy that exploited workers have of a world where work has been abolished, or feminists who conjure up a world without men, or teenagers who dream of a world without parents. "Such images of freedom perform mirror reversals of suffering without transforming the organization of the activity through which the suffering is produced and without addressing the subject constitution that domination effects, that is, the . . . social categories, 'workers,' . . . 'women,' or 'teenagers'" (7). Without the structure of injurious relations, the wound site risks destabilization. The subject of injury likewise risks being destabilized by the wound site's dismantling.

Other critics have argued that the citizen-victim serves a conservative agenda by displacing real differences onto the more banal and universal narrative of trauma. In her introduction to *The Queen of America Goes to Washington City,* Berlant expresses concern over a disappearing public sphere and its replacement with an intimate public sphere that turns trauma into a category of citizenship. Each citizen testifies to his or her own traumatic experience, which allows her to commune with the traumatic citizenry of the nation. Ahmed points out that even privileged white males now "secure" citizenship through testimonies of personal trauma, including the trauma of being denied privilege through programs like affirmative action (33). Such trauma-based citizenship can also be seen in Barbara Biesecker's study of how popular World War II nostalgia frames the "true American" in the singular image of a traumatized soldier. In her essay "Renovating the National Imaginary," Biesecker shows how movies like *Saving Private Ryan* and bestselling books like Tom Brokaw's *The Greatest Generation* create a kind of baseline for citizenship: the male body in pain. This body is willing to put aside its own safety, comfort, health, and even its life for the sake of a greater cause. According to the nostalgic narrative, these heroic figures put aside their own differences and individual stories in order to serve the nation's timeless ideals. This narrative calls for us, too, to put aside our indulgent differences and claims (race, gender, class, ability) and become true citizens, unmarked by public claims about the now. The true citizen is willing to suffer a private wound without public remark.

Each of these critiques says something important about injury claims and wound politics as productive forces. Injury claims do not only describe current states of being; they also make, produce, construct. In his careful study of injury claims, Carl Gutiérrez-Jones writes, "a focus on injury helps contextualize a larger rhetorical economy based on perpetrator/victim interplay" (77). By framing this discourse as an economy, Gutiérrez-Jones is not attempting to deny the very real material injuries faced by people who have experienced trauma. At the same time, this framework dares to recognize that the language of injury orients us toward certain kinds of discursive roles (and away from others). Gutiérrez-Jones's choice of words is especially fruitful for thinking about injury claims and the resulting discourse they sponsor as modes of production. What gets produced by injury claims?

On the one hand, what is produced through the economy of injury claims can be described as an invitation, or an entry point into public discourse. Although the two sides are waging a vicious fight, Kenneth Burke helps us to read them as working in a kind of cooperative spirit. Their ways are identified together. Burke's theories of interlocking cooperation and rhetorical identification suggest that the operation of publics and counterpublics can be read as an accumulation strategy. Burke explains the principle of rhetorical identification like this: "The fact that an activity is capable of reduction to intrinsic, autonomous principles does not argue that it is free from identification with other orders of motivation extrinsic to it" (*Rhetoric* 27). It is this notion of identification as shared substance that leads Burke to conclude that even war is a version of identification. He explains, "before each culminating blast there must be a vast network of interlocking operations, directed communally" (22). Even rival factions are said to be cooperating insofar as each "parry and thrust . . . can be said to cooperate in the building of an overall form" (23). Cooperation in war is a difficult concept, since we are used to thinking of war as the quintessential dialectic: one force against another. Yet, as Burke describes it, the opposing forces are working together in the production, design, and maintenance of a common operation. The cooperative production of any operation does not necessarily involve cooperation in the vernacular sense of peace and agreement. As Burke's case study reflects, even war is a form of cooperative productions. It does not involve intentional cooperation among parties, as a war might be said to do.

Rather than merely producing a dialectic, injury claims actually produce a collaborative site that guides our orientation to other people and to the world. The mutual parry and thrust coalesces into an entryway that we are invited to step into. Just as the mutual antagonisms between two forces gel into a recognizable scene we call "war," the dialectic of claims and counterclaims forms a recognizable site (topos) of debate. What emerges from the networks of nonofficial discourse, therefore, is a coherent entry point for orienting ourselves to the scene of crisis. Burke might describe this as the "building of an over-all form" through vernacular rhetoric. In another sense, however, the site of debate is also a placeholder for the crisis itself. A placeholder is always a kind of substitution, which means that something is deferred or lost in the act of substituting. Since the public crises of development and land transformation are lodged across many networks of various scales, what gets lost in this place-holding is the opportunity to engage development's complex networks. In short, the site of debate becomes the main topos for talking about development.

Topoi create public discourse by offering a site around which to gather our talk. Debate about injury was the main site where everyone could meet up. Claims about injury to Barton Springs and claims about injury to the Austin economy served as such gathering sites. At the same time, the debate also substitutes (holds a place) for the actual networks involved in development. By making the site of injury a primary topos (or placeholder), the work of public talk is removed from a space of alternative inquiry. Recall that Ahmed's criticism of the wound site's fetish is that a poor substitution takes place. Rather than seeing wounding as something that happens in time and space, it becomes something that simply is. Injury claims substitute a dynamic inquiry across time and space—or the networks of wounds—for a static one. The particular topos is thus a fixed point of gathering.

Likewise, consider how those who objected to Circle C's plans were themselves implicated in the work of land transformation. If we think about development as ongoing processes lodged in transspatial and transtemporal networks, then we might also see plans for Austin's newest development as part of a larger process. At some level, all Austin residents are part of the citywide (regionwide, globalwide) development process. Some residents made this argument in order to hinder criticism of the Circle C Ranch plans. As one letter writer put it, "Anyone who lives in a house, buys clothes and food at a store, drives on a road, has running water and flushes a toilet has benefited from development. Where would we all live today without our first major developer—Stephen F. Austin?" (Ayensworth). However, we are not precluded from critiquing unethical and unwise land use simply by thinking about development across its networks. The fact that we are implicated does not mean we cannot and should not intervene. On the contrary, it places a significant burden on us to critically engage those networks. Sustainable intervention requires an understanding of networks, including our own daily homelife-worklife nexus and the transhistorical/transspatial effects of physical places. Unfortunately, the focus on injury misses greater opportunities to interrogate and creatively intervene in those networks through ordinary vernacular public discourse.

In other words, the site of injury discourse that guides our orientation and invites us into public discourse only represents one way of thinking of ourselves in relation to crisis. As mentioned above, the example of a limb removal can show how topological claims of injury actually frame a situation, rather than accurately describe it. When a limb is removed, there are irreparable changes that happen. No new limb can regrow in its place. It is perfectly imaginable how someone might frame this situation as one of injury and harm. However, the limb may have been removed in order to save the entire body (as in the case of cancer or gangrene). In this situation, the claim of injury is not necessarily the only way we might read this scene. A different kind of rhetor may describe the irreparable change as an instance of health, prosperity, and benefit. The limb's expert removal, replacement, and healing may also be read as part of a progress narrative about medical surgery techniques. If my limb is removed, I am also likely to become part of new communities and networks that I had no access to before the surgery: physical therapy, support groups, and informal alliances among other survivors. All of these examples illustrate alternative modes of orienting to a particular event (limb removal, in this instance) that transcends the topos of injury and its discursive "gathering site." By allowing this topos to shelter our public discourse, we risk overlooking such alternative forms of orienting to the world and to others.

Even more troubling is the way that the site of debate cultivates distanced subjects as legitimate public modes. Ahmed defines emotion as a dimension of relationality: "Emotions are relational: they involve (re)actions or relations of 'towardness' and 'awayness' in relation to such objects" (8). When we talk about the affective dimension, Ahmed suggests, we are talking about relations. The reverse is also the case; relationality contains a directionality that can be read as emotion or feeling. The site of injury invites relations, which are also (re)actions of towardness or awayness. In short, the site invites us to feel something about it. Feeling injured is one obvious way that people relate to the site of debate. But, as I argue in chapter 2, the felt absence of injury (or benefit) is also an orientation toward that deliberative scene. The absence of a perceived injury might mean that I feel no compelling reason to join in the discourse against (or for) Circle C Ranch. However, my feeling about the collaborative site of debate still allows me to retain my public orientation. The lack of deliberative contribution does not negate my standing as a public subject.

Such a dual characteristic of public subjectivity brings us back to the space of exception. The exceptional subject is simultaneously outside public discourse while still retaining a relationship to it. Though this seems like a paradox, Agamben explains, "the most proper characteristic of the exception is that what is excluded in it is not, on account of being excluded, absolutely without relation to the rule. The rule applies to the exception in no longer applying, in withdrawing from it" (*Homo Sacer* 17–18). Imagine a resident in Austin who is reading the events surrounding Circle C Ranch's plans. She feels considerable distance from the dialectical site of injury claims. Rather than having no relation to this site, our distant resident is more like an exception or even an example. The example is outside a set without being unrelated to that set. The example is not part of the actual collection, but relates to it absolutely.

Similarly, our resident sets herself outside the set of injury claims without dissolving a relation. She withdraws from the discourse under the very conditions of that discourse. In the case of Circle C Ranch, the mutually produced conditions of the discourse make injury the rule of relation. Our resident, who feels no injury or benefits of any kind from the plans, is thus outside the discourse while still retaining a relation. One's public orientation does not depend upon participation in public discourse, therefore. (At least not as we might typically think.) For rhetoricians who want to encourage people to make difficult interventions in their ailing space and places, the trouble with such a mode of public subjectivity is obvious.

As the pattern of discourse in the Circle C Ranch case reflects, the mutually produced dialectic of injury claims is demanding. It demands interaction from its participants by offering the primary means of orienting to others and to the world. Furthermore, it demands a relation of some kind. It wants a feeling from you, even if you are setting yourself outside of its conditions for discourse. And where feelings of towardness do exist, there is an important substitution that takes place. The site of injury claims allows us to orient ourselves to public crisis in one way, while avoiding other ways of orienting to the public. We substitute one way of orienting to the world for another. In chapter 6, I advocate for an alternative mode of orienting to the world, not through feeling (or its distance) but through inquiry. But, in order to challenge the exceptional mode of subjectivity, we must first reconsider how vernacular commonplaces serve as rhetorically productive technologies.

Big Boxes and Better Living

Chances are good that you had never heard of the all-night city council meeting in Austin, Texas. Maybe you've never taken a dip in Barton Springs, or any other natural swimming hole that sits in the middle of an urban space. But there is a good chance that, like me, you drove by at least one big box store today: Target, Walmart, Costco, PetSmart, Home Depot, Office Max, or something similar. There is also a good chance that you've recently heard (or even made) some kind of criticism of these kinds of stores. Across the international stage, development is most visible in the construction of big box facilities that seem to exist in nearly every city. These chain stores are known not only for their identical patterns usually built upon formerly undeveloped land, but also for their business tactics that seek to drive out local competition. The giant big box store has been repeatedly analyzed, criticized, and vilified by people who see its presence as a death blow for local businesses. Anti-Walmart sentiment is especially strong across the world, as Walmart has become a kind of symbol of big box culture writ large. Protests against Walmart have cropped up across the United States and around the world. While the circumstances are unique to each anti-Walmart protest, the rhetorical gestures follow a similar pattern of injury claims that we saw in the Circle C Ranch debates above. There are numerous places to begin analysis of anti-Walmart rhetoric, but I will look closely at several development scenes that have attracted national attention. Like the Circle C Ranch debates, both supporters and detractors tend to rely upon claims of injury in order to articulate their deliberative positions.

The first controversy I wish to examine begins in one of the last Walmart-free places in the United States. When Walmart announced in 2004 that it wanted to open a supersize store in Vermont, many residents balked at this idea. Vermont protesters used a number of tactics to stall or prevent Walmart's construction, although the protests were ultimately unsuccessful. The anti-Walmart rhetoric emphasized the irreparable harm that a huge superstore would bring to Vermont's small town character and historical aesthetic. In an effort to stop the development, some officials successfully fought to place Vermont on the National Trust for Historic Preservation's list of endangered places.[4] It was the first state to ever be placed on this list. Trust President Richard Moe explained this drastic move as a way to protect an irreplaceable characteristic: "We know the effects that these superstores have. They tend to suck the economic and social life out of these downtowns, many of which wither and die as a result. I think it will drastically affect the character of Vermont, which I think is unique" (Belluck). Walmart opponents argued that these uniquely Vermont features transcend mere attractiveness. Development would destroy a special "something" that could not be rebuilt. In a speech to the Vermont Land Trust, historian Jan Albers put the situation like this: "Some politicians and developers will tell you that 'we can have it all' here in Vermont—the sprawl and suburbanization that characterize much of America's current development and the small scale and character we have long revered. They are wrong." The injury is so dangerous, went the protest rhetoric, because the harm is irreparable. Moreover, what is being harmed is more than beauty. It is the very intangible quality of Vermont life that is under threat.

In addition to the claims of injured civic space, other anti-Walmart Vermont groups pointed to the negative effects that Walmart would have on local workers and citizens. One of the most active citizen anti-Walmart groups, the Vermont Livable Wage Campaign, created a high-profile presence online and in local sites. The campaign's literature argues that Walmart's massive scale shows little concern for "the communities and people where they locate" ("Wal-Mart and Vermont"). Because Walmart has consistently shown "disregard for anything beyond their bottom line," the Vermont Livable Wage Campaign called for all Vermonters to demand legislation ensuring that Walmart "respects the people and places where they do business" ("Wal-Mart and Vermont"). Likewise, other critics insisted that the things Vermonters specifically care about will be destroyed by Walmart's presence in the state. Zachery Brown's editorial in the *Vermont Journal of Environmental Law* argues that Walmart will harm the ethical characters of Vermont citizens themselves: "Vermonters have continually asked for a livable wage throughout the state," writes Brown, "but this will not happen if Wal-Mart comes to town. The fragile economy, quaint downtowns, and local merchants cannot support this kind of social repugnancy. Therefore, we should ask ourselves if a cheap pair of underwear is worth damaging our social morale." In short, by allowing Walmart to build a superstore in Vermont, the character of Vermonters themselves risks damage that cannot easily be repaired.

Claims to injury of various kinds circulated widely in the Vermont case against Walmart. Yet, pro-development rhetoric also relied upon similar claims when making the case for why Walmart would be beneficial to Vermont. When asked about Vermont's unprecedented National Trust designation, one Walmart representative responded that the store was actually fulfilling many citizens' desires: "We've also heard from a lot of Vermonters who want a Wal-Mart closer to their communities. And customers have told us they like a larger store. It enhances their shopping experience that there's a wider selection and the aisles are large" (Belluck A1). Similarly, when interviewed by a local TV news crew, a potential local site developer in St. Albans, Vermont, explained that Walmart would contribute greatly to the community. "It's entirely different from just building a building somewhere," developer Jeff Davis told the reporter. Davis explained that Walmart's presence would mean badly needed jobs and economic growth for the community ("Wal-Mart Controversy"). Paul Beaudry, a local radio host, was one of the most vocal supporters of the St. Albans Walmart. Beaudry organized a pro-Walmart rally and signed up residents to voice their support for the store. "It's just going to be a boon to our community," he told a local news station. "We've been suffering up there for quite a bit, for quite a while. And we see this as a way out of that" (WCAX). Suffering (and its removal) is key to these arguments. Pro-development discourse did not challenge the injury claims made by anti-Walmart groups. Instead, it simply countered with claims of benefit that were meant to implicitly outweigh injury claims. In this case, Walmart's construction was framed as an end to needless suffering.

Many local residents articulated this same rhetoric of suffering and choice in support of Walmart. Two residents of St. Albans paid for a pro-Walmart advertisement out of their own pocket, and their subsequent letter to the St. Albans *Messenger* explained that their decision to create the ad was not encouraged by any corporate sponsor. Instead, wrote Ray and Eileen Gadue, the decision to support Walmart was due to a widespread desire for badly needed shopping options in the area. "Ever since we lost Ames and Woolworths we have been waiting for a new department store to come to town. Even before the price of gas really became an issue, the distance that we had to travel was." Furthermore, wrote the Gadues, the majority of the people they knew said they wanted Walmart in town. But a small majority of people seemed to be actively preventing the desired development. "The bullying is being done by those few small groups who seem to feel that the economic needs of the people of Franklin County come secondary to their own opinions as to the merits of Wal-Mart as a company," they concluded.

A number of resident letters to local newspapers sided with the Gadues. Their arguments were filled with a mixture of claims to benefit and injury surrounding Walmart's construction. For example, resident Nila Spaulding voiced similar complaints as the Gadues: "Every person against Wal-Mart has the money to shop in our downtown," Spaulding wrote. "My family is not able to buy our everyday necessities in Franklin County. I can't justify paying $60 for a pair of jeans for one of my children; let alone all four of them." Spaulding argued that Walmart would offer the many low-income people in Franklin County an affordable place to shop, as well as a place to seek employment. But the "tree huggers" protesting Walmart because they "think the corn field is pretty" do not care about these working people. Similarly, resident Sandra Bicknell wrote that while she loves Vermont, "God loves his people even more" (Bicknell). Bicknell goes on to write that Vermonters must care for one another's needs, which includes affordable shopping options. In another letter from a St. Albans resident, we find the appeal to love and care vividly illustrated through a parental analogy. "Let's look at this Wal-Mart issue from a much simpler perspective. . . . If the parents of this family don't provide for their children, they are considered dead beats. If a community and/or State does not provide for its citizens, what is it considered? I can tell you that we are the laughing stock of the northeast" (Beyor). These kinds of claims not only appeal to the economic and social benefits of building a Walmart, but they also imply a kind of injury from the development's obstruction. Indeed, injury claims take on a powerful punch when connected to the image of suffering children. If anti-Walmart forces are successful, argued the supporters, they will not only reduce options for working-class families, but they will also turn their backs on a moral duty to "provide" for citizens.

The patterns of injury claims in Vermont's fight over Walmart are hardly unique. In fact, when Walmart announced in 2004 that it wanted to also open a new superstore in Teotihuacan, Mexico—less than two miles away from the Aztec pyramids—the international discourse surrounding this development sounded remarkably similar to the Vermont case. Public opposition to the development was passionate; many citizens argued that the location of a huge store would irreparably harm a sacred Aztec space that united all Mexican people. The landscape held transcendent value, and the presence of a big box store like Walmart was likely to damage the sacredness of its space. This was the argument made by sixty-three prominent Mexican intellectuals and writers in an open letter to President Vicente Fox. "Mr. President, the archeological zone Teotihuacan is the symbol of our past," begins the letter, "the deep root of our national identity; the history that over time has been woven into and has built our social imaginary. It is . . . a sacred space of pilgrimage, a ceremonial center where worship was given to the ancient gods" ("Carta").[5] The lengthy letter's passionate argument against development appealed to an inability to ever replace or rebuild such sacred space. Moreover, the sacred space is connected with national identity. It is a space that links Mexicans with each other, as well as with the past. Walmart's construction was seen as a violent encroachment on this sacred publicness. The harm likely to come from this construction could not easily be repaired.

However, just as Vermont Walmart supporters countered this opposition with additional claims of injury and benefit, the Teotihuacan Walmart supporters also articulated the benefits of new construction. A spokesman for Walmart of Mexico told reporters that the new store was a welcome convenience for poor local residents, who had to pay high prices in the small markets or travel thirty miles to the nearest supermarket. He described the protesters as a small group who did not reflect the desires of the community (McKinley). When asked by a reporter what they thought about the new store, some local residents echoed claims about the convenience and cheaper prices. "For the poor, like me, the store will make life easier. It's good for us. It's cheap. You can buy in bulk for the whole week," remarked one local vender, who said she usually earns around seven dollars per day. Another worker told reporters that Walmart meant a "great job, with better pay than in other places. We want to buy so many new things we haven't seen before." Much like Circle C Ranch's response to the antidevelopment arguments in Austin, pro-Walmart rhetoric relies upon the claim that development represents expanded opportunity and benefits for more people than ever.[6] It isn't that the ancient pyramids are unimportant. Rather, adding increased economic opportunities in addition to the pyramids is even better. In this logic of accumulative benefit, development is both democratic and beneficial.

Perhaps neither of these situations is familiar to you, but you have probably heard similar criticisms surrounding the giant chain. Critiques of Walmart are not limited to individual cases of development, like the ones in Vermont and Mexico. National debates about big box development are often discussed in a more abstract way. In fact, several Web sites are devoted to both anti-Walmart and pro-Walmart sentiments, and social networking sites like Facebook feature both pro and con groups with large numbers of competing "fans."[7] Even so, claims of injury still organize a significant amount of the discourse surrounding big box development. Some of the most common anti-Walmart injury claims relate to the corporation's relationship to workers. An increasing number of popular books and documentaries have made a strong case against Walmart's labor practices and abusive working conditions. Robert Greenwald's highly publicized 2005 documentary, *Wal-Mart: The High Cost of Low Price,* argues that Walmart pursues a national policy of pushing workers onto Medicaid rather than providing decent health-care insurance. Greenwald also alleges that the company's aggressive antiunion tactics have led to such unethical and illegal practices as mandatory off-the-clock work, employment of illegal immigrants, gender discrimination against women in management, and deliberate underemployment of hourly employees in order to reduce the number of workers who are considered full-time.

Even beyond these kinds of detailed accusations, Walmart is simply read as cold and cruel by many people. When Walmart started offering their own brand of cookies that were almost exactly like Girl Scout cookies, for example, Jeffrey Goldberg remarked in the *Atlantic* that this move only proved the company was just plain mean: "Apparently, Wal-Mart wasn't satisfied with being the top . . . crappy-Chinese-products selling store in America. Now it's preying on Girl Scouts." One editorial cartoon literally illustrated injury claims by featuring "Wal-Mart Barbie," who is missing an arm. Walmart Barbie's unhappy owner turns to her playmate and says, "Great. Her arm came off and she can't afford health insurance." The cartoon is bitterly funny only because Walmart is often seen as callous toward its most needy employees.

Walmart's perceived cruelty was even lampooned in the off-Broadway musical *Walmartopia!,* a science-fiction tale of a world taken over by Walmart in the year 2037. The newly liberated independent nation of Vermont is under attack from the dark, sinister forces of Wal-America. Battling the monolithic powers is a single mother who works for Walmart, but who ultimately blows the whistle on her company's heinous working conditions. When the writers of *Walmartopia!* were featured on *Fox Business News* shortly after the play's opening, patterns of injury claims were plain to see during the somewhat awkward interview. The host began by asking the writers why they had adopted such an anticapitalist stance toward Walmart. She tilted her head to the side and asked, "Are you former disgruntled employees?" The play's authors, Andrew Rohn and Catherine Capellarro, smiled and explained that their critique of Walmart is not due to personal reasons, but rather due to Walmart's unethical business practices around the world. "But, my goodness," replied the host with an incredulous voice, "Why do you hate Walmart? It's so convenient and the prices are so cheap!" Rohn and Capellarro responded by citing Walmart's antiunion tactics, use of sweatshop labor, and illegal discrimination for female promotions. The host animatedly countered these critiques: "I'm from San Jose, California, an area that's, you know, low income. And when Walmart and Target came in, it provided jobs and maybe not the best health benefits, but these people weren't insured before. . . . Then we had Jamba Juice, then we had Starbucks. All of a sudden, there's a vital community because of these big chains coming in." She then turned the microphone over to the playwrights for response. "But there's also a community being destroyed by big box economies," said Capellarro. The host cut off Capellarro to interject, "But the communities I'm talking about are being helped" (*Fox Business News*). Watching the interview is cringe inducing because you can feel tensions mounting between the playwrights and the host. Through the bickering, however, it is plain to see that injury serves as a central topos that manages how development is discussed. Injury and its relief bring development conversations into focus for both sides of the debate.

In many ways, the *Fox Business News* reporter is repeating the same claims that Walmart itself makes in response to its critics. Rather than answering the accusations of unethical practices, corporate representatives tend to articulate claims of benefit that come from Walmart's presence. In a 2008 speech to Walmart leadership, CEO Lee Scott reaffirmed that the company's greater mission was to serve the people who shop at Walmart. Walmart is not simply a store, it is a service. "We have so much to be proud of here at Walmart," remarked Scott. "Perhaps more than ever before, we are delivering on our core mission to save people money so they can live better. And we are doing so at a time when people here in the U.S. and in all the countries we serve need us most." Scott also assures the employees that they are personally helping to better the world through their work: "There will come a day when you will be at home with your children or grandchildren . . . and you will look them in the eyes . . . and you will know that you made a difference in the world they live in. In the end, there is no higher calling for ourselves or our company." In another address to a Walmart employee convention, Scott conceded that many people fear Walmart's size and growth. However, he tells the audience, Walmart must not succumb to its critics because "Walmart is too important to individual families who are stretching their budget, . . . we're too important to our associates, for whom we have so much love" (*Wal-Mart: High Cost*).

This discourse of benefit is also visible in Walmart's revamped 2007 slogan: "Save Money. Live Better." This slogan coincided with its aggressive campaign to brand itself as a place of care and compassion. Walmart's campaign repetitively emphasizes the act of working together to bring people a better life. In a promotional video for the new advertising campaign, one Walmart executive explains that the company wants to "show the world what it's like to save and have a better life" ("Save Money"). Underneath these claims of benefit and care is also a competing claim of injury. If Walmart is the best hope for working families to have a better life, and if Walmart is the source for many communities to "live better" through lower-priced goods and abundant jobs, then the lack of Walmart is a threat to such better living. Without Walmart, a better life is out of reach.

Exceptional (Everyday) Values

Walmart's corporate discourse illustrates a point that Perelman and Olbrechts-Tyteca make plain in *The New Rhetoric:* arguments from values are complicated. On the one hand, an interlocutor cannot simply dismiss a value without appearing to be in favor of force. She cannot reject values out of hand, but must give justifications for why that value does not mean exactly what her opponent claims. When a value is in question, the interlocutor can "disqualify it, subordinate it to others, or interpret it," rather than rejecting it wholesale (75). Developers cannot simply dismiss counterrhetorics of injury that antidevelopment forces are making. Any denial that natural water sources or ancient pyramids are special would be a weak position. However, as Perelman and Olbrechts-Tyteca also point out, values can be subject to resubordination. "Most values are indeed shared by a great number of audiences," they write, "and a particular audience is characterized less by which values it accepts than by the way it grades them" (81). Herein lies the sophistication of claims and counterclaims of value. Developers do not need to challenge antidevelopment publics in order to be persuasive. That would almost certainly be an impossible goal. Instead, they must simply persuade an audience of the same claims against an encroachment or threat to something precious. Prodevelopment discourse tends to amplify benefits like quantity and greater access that are created through development: Circle C will make even more public parks, and Walmart will create even more opportunities for economic freedom. Encroachment upon these benefits, however, constitutes a threat.

What is happening here can be described as topological in two related senses. First, injury claims serve as a topos, or a guiding space, where public discourse is invited to happen. The protesters who objected to Circle C Ranch brought the various issues into focus by reading the scene as a matter of injury due to selfish encroachment. Likewise, developers were able to read the situation as an issue of beneficial community expansion potentially threatened by the stubborn complaints of a few "kooks" who held personal grudges against business people. In the case of Walmart, injury is conjured up by both sides who equally claim to be defending "the good life." In these scenes, the topos of injury becomes an invitation or an entry point to being public. Topoi generate arguments by focusing, or managing, the range of references and claims. This is why Rosa Eberly calls them "bioregions of discourse," since they are organic creators of discursive spheres (*Citizen Critics* 6). Topoi aid rhetors by placing coherent boundaries around potentially confusing and complex forces. As Carolyn Miller writes, "We may think of the function of the *topos* . . . as an aid to pattern recognition, specifically as a region that permits or invites the connection between the abstract and the concrete, between a pattern and the material in which it is instantiated" (142). In the instance of Circle C Ranch, an abstract value like injury or benefit provided some citizen rhetors with a meaningful pattern through which to read and make sense of the concrete details of a four-thousand-acre parcel owned by private developers who sought construction permits. Within the complex layers of local history, public memory, legal details, and geological facts, claims to injury offered a familiar pattern for both sides: this action will help, but that action will hurt.

The other sense in which the parry and thrust of such exchanges can be described as topological is that this discourse collaboratively creates a "site" of feeling. While pro-development and antidevelopment parties seem to be at odds, the dialectical cooperation of injury claims makes the crisis present to people in a particular way. This cooperative exchange frames the debate as being "about" injury and benefit. In other words, the topological pattern helps to thematize the complex scene in a more manageable way. They form what Perelman and Olbrechts-Tyteca call an accumulation: building up attention, even through contradictory elements (144–45). The claims and counterclaims of injury cooperate to create an accumulative site. Furthermore, feelings about that accumulative injury site are the means by which one steps into a public role. This site is precisely what orients our feelings of towardness or awayness.

However, the clamor of debate and deliberation does not tell a complete story of public response to the big box issue. We might also attune our rhetoricians' ears to the ways in which awayness is manifested in this debate. A kind of rhetorical shrug is performed by many who are located somewhere within this discourse. I may not feel injured by a new big box store, but I also may not necessarily feel benefited. I remain silent on the matter altogether. Indeed, our rhetoricians' ears may be highly attuned to ways in which spaces of deliberation contain silence. But by silence, I mean something different than what John Schilb calls "rhetorical refusals," which are purposeful violations of the audience's expectation. Schilb remarks that these refusals—the shape of which can certainly emerge in deliberate silences—are designed to advocate an alternative principle that the rhetor finds valuable (3). But the silences I identify here do not defy audience expectation. In fact, we expect a certain degree of apathy, even if we hate it. Perhaps the silences I mean are closer to Bartelby's "I would prefer not to." I do not feel hurt by Walmart's presence, but I also dislike its many weaknesses. Where the debate over development's encroachment is concerned, this silence simply announces: I would prefer not to decide.

These positions might seem like refusals. They do indeed refuse to actively participate in the deliberations over these issues, one way or another. However, I argue that we are better served by reading these silences as public stances in their own right. We have already seen that this rhetorical shrug is less of a turn away from the public, and more of an "alternative" mode of public orientation. They reflect orientations to public discourse as they have been framed by common rhetorical patterns, such as injury claims. Once again, this seemingly paradoxical relationship is made possible through the work of feeling. We feel our way toward towardness with others and with the world, and we also feel our way toward awayness with others and with the world. The exceptional subject is one who is related to the *koinos kosmos* through these feelings. Therefore, the exceptional subject finds himself or herself both inside and outside the scene of crisis. These figures do not refuse to think of themselves as publicly oriented, nor do they imagine themselves as abdicating their public role. Instead, their relation is one of distance.

Moreover, it is the dialectic of injury claims that produces the special something that invites towardness or awayness. Commonplaces of public discourse produce the spaces of exceptional public subjectivity. Consequently, because feeling has become the grounds for public subjectivity, we find ourselves in a strange position. Those of us who want to encourage more ethical and civic-minded responses to the serious crises facing us—including the crisis of place, as manifested partly in the current debates over development—need to consider what kinds of subjects are being produced by our vernacular techniques and technologies. Appeals to injury are not only lodged in institutional settings. The commonplaces of vernacular response are no less responsible for shaping how people think of themselves as public subjects.

Given that we are working as rhetoricians and as teachers, what does this lesson about rhetorical commonplaces (in this case, injury claims) and exceptional subjects teach us? We have seen that the claims and counterclaims are actually collaborative technologies that help produce key modes of public subjectivity. We have also seen that these vernacular patterns of discourse create a "site" that orients feelings in particular ways while avoiding alternative modes of public being. But this lesson has something else to teach us about the silence of civic apathy that rhetorical studies continues to hunt. One of the complications that comes from this analysis is a rethinking of what participation is/does/should be. Encouraging students to "take a side" in a controversy like big box proliferation may only reinforce the troubling dialectic we have seen above. This approach does not dismantle the structural problems within injury claims as a guiding topos. Consequently, "taking a side" may only reify the techniques and technologies of exceptional public subjects.

We can certainly read the silences that accompany and even underwrite Walmart's growth as an indication of what Peter Sloterdijk calls "cynical reasoning." Borrowing from Sloterdijk, Slavoj Žižek formulates a new definition of ideology as the state of awareness with accompanying changes in our actions. We know what we are doing (ideologically speaking), but we do it anyway (see Žižek 28–30). We know that Walmart is slowly encroaching on our landscapes and refusing to pay workers fairly, yet we drop in for a quick purchase anyway. Basic naïveté does not explain our behavior, though Marx imagined as much when he posed ideology as "Sie wissen das nicht, aber sie tun es" (They do not know it, but they are doing it). Such "cynical reasoning" may be an explanation for the silence and seeming complacency that is present in the midst of so much deliberative clamor.

As Marshall Alcorn writes, cynical reason explains why behavior is so hard to change, even after the "reality" of a situation has been revealed. Using a Lacanian framework, Alcorn explains that discourses are not like whole packages "placed" within a subject (or even throughout a given public). Although discourse is ideological, its mediating function is not without its own mediation. "Real-world experience suggests that something apparently within a subject mediates between discourse that seeks to change a subject's identity," writes Alcorn (17). Calling this subject mediation a matter of "libidinal investments," Alcorn argues that subjects have adhesive attachments to discourse. Indeed, these adhesive attachments are what grant discourse so much power: "We are moved by . . . libidinal attachment and loss of libidinal attachment . . . much more than by rational arguments. What we are in discourse is not evenly spread across all examples of discourse. We are in those discourse clusters that bind our emotion. . . . The rhetoric of discourse is libidinal" (26). Not only does discourse mediate culture and materiality, according to Alcorn, but those mediating discourses are themselves mediated through the libidinal attachments of a subject-body. Changing people's minds requires more than exposing ideological structures behind discourse; people's libidinal attachments to that discourse remain affectively bound. In order to change people's minds, you must also have an effect at an affective level, which is much more challenging.

The question of how to change people's hearts is one that has been masterfully addressed by some thoughtful scholars in rhetoric and composition, most notably Lynn Worsham and Sharon Crowley. Sadly, our ability to transform behavior at an affective level may simply be out of reach for rhetor-teachers who hope to spark changes through classroom encounters. Insofar as affect is structured at multiple points of institutional, cultural, social, and educational sites, the libidinal attachments to discourse may run much deeper than we even know. And they certainly run out of our reach. This is all to say that we cannot make students (or anyone else) feel differently about development or other public crises. Neither can we hope to make someone feel a different relation to a site of discourse. As much as I dislike thoughtless development, my job is not to unbind the libidinal attachments students come to class with. The rhetorical shrug of awayness that marks distant public subjects is not solvable through a teacher's emotional reassignment surgery.

But the rhetoric classroom is indeed a transformative space. Though we cannot make changes at the level of feeling, we can still make changes at the level of discourse. In other words, we can transform how certain discursive commonplaces are used topologically. As rhetoricians and teachers, we can encourage new kinds of vernacular discursive habits that help to shape a different kind of public subject. Instead of creating conditions that allow people to imagine themselves as exceptional public subjects of feeling who exist at a distance from crises, new discursive habits may encourage public subjects who orient differently to the world and to others.

4

Lost Places and Memory Claims

> Hell, I don't live in Texas. I live in Austin.
> —Jerry Jeff Walker

> Welcome to the new Austin. Hell has never been closer or more accessible.
> —James Montgomery

On New Year's Eve 1980, Austin experienced one hell of a farewell party. On stage in a loud and rowdy music hall were some of the greatest musicians of the time. Everyone had gathered together to say good-bye to the Armadillo World Headquarters, where people like Janice Joplin, Willie Nelson, Stevie Ray Vaughan, and the Grateful Dead regularly played. In the early 1970s, the Chamber of Commerce promoted the music hall as a "colorful but somewhat crude converted armory [that] is frequented mostly by young, long-haired progressive county fans." When its lease expired in 1979, property owners decided to tear down the music hall in order to build the One Texas Center building. The announcement of Armadillo World Headquarters was met with sadness, disbelief, and a touch of anger at what was perceived to be Austin's growing corporate ambitions. One writer for the *Wichita Falls Record* wrote an obituary for the music hall two days after its doors were shut: "Close the Armadillo? That was inconceivable. The club was an integral cultural facet of the Hill Country. The mind reeled. Of course, we wanted to believe anything that assured us it wasn't so. It could happen in Dallas or Houston, but not in Austin" (Reese A1). Meanwhile, when a local Austin radio station asked country musician Charlie Daniels about the closing, Daniels let out a sigh: "Just what Austin needs, another parking lot. But I guess that's the way things are going" (Daniels). During the 1980s, the question of how "the way things are going" in Austin was not entirely clear. The city had not yet experienced the digital boom that would follow in the next decade, and plenty of music and cultural places were still standing. Nevertheless, some residents claimed to see the writing on the wall.

Over the next two decades, Daniels's comment proved to be prescient. Armadillo World Headquarters was only the first of many landmarks to be torn down in the name of corporate development. Les Amis, Austin's legendary hangout for artists, intellectuals, and burnouts, also eventually fell victim to rising rents and unbeatable corporate competition. When Les Amis first opened in 1970, it quickly attracted a loyal pack of regulars who sat for hours in its smoky haze. The café served cheap food, wine, beer, and coffee by the potful. In spite of its attempt to adopt the look of a Parisian café, Les Amis never looked fancy. Nobody was ever underdressed for Les Amis. In fact, in its wilder moments, it was not uncommon for regulars and staff to strip naked and dance on the tables. While you could hear live music at Les Amis, most people hung out in order to read, write, and just talk. Just talking was what the café was perhaps best known for. Writer Scott McLemee recalls, "Les Amis was, so to speak, a non-academic outcropping of what Pierre Bourdieu called *skhole*—that is, the open-ended space-time of scholastic life, in which questions can be raised and explored in a free discussion that evades any outside demands." By 1997, rising rents in the city center took their toll on the café. The infamous and much-loved corner space was soon torn down and replaced by an upscale strip mall with a large Starbucks as its anchor.

Two years later, another popular music venue, Liberty Lunch, was forced to close when the city decided to sell its prime downtown location. Liberty Lunch was certainly not fancy digs. The music hall sat in a building that was over a hundred years old, with little renovation to suggest its contemporaneousness. Its hand-painted mural blended together a lion and lamb that were playing with a beach ball, a volcano erupting cherries, and a huge lizard with a cherry sitting on its long tongue (not unlike a tab of acid). In the early 1980s, Liberty Lunch attracted a diverse crowd of aging hippies, college students, and Austin residents who just wanted to hear some music. In one 1983 review of the club, local writer John Kelso remarked that you would appreciate this club if you frequently used the phrase "I'm hep" during the 1960s. "It just screams of superannuated hippie" ("Liberty Lunch" A26). Shortly after Liberty Lunch first opened in the 1970s, its owners explained that they wanted to be more than a music hall. They wanted to be "a minicultural center in the inner city area" ("Liberty Lunch" A26). Anyone was able to play music on stage, regardless of their style or ability. They also served as a public gathering space for such activities as Mom's Apple Pie Bakeoff, Huevos Rancheros Cookoff, and other community events. Liberty Lunch had been a local favorite for almost four decades. Students and nonstudents alike packed the tiny space to hear all kinds of music, from major bands to local artists striking out for the first time.

Much like Les Amis's space, the location of Liberty Lunch was prime real estate for developers. The tiny brick building was not much to look at, but it sat on top of a beautiful downtown space that was in close proximity to Austin's Town Lake and the capitol. The city owned this land and had rented to Liberty Lunch for many years. However, the city soon realized much more money could be made by selling the land than renting to the much-loved, but barely profitable, local business. By 1999, city officials decided to sell the space to the more lucrative Computer Science Corporation (CSC). The promise of such prime real estate successfully lured CSC, and Liberty Lunch's tiny brick shack was demolished to make way for two six-story office buildings. Johnny Walker, a deejay at KLBJ, reminisced, "What a great place. I drank more beer in Liberty Lunch than any other club, because they didn't sell tequila. It's sad that we're losing it. It seems like once again we're tearing down paradise and putting up a factory, all in the name of progress, and I think we might be moving in the wrong direction" ("Long Live"). In the two decades since Armadillo World Headquarters closed, the same fate befell a number of Austin landmarks, including Quack's coffee shop, Sound Exchange, Inner Sanctum Records, Empanada Parlour, Black Cat Lounge, Mad Dog and Beans, the Varsity Theater, the original Antone's nightclub, and many others.

Although these spaces are gone, their public memory continues to be a powerful force among Austin's residents. The memories of these spaces and the memory of their demolition are frequently retold as a public narrative. Many residents circulate a narrative of loss, displacement, and harmful development in a city that now sounds almost utopian. In this chapter, I consider the memory narrative that circulates widely throughout Austin. This narrative is not unified, of course, and neither is it coherent across its multiple manifestations. Nevertheless, there is a shared narrative of loss and public memory that is palpably real throughout the city. Just as we saw in chapter 3, this discourse helps to cultivate and encourage a certain kind of public subject, one that exists in a space of exception. It goes without saying that both the nostalgia and the critiques involved in this narrative are not always completely valid. But, as Kathleen Stewart writes in *A Space on the Side of the Road,* stories are sometimes powerful not so much by virtue of their references and meanings, but for the sense they generate. People's stories (and, truth be told, our own stories) sometimes go nowhere. Perhaps they are unrelated to the subject at hand, they meander, they do not finish, or they forget to reach a point. Yet these meandering stories do not necessarily lack rhetorical impact. As Stewart writes, "In stories like these the hierarchy of concept over event, or 'idea' (with its metaphysics of the theoretical, the internal, and the active) over 'example' (connoting the supplemental, the literal, the external, the passive) breaks down and is inverted" (80). The passionate narratives of "lost Austin" sometimes seem to lack a point beyond memorializing, yet the meaning of these stories accumulates in the growing body of individual stories.

Maybe someone publicly remembers the last time they set foot in Armadillo World Headquarters, which causes someone else to recall the way Austin traffic used to be light and almost unnoticeable. These narratives spark others to recall their own experiences in Austin's lost places. Others remember how the city looked ten, twenty, or thirty years earlier. In turn, these memories prompt other stories. The accumulated meaning of these narratives creates a world where "politics [is not] lodged in self, world, and action, but in the process of styles" (Stewart, *Space* 85). The validity of truth or personal veracity is not the issue, in other words. The validity and veracity is in the feeling and the experience they create between the storytellers. In my analysis of the lost Austin narrative, therefore, I am less interested in determining the truth of narratives than I am in examining how this discourse develops in response to ongoing development. How do memory claims help to construct and nourish certain public roles?

Wherever spaces are undergoing change, such as citywide development, memory claims often emerge. We may call these claims a form of epideictic rhetoric, for they engage in public memorializing while still retaining a deliberative relation. Aristotle is quite clear that epideictic is a form of social action, since the rhetor actually urges people to model themselves upon the qualities that are being praised. "Consequently," writes Aristotle, "whenever you want to praise any one, think what you would urge people to do; and when you want to urge the doing of anything, think what you would praise a man for having done" (*Rhetoric* 1.9.1368a). Thus, epideictic speech, which is often infused with memory claims and memorialization, is didactic.[1] It instructs the audience about what kinds of values and actions are considered worthy. As Bradford Vivian puts it, "Whether in somber elegies or celebratory tributes, epideictic organizes the terms of public remembrance in order to shape perceptions of shared values and commitments serviceable to future deliberative agendas" ("Neoliberal Epideictic" 2). Memorializing through praise is more than mere recollection of places that no longer exist. Public memory and epideictic also relate to current and even future actions among a public.

Memory claims become a very obvious way to enter public debates about ongoing development. By praising old Austin's qualities—smallness, tolerance, uniqueness—the memorializing rhetors are obviously urging a certain course of action. They are speaking out against further growth, overdevelopment, and the arrival of more chain stores that displace local business. In this way, memory claims fit a traditional model of public deliberation. Rhetors weigh in on the changes by praising the praiseworthy and blaming the blameworthy. However, I also see another public function for these memory claims, a function that does not fit any traditional model of deliberation. In fact, in this chapter I explore how memory claims also serve as a way for subjects to write themselves out of public debate. Memory claims create both possibilities for engagement, as well as spaces of exceptionality and nonparticipation. Yet, as we have seen in previous chapters, exceptional subjects are not wholly apart from the public. They are distanced from the scene of deliberation while simultaneously retaining their public orientation.

By reading patterns of memory claims that emerge in response to development, I hope to better understand how exceptional publics are constituted through public talk. That is, how does this kind of talk allow some speakers to remain rhetorically and actively distanced from public discourse, while never being outside of its discourse? Memory claims help to cultivate this kind of strange distance in three ways. First, memory claims surrounding urban development often imaginatively carve out a difference between the "old" space and a "new" space. By locating themselves in the old space that is now fading away, memory rhetors anchor themselves in a different deliberative scene than the one taking place in the new space. Furthermore, memory claims tend to characterize the old space as public, whereas the new space is privatized in multiple ways. This public/private distinction also explains why memory rhetors must locate themselves in the deliberative space of the old place. Both of these discursive patterns reflect the ways in which rhetors remain publicly oriented without directly intervening in the immediate crisis at hand.

A second way in which memory claims create a space of exceptionality is by shifting agency away from the rhetors and onto others who are marked by their lack of memories. Memory discourse about how things have changed often attributes the moment of change to the arrival of "outsiders." These outsiders are narrated as the agents of change, while memory rhetors describe themselves as the objects of change. Rhetors thus identify with the urban space itself—especially in its formerly public character. In this discourse, the rhetors and the city are both acted upon by outsiders/others, creating a complicated erasure of agency among rhetor-citizens who engage in memory claims. Because they mark themselves as objects, and not agents, these rhetors write themselves out of the scene of deliberation. Indeed, deliberation seems impossible for them, insofar as they are not the original agents of change.

Finally, the third way in which memory claims create a space of exceptionality is by creating subjects of nonmemory as well as a site of feeling. If memory is one entry point into the scene of public debate and deliberation, then those who lack memory would also seem to lack this way into public discourse. However, I will suggest that public memory is like a horizon that is available to everyone for orientation purposes. That is, everyone can measure his or her own towardness or awayness from this horizon. Regardless of whether you feel a relation of nearness or remoteness, you are in relation to those narratives of memory. As I describe in the previous chapter about injury claims, even those who are distant from these claims remain publicly oriented simply through the feeling of relation.

Although the stories and memories I relate in this chapter have strong tones of nostalgia, we can also read these discursive moments as strategic responses to the present scene of crisis. Public memory is about more than the past. Stephen Browne points out that public memory is a "shared sense of the past, fashioned from the symbolic resources of the community and subject to its particular history, hierarchies, and aspirations" (248). In other words, the public creates a shared sense of the past from its present rhetorical resources. Moreover, Browne reminds us that public memory is embedded in the living structures of the present; memory is enacted in the immediate needs, wishes, and beliefs of those bodies engaged in the act of memorializing. This certainly seems to be the case with the public memory of a lost Austin. The narratives are ways of orienting to the current call for public deliberation about urban change. My interest in public memory is perhaps less related to the politics of remembering (how it happens, what it forgets, and so forth) and instead more focused on what it allows its users to do. Memory claims have a strange ubiquity around scenes of urban change and development. At the same time, this ubiquity does not necessarily mean more public intervention in the crisis of place.

Old Place Is Gone

One of the most common versions of the lost Austin narrative might be summed up as: "Old Austin is gone." It seems to offer both an epitaph and evidence that what was once a great city has now morphed into a very different place. For many people, Austin was once a city where beauty, tolerance, and creativity was unmatched by any other place in the world. Austin resident Don Clinchy extols the virtues of "old Austin": "Austin is to Texas as San Francisco is to, well, Oklahoma. It is a nation-state of progressive politics and culture surrounded by 700,000 square miles of provincial, backwatery fear and loathing. It is . . . raucous bars in 19th-century storefronts and cafes in old houses and vintage clothing stores in pleasantly shabby 1950s strip malls. It is Willie Nelson and Jerry Jeff Walker and memories of when they played at the long-gone Armadillo World Headquarters. . . . More than anything, Austin is the vague and pleasant notion that everything will be all right" (387). Echoing Clinchy's words, many other narratives of life in Austin take on a kind of cultural salvation twist. Compared to what Clinchy calls the "provincial" spirit of other Texas cities, Austin is often held up as a space of liberalism, progressivism, tolerance, and (in some versions) even hedonism. Local writer Robert Draper remarks that Austin once had a single raison d'être: "to be unlike Dallas and Houston. It was the place that never was, nor ever could be, Dystopia" (353). James Tynes, another Austin resident, tells a story of his first visit to Austin in 1975, when he was serving in the army. After being told about the vibrant music scene in Austin, Tynes decided to make a trip to see the city for himself: "Most of the bars on the coast were off limits to soldiers because of the 'bad vibes, man.' Austin was different. No one seemed to care where I came from or what I was doing before I walked into the bar. The music was what was important. No one asked me to leave because my hair was too short. The people and the music seemed to say: 'If you like this, then maybe you belong here'" (363). Perhaps it is less crucial for us to determine the validity of these stories—whether or not they are "true" reflections of Austin's civic spaces—than to notice the fact that they circulate throughout the city's spaces. They are real insofar as they have real impact.

In the days before Armadillo World Headquarters shut its doors forever in 1980, author Craig Hattersley wrote a version of this narrative for the *Texas Observer*:

> The revolution is mired in mortgages, drugs, the seventies' deadness— who knows? And in the meantime, Austin has gotten fat, sniffed success. There's no turning back. The Armadillo is history. Perhaps, today or tomorrow, you might happen to note Austin's air-pollution index climbing. You might curse the snarling traffic. You might wonder why your rent went up again . . . , why the music is what it is and the people what they have become. You might stop and think back with kindness on that funky old hall and its rancid carpets. It served a purpose, and well. (7)

Hattersley's narrative of a newer, fatter, and unfunkier Austin has only become more popular with each closing landmark. Austin musician Tim Abbot dubbed these lost Austin businesses "condo fodder," a moniker that aptly describes a popular perception among local residents that sees local businesses as actively destroyed by greedy developers who want those spaces for more profitable enterprises. "The things that attracted people here, all the beauty and the magic, we've sold those things out to the highest bidder," complains Abbot (Kelso, "Savor" B01). Austin's narrative of loss has become an important part of the larger public discourse on urban development.

Indeed, even before the technology boom of the 1990s, the city's cultural feel had long been made opaque through stories people told about Austin. Whereas Dallas and Houston were seen as ultraconservative and dull, Austin had seen itself as more progressive and unique. Austin was commonly described as an oasis within Texas. With the changing population of the 1990s, however, some Austinites began to complain about the "immigrants" from Dallas and Houston. The complaints reverberated with fears of colonization from the bland image of fast-paced, corporate-minded Dallas. As journalist Mike Perry laments, "I lived [in Austin] and went to school back in the '70s (yep, that's my dirty little secret) and I'm not sure there ever was a better town or city. Now? Well, there's still a lot to keep you interested over there on the Colorado, but to my mind it's turning into Dallas." Whatever Austin was at one time, it is no longer the same place. The golden days of Austin are gone, or so goes the narrative. This is a changed city.

Even traveling the streets takes on a new pace, direction, and movement. William Scheick's short story, "Gridlock," begins in a typical scene of Austin's daily traffic. "A trip that should take fifteen minutes now requires at least thirty-five, on a good day with no accidents. The new Austin—Gridlock City" (443). Landmarks that used to be standard gathering spots are being replaced by chain stores. Lifelong resident Rob Hill half-jokingly remarks, "In the last decade or so, Barnes and Nobel's [sic], Chili's, Beds, Baths and Beyonds, Best Buys and other stores were cloned in secret corporate labs in Montana, airlifted by flying saucers, and dropped like cluster bombs, cratering the Austin landscape" (408). But, in a more serious lament, plenty of other residents lament the city as if it were actually a dying body: "Austin is a fading beauty whose glory days at the sweethearts ball are far behind it," writes one resident, "but still insists on obsessing over herself. . . . Maybe somehow she can accept herself as she is now, and try to make the best of things. You're a big girl now, you ain't so special as you used to be" (Wilder).

In 2003, the *Austin Chronicle* ran a special issue devoted to "Lost Austin" and the places that are either gone or (almost) forgotten. The editors introduce the issue with a familiar story about old and new: "As this city has transformed over the last decade—or two, or three—more clear divisions can be seen between Old Austin (you know: hippies, funky live music bars, mom & pop shops) and New (techies, traffic, chain stores). . . . The new simply grew in the midst of the old or, too often, on top of it" ("Get It While You Can"). For many people, the "new Austin" that emerged from the ashes of old Austin was a direct effect of the technology boom. "Today Austin's Old Guard mutter among themselves in the margins of coffee shops and Tex-Mex dives," writes Draper. "The rest of the city has been subsumed into generic colossus of Greater Silicon Valley, a wasteland so smug and culturally vapid that Dallas circa 1963 seems flamboyant by comparison" (357). Draper's words repeat a common theme heard in the lost Austin narrative: a new vapidity has been ushered in by high-tech ambitions. On local blogs, comparisons between old Austin and new Austin are ubiquitous. One blogger sums up his perspective like this: "The NEW Austin has expectations, the NEW Austin is a more sophisticated, urban, urbane city. Old Austin is Armadillo World Headquarters, Jeffrey's and Threadgills, keg beer and salsa. . . . Old Austin refuses to embrace NEW Austin and wants to Keep it Weird. NEW Austin thinks Old Austin should just join the 21st Century already" ("Pray You Now").

Of course, laments about old versus new Austin do not emerge from a neat, linear narrative. Stories about the new Austin have emerged and reemerged numerous times. In 1985, the *New York Times* wrote a story on a new Austin that was troubling some locals. "Much to the dismay of many old-timers, a new Austin is emerging, a boom town based on computers and high technology. And, despite efforts to 'manage' growth, that boom has brought traffic jams, pollution and high prices" (Reinhold). Fifteen years later, the paper ran a nearly identical story. Journalist Helen Thorpe wrote, "Austin has always been a city of distinct worlds—a college town, a state capital and a live-music center all in one. But lately the number of worlds that Austin contains has been multiplying, and now, everywhere you look, there is the spectacle of worldviews clashing. . . . Because of all the new people, Austin now suffers from world-class traffic jams, polluted air, a serious lack of affordable housing and a school system in disarray." In fact, this same theme about Austin's anxiety has served as the backdrop to several *New York Times* stories since 1990. One 2002 story profiled the "weird" (and not so weird) characteristics across Austin, and a 2004 story told about a changed city where "tract mansions filled the hills surrounding the laid-back college town, music saloons were torn down for office buildings and lofts, and exotic martinis were ordered in places that used to serve only cold beer and shots" (Lewis). For at least twenty years, the lost Austin narrative has been a national story, not just a Texas one.

When I first moved to Austin in 1993, I was already hearing the nostalgic laments for a lost Austin that had disappeared. People were eager to repeat stories about Austin in the 1980s, 1970s, 1960s. Austin used to be smaller, more tolerant, less corporate, and more irreverent. Now it looks like any other place. As a teenager who had grown up in suburban Dallas, the stories did not ring very true to me. This place was very unlike the Texas suburbs I had known for most of my life. People stood on the sidewalk singing and handing out literature about their communes. I saw people with tattoos all over their bodies, piercings everywhere, with hair that looked wilder than anything I had ever seen. I met anarchists, hippies, militant vegetarians, artists, ultraserious Marxists, and old men who would talk to me about government conspiracies as I waited for the bus. In 1997, I left Austin for three years and returned again in the late spring of 2000. My first stop in town was a drive down Guadalupe Street, Austin's main street affectionately called "The Drag." I noticed how many local businesses had been closed. An independent bookstore was gone and a Barnes & Noble now sat in its place. Coffee shops were closed, replaced by corporate chains. More cars were on the road and I noticed fewer bicycles. As soon as I arrived at my friend's house after a long drive into town, I took my turn at the narrative. "Everything has changed so much," I complained. "It's like my Austin is gone."

In the course of writing this book, I have had many encounters with Austinites who launch into their own version of the narrative as soon as I tell them about my research. On one research trip to Austin, a waitress asked about my work that was spread all over a diner table. When I explained that I was writing on how we talk publicly about cities' changes, she smiled and said: "I used to love Austin. But I don't know what this place is anymore." The lament is so ubiquitous that it has become the butt of many local jokes. One local zine mockingly created "The Genties," awards in the style of the Academy Awards. The winner in the Best Gentrified Coffee Shop category was Les Amis. Writers jokingly observed, "The saddest thing about losing this ill-managed hippy mainstay is listening to old-school Austinites complain about how their favorite hangout is gone" ("The Genties"). The stories have circulated so much that they are a running joke.

The lost Austin narrative often emphasizes the transcendent magic of old Austin and its places that no longer stand. Just as people described the Barton Springs pool as a pseudodemocratic and mystical space where race, age, gender, and class were transcended, the places that are now "lost" tend to be remembered as equally magical. This storyline began early in Austin's mythology, so it is not surprising that it returns today as a tale of loss. In 1983, the *Dallas Times Herald* wrote an exposé of the Drag as a strange (and strangely magical) place: "Up the Drag you can, and often do, find anything. Books, sandals, dresses, jeans, calculators, . . . panhandlers, petition-seekers, blue-eyed Hindus and people with funny eyes" (R. Davis A19). When Liberty Lunch shut its doors, Robert "Beto" Skiles, a local musician, remembered its space as open to everyone: "Liberty Lunch opened up Austin's music gates to African music and to reggae and ska and so many other kinds of things. It was a truly alternative place. You had politicians and you had symphony people and you had children and you had punks and you had bikers and just anyone who wanted to dance. It's sad that it's going down. I had the same feeling when the Armadillo was taken down" ("Long Live"). Skiles characterizes the music hall as an "alternative place," a name that is quite appropriate in this instance. In this lost Austin version, the music halls, stores, and coffee shops that have closed are narratively framed as "alternative" to the harsh realities of the outside world. Class, race, and gender were temporarily suspended (or so goes the narrative), and a new zone of community was created in this space.

Part of the transcendence of old Austin was transcendent weirdness. Austinites have long considered their city to be weird. That is no knock. Austin is a city that thrives on being strange. As early as 1974, local writers like Bud Shrake were already writing obituaries to old Austin and its transcendently weird character. In a short piece for the *Texas Observer*'s twentieth anniversary issue, Shrake wrote, "There are precious few places in the whole of the USA that have got the odd magic that Austin has got. Some of the very things that make that true—cedar hills, Barton Springs, unexpected vistas, a sultry mañana way of moving—are the things that have to get torn up to make room for the people they seduce" (74). The odd magic seemed to range from Austin's natural beauty (hills, springs, trees) to its small commercial spaces. In the decades since Armadillo World Headquarters closed, the narrative shifted to the unweirdness of new places that were cropping up around Austin. The man known simply as Newman, former manager and quasi-celebrity of Les Amis, reflects on how Austin has changed: "Over time, as things become more prosperous, they become less peculiar and interesting. That's evident in no place more than here [in Austin]" (*Viva Les Amis*). Even the question about whether closed landmarks could relocate was largely met with skepticism. Eddie Wilson, owner of Threadgill's, was doubtful that the "odd magic" of places like Liberty Lunch could be recreated in a different location: "The Lunch is what it is in the minds and memories of a lot of people because of who was there and where it was and what was going on. You take a name, relocate it, and it becomes a little bit more like a car dealership. It's like moving a gift shop from the Grand Canyon to somewhere else. You can still get postcards, but it's not the Grand Canyon" ("Long Live").

Many Austinites became quite vocal in their displeasure over these changes. *Austin Chronicle* journalists Chris Walters and Jim Shahin articulated this unhappiness in a lament about Austin's transformation: "Austin was a place for misfits and dreamers and rebels, a work in progress toward some endearingly flawed bohemian utopia or, as the late Doug Sahm would have it, Groover's Paradise. It was smug, self-righteous, and never as progressive as it pretended—Where's the mass transit? Where's the minority mayor?—but it was also free-spirited, socially tolerant, and culturally exciting. It was different, and it was special. And it was special because it was weird." The weirdness of local businesses was seen as being lost in the onslaught of big box stores that carried the same products as a similar store in another city or state. It became more difficult for local artists, writers, or musicians to speak directly to the store owner about carrying their products. Even the larger and more established local businesses found it difficult to compete with big box stores that began to open in direct proximity to their sites. But it was the lost weirdness that seemed to stick in public memory.

In 2002, local businesses began to take more aggressive measures to fight this trend. Two businesses in particular, BookPeople Bookstore and Waterloo Records, changed the shape of the city's rhetoric after they borrowed a phrase from a sticker that had been appearing sporadically around Austin: "Keep Austin Weird." This phrase gained popularity after independent bookstore BookPeople and music store Waterloo Records decided to fight the city's incentives to a large Border's bookstore, which was to open directly across from BookPeople and Waterloo. The owners printed bumper stickers with the phrase "Keep Austin Weird" and the store logos. They initially printed five thousand stickers, which were immediately snatched up. The stickers were so popular that the stores immediately ordered another ten thousand and then twenty-five thousand. Almost a year later nearly sixty thousand stickers had been distributed. There were enough "weird" stickers for every one in fifteen Austinites. While BookPeople and Waterloo (and their supporters) successfully and aggressively used the campaign to block the construction of Borders, the sticker and phrase continued to circulate as a synecdochical cry against the onslaught of the corporate homogenization of Austin. Soon enough, other Austin businesses joined the call to weirdness. Local businesses—everything from Amy's Ice Cream to Shady Grove restaurant—began to sell T-shirts that featured their individual logos on front and the same "Keep Austin Weird" logo on the back.

The phrase "Keep Austin Weird" quickly passed into the city's cultural circulation, taking on the importance of a quasi-civic duty. One pledge pitch for a local public radio station told listeners, "You too can work towards keeping Austin weird by pledging to keep KOOP Radio 91.7 FM on the air." In certain parts of Austin, it is nearly impossible to go for very long without finding some display of the slogan on a T-shirt, a car's bumper sticker, a tote bag, a mug, or a local business's billboard vowing to "keep it weird." Though the slogan is a kind of bonding experience, it seems to suggest that weirdness is under attack in Austin. The city's "odd magic" is on the endangered species list. Red Wassenich, who is largely credited with creating the slogan, admits that the phrase does contain a certain amount of nostalgia. "If we have to make this plea," he writes, "that means the battle is being lost. Sadly, that's correct" (1). This popular narrative thus sees something beyond the independent stores themselves as disappearing from Austin. Something magic, odd, different, "weird" is also being lost.

The more the weirdness disappears, the more Austin turns into "Anyplace, USA." At least, this is the fear that is expressed by people who participate in this narrative. "Just what the hell is happening to Austin?" asks one resident in a letter to the *Austin Chronicle*. "I've lived here 14 years and seen some major changes: the buildup of the "warehouse" district and downtown, the meteoric rise of loft apartments and property taxes, the proliferation of tech companies, and, consequently, the loss of some of my favorite places. . . . We are giving up that old local Austin hippie feel of 'peace and love' in exchange for the dull, lifeless material growth of the corporate machine" (Swanner). When the city council asked for public comments on their commercial development plans, they received hundreds of letters begging the city to curtail the pace of development across Austin. Development is inevitable, one resident writes, but "please just don't let Austin become a Houston/Dallas strip mall hell." Another respondent put this sentiment in slightly stronger language: "The city council seems to be happy to let Austin become a strip mall. It's already lost much of it's [sic] flavor, but might keep some semblance of a nice town if something is done now." Many other writers asked city council to take a more active role in controlling the rise of commercial developments: "Please control the big box stores. We do not need a Lowe's, Home Depot, Target and Wal-Mart in every neighborhood. It seems particularly unnecessary to have duplications like a Lowe's and Home Depot both in the same proximity," writes a concerned Austinite (Austin Planning and

Development). It is not that Austin had no strip malls before massive development happened, of course. But many locals argued that Austin had a uniqueness that kept it from looking and feeling like any other place in the world.

In 2005, one resident gathered the memories of old, weird Austin into a three-hour stage play. Dave Steakley wrote and directed *Keepin' It Weird*, which dramatized interviews with over two hundred Austinites. The monologues combine to give a sense of Austin's spirit and its one-time uniqueness that some see as forever displaced. Steakley's quasi-ethnographic play emphasizes the strange, unique, and utterly Austinish character of Texas's capital. The play ran for several months, and many reviewers saw it as a paean (even if an overly nostalgic one) to something magical that is now missing. The self-referential nature of this play was not wasted on at least one reviewer, who chastised the production for being too indulgent: "What does it say about a city so in love with itself that its leading professional theater creates an original production about a slogan about itself, oftentimes performed in front of the very people who spoke the words that make the script?" (Beach). Although the reviewer does not answer his own question, we might see the play as evidence that the lost Austin narrative is accepted as true partly because of its frequent testimonies. The play calcifies these narratives, which hardens them into a type of rhetorical evidence.

At least one formal study examines the level of awareness among residents in regard to the "weird Austin" phenomenon. Cultural geographer Joshua Long conducted formal interviews with almost a hundred informants in Austin. Around thirty of these were considered "key informants," closely involved with the city initiatives in some way. But many more were simply Austin residents who had different levels of awareness about actual plans and developments. Long discovered that the kinds of knowledge differed among informants, yet a majority of interviewees expressed some strong opinions about Austin's development: "Despite the flexibility of sampling criteria, almost all interviewees exhibited a significant level of awareness of the 'Keep Austin Weird' phenomenon and about the situation of the city of Austin in general. In other words, it seemed that most Austinites were well aware of the growth and transformation of the city they called home, and there was no shortage of opinion. The passionate attitudes and well thought-out responses suggested that 'Keep Austin Weird,' local business promotion, downtown revitalization, gentrification, and the 'homogenization' of the cultural landscape were topics of frequent discussion" ("Sustaining" 211). Throughout hundreds of interviews, Long discovered that residents "repeatedly voiced concern over the loss of the city's cultural character and a sense of detachment to the changing cultural landscapes of Austin. Interviewees employed several terms to describe these feelings. They spoke of the city's 'soul,' the loss of 'weirdness,' the commercialization of the Austin 'vibe,' and the 'homogenization' of the city landscape, an important symbol of the city's nonconformist attitude" ("Sustaining" 215–16). Long expresses some surprise that very few interviewees strayed from the central line. More remarkable yet, he notes, "even recent arrivals regularly claimed solidarity with the 'Old Austin' or 'Keep Austin Weird' mentality" ("Sustaining" 216).

These laments are both epideictic and deliberative. These memory narratives make claims about the quality of changes in Austin. To put it mildly, most of them pronounce the city's recent development a bad thing. By looking closely at the patterns of claims, we might also locate a complex sense of deliberative space being created through these memories. The stories carve out two kinds of spaces: a new Austin and the old Austin. The new Austin has replaced the old Austin physically, emotionally, and spiritually. Memory claims and "lost space" narratives allow the speaker to place herself in a different place altogether. Deliberations are about that place, the one that once existed long ago, not this place. Of course, plenty of Austin residents do debate about current development practices within Austin. However, by engaging in this specific kind of memory claim, the speaker makes themself somewhat distant from the place that is here right now: new Austin. Therefore, the deliberative possibilities only go so far. If memory claims place the rhetor and the audience in the "space" of a different place (a place that is inimical to the space they now find themselves), then the very rhetorical situation is shaped differently. The audience, exigence, constraints, and relevant scene are situated within that old space of weirdness, transcendent community, and uniqueness. In this way, rhetors of memory claims write themselves out of deliberations concerning the actual space in which they find themselves.

There is another way that these claims create an excluded public subjectivity. Within these particular memory claims, old Austin is retold as a space where public discourse seemed to thrive. Many of the narratives and memories bring up the old Austin in terms of its interaction, engagement, and publicness. Stories about the now-defunct Liberty Lunch and Armadillo World Headquarters tend to emphasize the different kinds of people who all gathered in one place. These were spaces of encounter among people who might not normally interact—yuppies and hippies all happily grooving to the same sounds. The new Austin is the opposite of all that. In this way, the lost Austin narrative draws upon the tensions of private and public. Many of the stories point to the public character of coffee shops, music halls, and independent stores, while the replacement office buildings and chain stores seem to have a private character. Some local residents see the changes as a concerted effort to privatize Austin in accordance with a city master plan. Craig Koon, the longtime manager of the independent record store Sound Exchange saw Liberty Lunch's closing as an example of the privatization plans: "I think it's perfect that a computer company is going in there. It's part of [Mayor] Kirk Watson and his minions' message to Austin: Be part of my future or get out" ("Long Live"). That many people described feeling "pushed out" of Austin captures this tension between virtuous public spaces and loathsome private spaces.

Whether or not this distinction is cultivated partly out of idealistic nostalgia, the perception of its reality is palpable throughout the city's discourses. Brad Buchholz's homage to the (almost closed) Hole in the Wall, a seedy dive bar that had been a local favorite since 1973, noted that places like these Austin establishments were almost public spaces: "Yeah, the Hole in the Wall was a nasty, smoky place on any given midnight, with some of the grungiest restrooms this side of Istanbul. It was hard to park. There was never enough room—to sit or to stand—on the night of a special show. And God, the smoke. . . . And yet, the Hole in the Wall belonged to us. Musicians who played there knew it, and the people who went there knew it" (Buchholz). Buchholz goes on to name the places that have replaced the Drag's many landmarks: a Starbucks, Eckerd's, Gap, Tower Records. They are simply places with "a lot of money from national chains, with no connection to Austin or its history" (Buchholz). More than a missing connection, however, these new places are not seen as public in the same way. Writing about the Starbucks that has replaced Les Amis, McLemee remarks, "You can't imagine a poetry reading taking place in such an environment. No doubt it is more efficient and profitable than Les Amis ever was. But the drive to uniformity and perfect top-down control seems joyless, no matter how much Bob Marley they play over the loudspeaker" (McLemee). That places like Les Amis and the Hole in the Wall allowed members of the public to read poetry, play music, and even hold political meetings in their spaces made them more than a business. Regulars like Buchholz believed that these places "belonged to us."

This argument about old Austin as public and the new Austin as private also creates the possibility of exclusion from deliberation. We cannot deliberate about private spaces in the same way that we talk about public space. Of course, we do argue about private corporate decisions all the time (Should BP be held responsible for its unethical practices? Should Walmart treat its employees better?) However, the demarcation of space as private or public does change the way we argue. In fact, by dubbing a space as private, we alter the exigence altogether. The deliberative track pursued in the lost Austin narrative seems to debate whether or not the so-called private spaces are good or bad for Austin. This focus of deliberation siphons away attention to a different kind of deliberative question, namely, how should Austin continue to develop in conjunction with these new corporate spaces? While plenty of people are having this very debate, it is often not happening in the same rhetorical space as memory claims. In other words, these rhetorical scenes are working from two very different questions.

Furthermore, the arguments about public versus private spaces have an interesting flip side. One counternarrative actually imagines Austin's development as a public gesture, insofar as it provides more jobs, more money, and more opportunities for more people. In one online debate about development's drawbacks and benefits, one comment chastised other readers for their overwhelming criticism of development: "Scream all you want at all the new development, but it's merely concrete evidence that you're probably way better off economically (jobs, tax revenues, etc.) if [you're] here in Austin than in most of the country right now—and it's been a long time since anyone could honestly say that 'round these parts" ("Development Forces"). Another online comment from an Austin resident likewise testifies to development's quasi-public character: "I've lived downtown for over 5 years, have owned a condo for 4.5, and have walked to work downtown (in the tech industry) for over 2 years. . . . I know plenty of other professionals in other downtown condos who also walk to work. A couple of them work with me. I can name quite a few tech companies with office spaces downtown and some of them are hiring. Perhaps you've heard of one called Google? They're looking for dozens and dozens of software engineers last time I checked" ("Condomania"). Corporate development and technology booms do not necessarily cut off people from public encounter, or so goes the powerful counternarrative.

Even in the emotional debate about tearing down a longtime Mexican-American restaurant and low-income bilingual daycare in order to build a hotel, counternarratives offered a defense remarkably similar to the arguments we saw in the previous chapter. "While sad to see another homegrown Austin business have to move or close, the fact of the matter is that change is inevitable," one commenter to the *Austin American-Statesman* wrote with a resigned tone. "The hotels will bring in much more tax revenue which is better for all of us" ("What Local Businesses"). Another resident chimed in with even stronger sentiments: "The hotel will create a huge tax base. Thousands upon thousands of Austinites will reap the benefits of this tax base for parks, roads, social services, libraries, hospitals and a multitude of other public services. Hundreds upon hundreds of jobs will be created by this relatively pollution free business. Multiple businesses located in the downtown area will benefit as well" ("What Local Businesses"). In the spaces between these narratives and counternarratives exist a question about what kinds of places serve the most people. What is public, and what serves the public good? The confusion between public and private places can also be seen in one young woman's response to a question about local businesses disappearing. The documentary film *Viva Les Amis* features an interview with a young woman who is asked what she thinks about places like Les Amis being displaced in favor of Starbucks and other corporate chains. "As far as corporate versus private, it's very much a capitalist society," she explains. "Corporations are able to give their employees benefits. But I still don't think there's a replacement for the feeling of family that comes from a local coffee shop" (*Viva Les Amis*). When asked if she knows what used to be in the space before Starbucks, the woman answers tentatively. "I think it was a private coffee shop. Is that right?" Her distinctions between corporate space (like Starbucks) and private space (like Les Amis) mark another interesting distinction between what counts as a public space. In this counternarrative, public takes on the characteristics of "more for more people." While a "private" space offers independence and creativity, "public" spaces offer the security of jobs, benefits, and economic stability for all citizens—even those who openly dislike the new corporate presence in Austin.

Memory claims about old Austin work in multiple ways to generate two different conceptual spaces. One effect of this spatial conceptualization is that the deliberative exigence also changes. By locating myself in the old space of lost Austin, I may actually write myself out of the new scene of development's changes across the city. My deliberative focus is entrenched in the old space, where different actors and exigencies exist. The new space contains new sets of rhetorical elements that do not involve me. Though I may live in this physical space, therefore, I am rhetorically exceptional to it. That is, I am outside of its rhetorical situation. In this way, the memory claims about lost Austin create a public subjectivity that resembles the exceptional subject: those who are both a part of and apart from the system they find themselves within. Another way of saying this is that memory claims help to shift agency away from oneself and toward another body. This shift also removes the call to deliberate and debate, since the excluded subject does not seem to be the one who is affecting change.

Shifted Agency

Another version of the lost Austin memory claims focuses on the others, the outsiders, who have flooded into the city. This version emphasizes a trope of displacement and replacement. Many of these claims highlight how outsider corporate development is now creating a new kind of city. Local businesses that were once landmarks suddenly seemed to be replaced by "chain stores," a category that carries an outsider connotation. When the notorious coffee shop on the Drag, affectionately called Quack's, closed its doors in 1999, sentiments quickly turned to fears about the future of corporate development. As one longtime Austinite told a reporter, "Before we know it, the funky Austin Drag will be just like any other strip mall in America, totally devoid of local character." Although another business would almost certainly replace the beloved spot, many people marked the closing of Quack's as a sign of old Austin's disappearance. As one editorial commented, "And so another small piece of the places and people that made Austin Austin is going, going and eventually gone" ("Quack's, Coots"). Similarly, one Austin musician commented, "The most insidious thing is that the developers and landlords are cleaning up replacing these beloved places with chain or chain subsidiary operations designed to look all Austiny and unique." Whether or not the chain stores actually look "Austiny" or not, many people saw these places as symptoms of their city's sickness. Some writers, like Reid Worth, blamed the city's determined effort to win high-tech corporate residents. "The ripple effect of Smart Growth coupled with the tech boom raised rents for residents and local businesses alike as well," writes Worth. "The result is a Starbucks where Les Amis used to be, whatever the hell is violating the space formerly occupied by Quack's, and the loss of Hole in the Wall. And that's just the Drag." Chain stores were not only reviled because they displaced much-loved landmarks, but also because they were simply not Austin.

It was not only outsider chain stores that stirred up such loathing. The "newcomers" also seemed to be a perennial thorn in Austin's side. In the early 1970s, even singer Willie Nelson had a suggestion for how to keep growing numbers of outsiders away from Austin: "Build a big tall electrified barb wire fence around the place and give out numbers to the folks inside. I suppose I would probably be about number 217,156. Anybody with a number higher than 250,000 has to leave town and can't come back" (quoted in Shrake 27). Of course, Austin never did build that fence. And the city quickly shot past the 250,000 mark. In 1980, Austin's population was around 585,051. By 2009, that number had reached 1,705,075.[2] The steady influx of new residents raised charges of "carpetbaggers," since the latest newcomers seemed to arrive in the city strictly for the promise of good money in the growing tech industry. Even relatively new Austin residents participated in this screed against newcomers. Novelist and journalist Robert Draper had some fun with this narrative in a tongue-in-cheek farewell to old Austin: "Each of us could calculate to the day when Austin went to hell. It was when some ethos-drenched five-year-old local institution . . . fell prey to the evil spirit of capitalism and expired amid bitter eulogies. It was when Don Johnson began flying to town to strafe the local titty bars. . . . More likely, it was when your carpetbagging ass moved there, one month after mine did" (355).

Perhaps the bitter sentiments from residents are easy to understand. Traffic, smog, and sky-high rents became a problem in a relatively short period of time. Average home prices increased 40 percent between 1999 and 2009, from an average of $170,000 to $240,000. Rents also shot up for everyone across Austin. Local businesses also found themselves paying almost twice as much for the same space. Sound Exchange, a popular local record store that sat in the heart of central Austin for twenty-three years, is one example of a business that was forced to shut down its operation due to higher rent. Whereas Sound Exchange's rent had previously been $2,800 throughout the 1990s, the new lease in 2003 climbed to $4,369 per month (J. Gross). After serving as one of the most unique record stores in Austin since 1977, Sound Exchange finally closed its doors in January 2003. The business was quickly replaced by Baja Fresh Mexican Grill, a national fast food chain. With bitter humor, former Sound Exchange manager Craig Koons concluded that "there simply wasn't room for Sound Exchange in 'New Austin.'"

High rents and traffic jams were not the only reason newcomers posed such a problem. The fact that they lacked public memory also seemed to be a source of contention for rhetors of memory claims. Local writer John Kelso laments the changes in Austin, yet he sees the lost Austin narrative as a lost cause. Speaking about memory claims, Kelso writes, "My problem with this theme is that I'm afraid most new Austinites don't really care if the old Austin is taking a hike. And why should they? If you didn't see Stevie Ray Vaughan play at Hut's, how would you know what you missed?" ("Savor"). Local documentarians dramatized the problem of memory loss among newcomers in their film *Viva Les Amis,* which interviews young residents about the history of Austin's spaces. Early in the documentary, we see an image of a large and highly stylized Starbucks that now stands on the corner where Les Amis, with its unique take on a Parisian café in Texas, used to be. The filmmaker stops a young woman on the street and asks her if she knows what was here before Starbucks. "I've never seen it," she says, "but I heard that this location was, uh, what do you call those shops that sell pipes and things?" Another young woman is asked the same question: "People I talked to said this used to be another coffee shop, a private coffee shop, called, um, oh I don't remember." She laughs and waves her hand in a dismissive gesture. Others who are stopped at random make guesses ranging from "head shop" to a genuine puzzlement that anything was here before Starbucks.

In recent years, some of this anticarpetbagger discourse has turned to a specific kind of outsider: the Californian.³ Newspaper editorials, letters to the editor, and plenty of online message boards frequently feature comments about the "Californians" who are changing the Austin landscape. More than a few comments encourage these newcomers to go back to California, as if their presence is an intrusion or an invasion. One letter writer said, "What I love the most about living in this part of Texas is that it's so unlike Houston, San Antonio and Dallas. If the 'New Silicon Valley' and influx of Californians who are moving here is one reason for the new homebuilding, my suggestion is for land development to move elsewhere around our city to house these people. Or, better yet, why don't they all just go back home? If Texans will remember, they never liked our state anyway" (Boone). Other residents directly attributed Austin's rapid development changes to the ex-Californians who flooded the city. As another letter to the *Austin American-Statesman* exclaims, "The Austin I know and love is losing the charm with all the transplants coming in trying to turn a funky college town into a cosmopolitan big city. We should have shut the gates a long time ago!" ("What Local Businesses").

The anti-California attitudes in Austin have taken on a life of their own, though it is unclear how many developmental changes can actually be attributed to an influx of Californian people or ideas. As Joshua Long, "The perception that Californians are creating the demand for downtown condo development, increasingly cosmopolitan food and drink choices, and a valet-parking lifestyle is common. Yet, reliable statistics that might confirm these perceptions have been difficult to find" (*Weird* 88). Nevertheless, the Californian (a figure that Kelso dubbed the "espresso-suckin', SUV-drivin', no-dairy-eatin', kumquat-chokin' Californicator" ["Savor"]) continued to serve as a synecdoche for the detested changes happening across the city.

Although many residents saw outsiders as the cause of Austin's rapid changes, others blamed a combined partnership between the city government and high-tech industry. When Intel announced that it would not complete its half-built high-rise downtown as a result of the economic collapse, some locals saw this as another example of how high-tech was turning the city's soul into its own empty shell. Austin resident Dave Lambert remarks, "It certainly is amusing to see the concern over Intel's choice to not finish its building. What disappoints me is the lack of public concern over the non-resurrection of Liberty Lunch. It was bulldozed in the name of the [Mayor] Watson Memorial Digital Downtown, despite the fact that it was a vital, vibrant part of the quality of life in Austin long before high tech. This is just another sign that Austin has become a vapid, soulless, polluted, expensive, crowded clone of Anytown, U.S.A. I guess I'll go to Starbucks for a latte to soothe my nerves." If old Austin was a unique place that stood apart from any other American city as a "funky" place, new Austin was becoming bland and unoriginal. The culprit could be traced back to the city's overzealous welcoming of the technology sector, a different kind of outsider. Some residents were more cautious in their assessment. "I'm not certain if High-Tech is to blame or if it is just greed that it is the true culprit, but something bad is afoot here," wrote Mike Thomas in a letter to the *Austin Chronicle*. Similarly, political commentator Jim Hightower saw the arrival of outsider technology businesses as an intrusion into a formerly open city:

> A few years ago, our mayor gave taxpayer subsidies to lure something called CSC Corporation to town, giving it the spot of city-owned land that Liberty Lunch had rented for years. So now we have a cold, six-story building housing a high tech military contractor that has no roots in Austin, is not in character with our city, and offers nothing to our way of life. What we do not have are the good eats, good sounds, and good spirit that emanated every night from that spot, drawing thousands of enthusiastic customers and helping define Austin for people everywhere.

In this narrative version, then, it is not simply transplants from California who are killing the old Austin. City government had encouraged companies to arrive on the scene and had displaced longtime businesses either deliberately or inadvertently. Either way, it was the arrival of outsiders that precipitated the transformation of Austin into a "vapid, soulless, polluted, expensive, crowded clone" of any other town in the United States.

By shifting attention to the "real" agents—corporations, Californians, greedy city officials, the high-tech industry—the rhetors who make memory claims can write themselves out of a more complex scene of agency. Again, these memory claims locate their speakers in a specific space (old Austin) that has experienced changes. These changes appear to come from the outside, whether it is the encroachment of new populations or new commercial spaces. As one longtime resident lamented, when these outsiders moved in, "our city was being so coldly snatched from [our] clutches" (Darr). The sense of local that infuses this discourse is carefully produced and made distinct from global flows of capital. However, Arjun Appadurai points out how the local and the global are not distinct from each other, but exist in a dialectical tension that is not isomorphic (198). Neither is the local distinct from the hierarchical nation-states and global flows. Localities can even be seen as contextual responses to these hierarchical forces.

Within the narrative of lost Austin, many speakers point out that the feeling of Austin is not the same feeling of Dallas or Houston. Both Dallas and Houston are cities that are deeply entrenched in global flows of capital, with their highway systems, suburban rings, and corporate office parks aimed at pursuing a smooth space of international commerce. While some Austin residents may resist the city's redesign as a space of global production, we can all locate ourselves within these dialectical tensions. Just as localities cannot remove themselves from the force of global capital flows, individual subjects are not outside of this system. To use a somewhat worn-out term, we are thoroughly networked beings. As Steven Shaviro points out in his science-fictionalized theory *Connected*, we live in a networked space of flows and connections, not fixed sites. "The predominant form of human interaction . . . is networking," he writes (131). Nevertheless, by attributing urban changes to "outsiders," rhetors reimagine their agency as existing outside this network. The flows of global capital that stimulate urban redevelopment are somehow outside of their own daily form of human interactions.

The work of attributing changes to an outside agency allows subjects to exist both inside and outside the system in which they currently live and work. Residents and lovers of old Austin experience the changes as happening to them, without their own participation in the network. They bear no responsibility for these changes. This rhetoric resembles what Patricia Roberts-Miller (following Kenneth Burke) calls a scapegoat device, which allows rhetors to project agency for unhappy events onto another body. By projecting agency, rhetors turn themselves into objects who are being acted upon by another body (38). Furthermore, writes Roberts-Miller, "Projection is distracting in a politically useful way, in that it shifts the stasis" (38). This rhetorical maneuver shifts the stasis question away from the rhetor's own potential actions. Instead, the stasis is now centered upon the scapegoat. In the example of lost Austin's memory claims, rhetors have turned the focus away from their own complex involvement in the system of global capital flows.

Development discourse often contains rhetorical gestures of shifted agency. One of the most illustrative recent examples of such shifts, and the problems that come from engaging in this discourse, is captured in Nathan McCall's novel *Them*. McCall tells the story of longtime residents in a historically black Atlanta neighborhood that is experiencing gentrification. In an early scene, two men sit outside on a porch, talking about sports and the upcoming boxing match. As they make a friendly wager over the fight's outcome, they notice one of the new neighbors walking down the street. The men are troubled by the sight. "Lately there had been rumors," McCall's narrator explains, "all kinds of wild rumors, about them coming through the neighborhood, snooping around for who knows what" (38). For several minutes, the men sit quietly, lost in their own thoughts. Finally, the younger man voices what both men are thinking: "I think we better get ready, Mr. Smith."

"I know," his neighbor replies, "They coming" (39). Throughout McCall's book, change is catalyzed by them: the people who seem to sneak into a space that does not belong to them. They—the people who will inevitably bring change—stand in contrast to the majority of us. We are the people, and they are a small band of individuals who seek to attack the life that we have made here for ourselves.

Something is missing in a shifted focus on them. Most troubling is a missing space for imagining how we are all situated within many local, regional, and global networks. There is no room to consider how our own agencies are spread across temporal and spatial networks, so much so that we ourselves are implicated in the very processes of change that development critics find so abhorrent. When changes come to our neighborhoods and our cities, we risk adopting a distanced public role if our discourse focuses primarily on them: the ones who invade us from the outside. In fact, as Roberts-Miller points out, the stasis itself shifts during this act of scapegoat projection. Rather than considering future problems of sustainability, questions of a deliberative nature, this kind of discourse is rooted in the present and the past. Discourse takes on a more judicial, even epideictic tone.

Other problems of shifted agency can also be found in so-called NIMBY (not in my backyard) discourse concerning unwanted sites like dumps, electrical plants, and prison facilities. By shifting agency to those bodies that would bring such sites into close contact with residents, NIMBY rhetors successfully avoid the question of their own culpability within a system that needs to increase dump sites, electrical plants, and prison facilities. How do our own daily activities contribute to the system? By shifting the agency to outsiders and others—them—who want to bring such unwanted sites into our neighborhoods, we deftly avoid this conversation. Likewise, although Austinites are complicit with everyday corporate activities (including the cutting-edge wireless technology sector), many residents contend that they are brutalized through these very corporate spaces. Herein lies a particularly powerful mantra of excluded subjects: the system affects me, but I do not affect the system.

Memory as Orienting Horizon

As we have seen in these narratives of lost Austin, public memories of landmarks have become a kind of discursive currency. They are a synecdoche for the city as a whole. When director Richard Linklater was recently asked to reflect on the city's changes over the past two decades, he remarked that his Austin-based film *Slacker* was "documenting the end of something." Linklater's 1991 cult classic film follows a number of unnamed characters and their unrelated narratives around the streets, small stores, and public sites in Austin. Rather than telling the story of any particular character, *Slacker* actually tells the story of Austin and its one-time "slacker" culture of drifting, underachieving college-aged oddballs. The camera follows various people around the streets of central Austin, up and down the main streets, into local bookstores and coffee shops, through parks, and into small diners. The characters, for the most part, are constantly walking the streets of Austin at a slower than slow pace. Like the "slacker culture" itself, the movements are plodding, sometimes aimless, and never rushed. For Austinites, *Slacker* became the mark of the city's spirit. As we have seen in this chapter, however, Austin lost many of the very landmarks memorialized in *Slacker,* replaced by chain stores, franchises, or nothing at all. For many locals, *Slacker* became a mark of something lost—an almost personalized "individual" who was gone, but not forgotten. As *Austin Chronicle* writer Mark Savlov states: "Much of what you see in *Slacker* today is long gone, but like a good friend since passed, the memories of the fundamental locales linger in the minds of those who were present at this magical, formative time. And, of course, depressed, aging slackers such as myself can always pop in the *Slacker* tape, crack a cold Shiner Bock, and return to the old school." Unlike the (perceived) fast-paced, freeway culture of Dallas, Houston, or other Texas cities, Austin was seen as a place where you could drift. Perceptions of Austin often imagined the city as a walking culture, a community of familiar faces. It was, in a word, small-scale—a feeling materialized in the drifting imagery of *Slacker.*

The fashion retailer Anthropologie recently showed how public sites can evoke an entire city, when it featured Austin as a backdrop for its summer 2009 catalog. The *Austin American-Statesman*'s fashion reviewer points out this high-profile showcase, yet he notes that only a certain version of Austin is revealed. The catalog "doesn't concern itself with New Austin (tall condo towers or the Domain). The storyline is signature Old Austin" (Harper). Models are photographed beside Austin's oldest and funkiest buildings that any longtime resident would recognize. The images look quite like what people call "old Austin," with a careful avoidance of more generic lofts, high-rises, and newer downtown nightspots that sum up what people mean by "new Austin." The Anthropologie catalog illustrates how such memory spaces serve (quite literally) as rhetorical currency. Not only does it evoke a sense and meaning for people who are flipping through the images (whether images of a catalog or a film), but it also serves as an entry point for people who want to talk about urban development as a crisis.

Consequently, public memories of lost Austin create what Edward Casey calls an external horizon for the Austin public sphere. Casey claims that public memories are actually an external horizon of the public domain. Public memories become the sense-making limits of our mutual understanding. Just as the physical horizon gives coherence to the environment around us, so do public memories help to organize and limit our sense of public space (30). Public memories are more than simple recollections, therefore. They actually help us to reflect and make sense of our present and future. The public memory of a lost Austin certainly appears to serve as an external horizon. Members of a public use these memories as "an active resource on which current discussions and actions draw" (Casey 25). People's memories of music halls and gathering spaces provide them with a measurement, and a way to describe the quality, of Austin's development. It is an active resource from which to draw and create meaning. Although the horizon is socially constructed, it does provide a means of comparison. Therefore, while public memories, such as those we have seen so far in this chapter, may appear to be backward looking, they are actually focused on the present.

Compare Austin's narrative to a much different kind of public memory in another rapidly developing space: Branson, Missouri. Nestled in the Ozarks, Branson is home to Old West theme parks, family-friendly music shows, and plenty of stores that feature authentic products like handmade soap and woodcarvings. Jerry Rodnitzky writes that Branson, with its simulated images of "old fashioned values" and a "historical America," draws upon public memories of country-and-western musical reviews, hand craftsmanship, and a less divisive country (which Rodnitzky reads as code for a less ethnically and racially diverse country). The public memories of a more bucolic America are dubious as facts, of course, yet they still serve as an external horizon for many people. Rodnitzky points out that Branson's rapid development as a corporate entertainment makes it more like Las Vegas (not the place of old-fashioned values). Yet the horizon of public memory allows its participatory public to read its development as moving toward that nostalgic horizon. "Branson," writes Rodnitzky, "for all its glitter and hype, is clearly not postmodern; it is premodern. Its attempt to escape the present makes it reactionary rather than conservative" (105). Ironically, Branson's supporters see increased development as a step (back) toward something greater.

If it seems like public memory constructs the context for the very thing that is being examined, that is because this is precisely the role played by public memory. As Casey puts it, any horizon "is a constituent feature of the phenomenon for which it is the horizon" (30). Strong public memory of landmarks can create a context that makes development seem troubling, destructive, or harmful. Or, in the case of Branson, as something that is good, productive, and desirable. The memory of Armadillo World Headquarters creates an external horizon of what many consider to be good and positive about the city. Change is thus measured within and by this context of public good. Because development sometimes means that landmarks and beloved sites will be displaced or altered, pro-development discourse cannot dwell too much on the public memory of lost places.

Even when such sites are remembered in official discourse, the trauma of crisis is usually downplayed. In 2006, for example, the city of Austin dedicated a historical marker at the former site of Armadillo World Headquarters. The plaque tells a story of the music hall's cultural significance to Austin and the country. Many famous musicians got their start in this very place, announces the plaque. But "music was only part of the show. The rest was the people of Austin who packed the 'Dillo night after night. The music, art and spirit of Austin flourished here, and reflected an era in Austin." One sentence briefly mentions that the hall was torn down in order to construct the office building that now stands on its site. "The Armadillo has been gone for many years now," concludes the plaque, "but the spirit lives on in today's Austin. Remember the Armadillo." Remembering the Armadillo in this context is not equivalent to the public memories circulated above. The city's official version asks residents to see the Armadillo's spirit as recreated in a new Austin—today's Austin.

Therefore, subjects who claim to have memories are not the only ones who are affected by this horizon. We can think of memory claims and their horizons as rhetorical orientation devices. As the Branson example shows, the horizon of memory may not even be real. Bradford Vivian writes that public memory is not a perfect copy of authentic or original events. Public memory is not a vertical line that attaches its memorializers to the authentic point of origination. Instead, Vivian proposes that public memory is lateral. Memory "is not the echo of an origin," but multiple iterations across time and space that cannot help but mutate in each emergence ("Jefferson's" 299). Vivian continues, "[Public memory's] sheer repetition across changing contexts, in response to new exigencies, transforms its character and brings about new iterations, new desires" (299). Lacking public memory does not mean that you lack an authentic artifact that others can claim. Perhaps it is more like an experience of the iteration that differs from those who claim to "remember." In this way, memory and nonmemory are both responses to a single event: an iteration of repetition. Both of these responses are co-produced by the same happening. Consequently, it would be difficult to claim that one response is more publicly oriented than another. They both are produced by an emergence of public memory's horizon.

The ubiquity of lost place narratives creates a horizon for people who can claim to remember and for those who cannot. Newcomers, young residents, temporary residents, and transient visitors may feel distant from that horizon. They have no memory of places like Armadillo World Headquarters, Les Amis, Liberty Lunch. However, that distance becomes its own relation. It is its own means of orientation to public deliberation. In other words, memorializing creates the horizon by which everyone can measure some kind of relation, whether it is one of towardness or awayness. And so, the experience of "not remembering" forms its own mode of publicness. For subjects who are distanced from the memory horizon, there is little at stake in relating differently to the "old" space.

Moreover, neither form of towardness or awayness helps to cultivate the kind of subject who asks different kinds of questions about changing spaces. The true public subject of feeling does not feel compelled to survey the networks within which a crisis is embedded. This is not because memory claims are primarily backward looking, rather than forward looking. Such a critique would presume that memory rhetoric cannot accomplish work in the contemporary deliberative moment. Instead, the problem of exceptional subjects is sparked by a feeling-full relation to public memory's horizons. To feel closeness or distance from these memory claims is to affectively fulfill our role as public being. I feel it; the feeling makes it so. With that, the opportunity for a subject grounded in inquiry is lost.

Other Memory Claims

This chapter looks at one city's memory claims that have emerged around urban development, but there are plenty of similar examples happening across the nation. Consider the way Times Square and its changes have been documented in national conversations. Samuel Delany captures some of the most pronounced memory claims in his *Times Square Red, Times Square Blue*, which documents the Times Square Development Project in New York City. Delany recounts how the city's dramatic demolition and redevelopment of Times Square destroyed what had become one of the best-known urban public spaces in the global imagination (xiv). Delany also remembers the old Times Square, with its combination of porn houses and marginalized figures, as a unique space of livability for gay men of color. During the mid-1950s and 1960s, Times Square served as a place of encounter among gay strangers who were otherwise forced to live in a kind of hiding. They could not act upon their sexual urges with strangers in "straight" places for fear of being discovered. Yet, in the dark porn houses in Times Square, the world was different. The theaters were spaces of all kinds of public encounter, Delany writes. In Forty-Second Street's theaters, people of all nationalities, races, classes, and backgrounds could get together. "I've met playwrights, carpenters, opera singers, telephone repairmen, stockbrokers, guys on welfare, guys with trust funds, guys on crutches, on walkers, in wheelchairs, teachers, warehouse workers . . . [and] Hasidim" (15–16). This was the old Times Square, a place where the "seedy" establishments actually created a kind of public sphere among people who were otherwise disconnected from each other. When New York City began its redevelopment project, the adult theaters and bookstores were the first to go. Times Square's many porn houses were replaced by "family friendly" stores that also happened to be more profitable for the city.

Similar to the discourse surrounding the old and new Austin, Times Square's memory rhetors often carve out two different spaces when talking about development. "The old Times Square and Forty-Second Street was an entertainment area catering largely to the working classes," writes Delany. "The New Times Square is envisioned as predominantly a middle-class area for entertainment, to which the working-classes are welcome to come along . . . if they are willing to pay and are willing to blend in" (159–60). Delany's vision imagines almost two different spaces created on top of one another. They are perhaps not even the same place. Similarly, architect Rem Koolhaas writes that Times Square died a kind of unnatural death, only to be resurrected in the "embalmed cheer of Disney" (qtd. in Eeckhout 379). Writer Luc Sante also captures this feeling of two places in the title of an essay that bemoans old New York: "My Lost City." What was once a public space that encouraged encounters among strangers has now become a privatized space that discourages strangeness. At least, this is the theme of many memory claims about Times Square's development.[4]

In many vernacular accounts of this transformation, the construction of a megasized Disney Store has become a kind of synecdoche for the new Times Square. The problem with Disney's replacement of long-standing theaters as the New Amsterdam Theater is that what was once public space has turned into a space where "Disney consumers can participate in (consume) a Disney event with other Disney customers, helping to establish in person a temporary Disney consumer community" (Bell 27). The space is thus transformed into a private zone of consumption, not engagement. Of course, as Bart Eeckhout correctly points out, Disney was not the driving force behind the redevelopment. A complex number of city and private-public organizations had planned to overhaul the area since the 1970s (397–98). Regardless of whether Disney or civic bodies can be blamed for Times Square's changes, this discourse shifts agency onto the "outsiders" who sweep in to transform what was formerly a welcoming public space. In fact, the major outsider who is most often identified in this discourse is a literal outsider, the tourist. The tourist family (imagined as non–New Yorkers, nonurban) are frequently posed as the primary targets for these sweeping redevelopments. When Forty Second Street was redeveloped, writes Sharon Zukin, the audience was not local New York residents. Instead, "42nd Street was reborn as a public space for tourists, suburban residents, and families on vacation." Tourists are the reason the homeless and troubled teens on the streets are being displaced, not to mention artists and lower-income New Yorkers (Trebay 34). These suburban family tourists are the ones who create the demand for such wild changes, and they are the ones who sustain a new Times Square. At least, this is how the narrative goes.

Within these memory claims about the old Times Square lie rhetorical patterns similar to the old Austin memory claims. Writers like Delany are certainly participating in public talk about Times Square's development, although they simultaneously evade making rhetorical interventions into the current exigence of New York's development (let alone national development). Their discourse writes them into a position quite similar to the demolished buildings themselves: they are objects who have been acted upon by outsider-others. At the same time, they have no "location" within the new space that has been created on top of the old Times Square. Intervening as an active agent—part of the network that created and sustains the development—is outside the scope of their rhetorical position. They are excluded subjects who nevertheless retain a public orientation.

Beyond the visible development in Times Square, however, these very same patterns of memory claims can be found in a number of places across the country. In fact, when I tell people about this book, I usually get at least some small recollection of a place that is now "lost" through development. I have been told personal stories about the changing shape of Milwaukee, Baltimore, Washington DC, San Francisco, Boston, St. Louis, Brooklyn, and Omaha. Each memory is unique from the speakers, yet they tend to echo one another in some interesting ways. I have also told similar stories about my memories of a younger, less developed Austin. To be sure, there is nothing wrong with these memorializations. We have already seen that epideictic discourse of this kind actually has a deliberative function. Yet, it is also important to see how this kind of popular response to development can remove rhetors from intervening more directly in the contemporary national crisis of development. Furthermore, memory claims can also skew our perceptions of the rhetorical situation. We risk writing ourselves out of the agentive position and into a position of excluded subjectivity.

5

The Good and the Bad

GENTRIFICATION AND EQUIVALENCE CLAIMS

> Where it breaks Austin into two
>   unequal sides,
> The sun, declining, dazzles on
>   the Interstate.
> —Wayne Pounds,
>   "I-35 Seen from Manor Road; or,
>   All Austin is divided into two
>   unequal parts"

The story of east Austin has been a remarkable example of development rhetoric in action. At one point, east Austin was considered a dangerous place. Many years ago, I found myself sitting in an apartment hunter's office in Austin, Texas. The agent had spread open a large map in order to show me the neighborhoods in Austin where affordable housing could be found. "Of course," he said, "you don't want to live east of I-35." He pointed to the highway on the map, and then to the neighborhoods running east of the thin line representing the freeway. "It's just not a very nice place to live." I would later hear the same kind of warning many other times throughout my years in Austin. Even after I rented a house on the East Side, friends would take comfort in knowing that I was not living "too far east." No signs announce the East Side as a bad place. However, this rhetoric works its way into the ordinary speech of many Austinites, whether they are working for or against such a description. As one longtime resident put it, "East Austin has a connotation that doesn't have so much to do with directions" (Jackson 70).

Long before I stepped foot into that apartment hunter's office, the East

Side's imaginary as "not a very nice place" unfolded in everyday discourse for local citizens and beyond. In 1984, the Guardian Angels conducted a "test patrol" in east Austin. Founder Curtis Sliwa told reporters that he wanted to "determine whether crime problems in east-side neighborhoods are as bad as he has been told." Journalist Robert Jensen remembers that even the most consciously antiracist Austinites circulate this rhetoric. "When I came here in 1992," says Jensen, "well-intentioned white liberals, colleagues of mine here at the University of Texas, quickly advised me don't bother looking for a house on the east side of the interstate. These were people who thought of themselves as anti-racist, thought of themselves as liberal" ("East Austin Gentrification"). Without a doubt, east Austin was different from the rest of the city. According to the 2000 census, median household income for East Side residents was $15,678 versus $48,950 for the rest of Austin. Over 40 percent made less than $20,000 per year, and almost 60 percent made less than $30,000. East Austin's unemployment rate hovered at 12.5 percent versus 4 percent for the other sections of Austin. The East Side's ethnic makeup also failed to mirror other parts of the city. Residents were 58.9 percent Hispanic and 30.7 percent African-American.

Today, gentrification in east Austin is visible nearly everywhere you look. As more people began moving into Austin, real estate prices soared to almost unaffordable levels. Central Austin and south Austin quickly became hip and desirable. The last remaining space of affordable housing was on the East Side, where houses could be purchased for a mere fraction of what similar houses would cost only a few miles away. In my old neighborhood on the East Side, the median sale price of a house in 2000 was $77,000. In five years, the median home price rose to $195,000. This marked a 250 percent increase in sale prices, which affects the property taxes of all houses in the surrounding area (Gregor).

When I visited my old neighborhood after moving away for several years, I was surprised by the cultural transformation of east Austin from a "no-go area" to a haven of hipness. People suddenly proclaimed their love for the area and its culture scene. One national story covered the "extreme makeover" of east Austin, "from a heritage of taquerias and party shops to upscale condos and bars galore" (Smithson). The upbeat news story features a recent University of Texas graduate, who declared, "I love living over here. Walking down any given street, you run into a thirtysomething hip crowd, although we did have drug dealers living close by at one point. It's prime real estate . . . and the culture makes the whole experience that much better" (Smithson). The student certainly was not joking about prime real estate. Everyone wants to live here. But "prime real estate" also affects East Side residents like Ora Houston, whose property taxes jumped from $1,500 in 1996 to over $6,000 in 2005 ("Gentrification").

When driving down my old street, I found a house for sale that looked like a renovated version of the house I lived in against the railroad tracks. I pulled my car over to get a better look at the flyer. Bold letters proclaimed, "East Side Modern!" The flyer went on to describe the house's upscale renovations: stained concrete floors, Brazilian brushed granite, designer lighting, and vessel sinks. Below these descriptions, the flyer also boasted that the house would allow its owners to enjoy "everything that the East Side has to offer! Walk to award winning restaurants . . . or stop by Clementine's for coffee and conversation!" Finally, at the bottom, was the price: $445,000. I swallowed hard at the thought that East Side homes were going for half a million dollars.

These changes came as a surprise to those who lived on the East Side prior to its development. Many years ago, I rented a tiny one-bedroom house in east Austin. The house was extremely affordable, even by my (less than) minimum wage salary. Rent in another area would have easily cost me twice or even three times what I was paying for my older, smaller house on an ungentrified street. My neighbors were an eclectic mixture of students, blue-collar workers, and retired people who had lived in the neighborhood for decades. Living on the East Side meant that I could have a house of my own, without sharing walls in an apartment. I could sit on my own porch and have a cigarette while taking a break from writing and reading. Today, I can afford very few houses in this neighborhood. People who still live on the East Side are reeling from the sudden development. Property taxes shot up in a very short period, thanks to the arrival of new loft developments and "flipped" houses. The ethnic makeup also changed, along with the economic makeup of East Side neighborhoods. In central east Austin, the African-American population actually decreased 16 percent between 1990 and 2000.[1] The numbers of white residents increased during this same period.

You do not have to look far to hear how passionate people are about these changes. Many people vocally oppose the new lofts and expensive housing flips. Other people across the city strongly support these changes, for a variety of reasons. While these two responses are interesting to consider, I am more interested in a third kind of response. Beyond antigentrification and progentrification claims is another common response that I will call "equivalence claims," or claims that read the scene of gentrification as undecidable. These claims take the position that gentrification is both good and bad, a paradoxical position that effectively writes itself out of any interventionist role. Equivalence claims help to create exceptional public subjects by substituting the feeling of undecidability for judgment (*krisis*). In short, undecidability becomes the *krisis*. The troubling effect of such discourse is that patterns of equivalence rhetoric serve to cultivate subjects who retain a public orientation without writing themselves into the scene of public change. In short, legitimating equivalence claims help to maintain a space of exception.

East Side Story

The East Side's "othered" status can be traced back to the city's official master plan of 1928, which created a totalizing vision of a beautiful and productive southern city. According to the master plan's design, Austin's structure was to be reorganized in order to encourage progress and industry without taking away from the natural splendor of the city's center. Dallas-based planners Koch and Fowler were passionate about preserving Austin's beauty as a resource. Not only was Austin built along a beautiful river, but the state capitol and university sites were aligned with each other as if in perfect harmony. For this reason, proclaimed Koch and Fowler, "the capitol building should be conspicuous and visible from all parts of the surrounding territory. It should predominate and other structures should be subordinated to it" (*A City Plan*). Skyscrapers and signs of industrial work were dismissed in favor of showcasing Austin's picturesque views. Nevertheless, the city planners also recognized that Austin was a city filled with the promise of growth and industry. In order to both preserve Austin's natural beauty and pursue industrial development, the master plan looked to the East Side as an answer. East Austin was officially designed as a space of removal for all unwanted and undesirable elements that were still necessary for the city's operation. It was designed as a place of operative invisibility.

In order to remove the sites of industry from the central heart of Austin, the master plan recommended that city officials designate the area east of East Avenue as a space for industrialization. Transportation facilities were rerouted through the East Side in order to avoid the accompanying noise and traffic in the central business districts and western residential areas. The Houston and Texas Central Railway line already snaked throughout the East Side, and city officials proposed to build a connection that would take the I&GN trains that currently ran on the West Side and move them to the newly proposed industrial district past East Avenue ("Community Change"). More significantly, the area was officially designated as the city's only "unrestricted industrial" area, which meant that the city's "nuisances" could be located in this area and no others (Moore 180).

But most significantly of all, the 1928 master plan also designated the East Side as the only area in which African-Americans could live. In the years prior to the massive rezoning, African-Americans lived in central Austin neighborhoods like Clarksville and Wheatsville. These neighborhoods had been long-standing freed-slave enclaves, and generations of black families lived in decent housing. Yet, as Austin's population grew, white residents began to move into these neighborhoods, and they quickly demanded that blacks be forced out. This situation formed part of the civic "problems" that Koch and Fowler's firm addressed. The planners acknowledged that Austin could not legally relocate blacks into a specific part of town through force or through decree, yet the city could force this relocation through public policy of utilities. In the language of the master plan itself, "In our studies in Austin, we have found that the negroes are present in small numbers, in practically all sections of the city, excepting the area just east of East Avenue and south of the City Cemetery. This area seems to be all negro population. It is our recommendation that the . . . district [be designated] as a negro district; and that all facilities and conveniences be provided the negroes in this district, as an incentive to draw the negro population to this area" (Koch and Fowler). This intentional zoning of industry into the East Side not only created poor living conditions in the area, but also severed east Austin neighborhoods from the larger circulation habits of middle-class residents. The original decision to designate the East Side as both an "unrestricted industrial" zone and a "negro" district was partly due to the fact that east Austin was less developed than other areas. Roads were un(der)developed, curbs did not exist, and utilities often came long after residents had built their houses on land purchased without the help of bank loans.

East Avenue became an important marker for the policy decisions in Koch and Fowler's 1928 master plan. The planners used it to demarcate where one version of Austin ended and another one began. But the wide avenue also became much more than a policy symbol. It served to physically divide middle-class white areas of the city from the only areas where blacks, Mexicans, and poor whites could reasonably live. East Avenue was a wide street running north-south, perfectly separating the East Side from the central areas. The official division would become technologized after the paving of East Avenue in 1933. By 1951, the dividing line was federally subsidized when it became Interstate 35, and the only way to travel from Austin's center to the East Side was literally by way of an underpass. The massive gulf that East Avenue created made it an obvious choice for highway construction only thirteen years later.

Only a few decades after the city officially pushed African-Americans and Latinos onto the East Side, the city began to covet the very land that was originally designated as "undesirable." Thanks to a growth in industry and the university, Austin's urban core began to expand. Suddenly, land on the East Side looked more attractive than ever. Under the heading of "urban renewal," the city approached east Austin residents with the opportunity to sell their property back to the city. In the 1960s and 1970s, Austin launched an aggressive campaign for urban renewal. The city's claims were simple and unequivocal: urban renewal is good for everyone. In fact, urban renewal was sold to all Austinites as a solution to many problems. In a pamphlet dating back to the early 1960s titled "Rx for Cities: Urban Renewal," the city declared that urban renewal "offers the means to treat to 'sick spots' of cities and urban areas." The pamphlet posed blighted areas as a suffering human body whose future depends upon surgical removal. "Corrective treatment must be administered where it is possible and surgery performed where an area cannot be otherwise saved" (2; Austin History Center). By removing and clearing away entire neighborhoods, therefore, the whole body would be benefited. Likewise, a pro-urban renewal pamphlet dating to the late 1960s (posed to "Mr. Austin Citizen") was designed to win support for a zoning ordinance that would have made development much easier. Even if your house is "fine and dandy," reads the pamphlet, urban renewal will still benefit you. Not only will the development save tax dollars by reducing the cost of health problems, police, and firefighters in the poor areas, but "you will take pride in the uplifting of human values relative to improved living conditions and in making all of your city a pleasant as well as a wholesome place to live" (Austin History Center, "What Does").

Residents did not easily accept the rhetoric of urban renewal. East Side residents fought urban renewal (or urban removal, as some called it) throughout the 1960s and 1970s. In a typewritten booklet from the late 1970s found in the Austin History Center, one East Side group warned Chicano neighbors that developers would soon be coming for their neighborhood. "Los 'Land Developers' quieren que todo el mundo se marcha del barrio," warned the newsletter. The land developers want everyone to move out of the barrio (east Austin). The group continues to describe how developers will one day buy property from under the feet of poor East Siders in order to get rich by turning neighborhoods into profitable business areas: "Y esto quiere decir que East Austin no sera un barrio Chicano-Mexicano nunca jamas!" (And this means east Austin will no longer be a Chicano-Mexicano barrio!) In the spring of 1980, a story from the *Texas Tenants Union News* spotlighted the gentrification that seemed to be looming on the horizon. "Whether it's public or private," warned the story, "they end up moving you out" ("Inner City").

Many people fought bitterly against losing their homes in the face of "healthy benefits." One East Side group threw a "Not-Going-Away Party" in order to protest the inevitable changes. A flyer for the party began by announcing, "We are not going away, but we are being displaced by runaway development.... If you are a tenant who has been or anticipates the likelihood of being thrown out on the street, the party is in your honor." Protests like the Austin Not-Going-Away Party especially emphasized the struggles of renters who would lose out when landlords saw an easy profit in urban renewal dollars. "Eat, drink, and be merry," announced the flyer, "for tomorrow we may be evicted" (Austin History Center).

The story of the East Side's Blackland neighborhood is a particularly dramatic example of Austin's aggressive urban development in east Austin. When the university wanted to expand its campus, one of the only directions available to them was east. Together with the city, the university relentlessly attempted to secure "blighted" homes in order to bulldoze them for more space. Almost sixteen blocks were scheduled to be annexed by the city, although neighbors refused to give up without a fight. Longtime resident Katherine Pool remembers working and raising her family in Blackland, all while speculators from the university constantly tried to buy her land. At one point, recalls Pool, "they even sent black realtors out with tales about foreigners interested in buying property in Blackland" (391). When some neighbors did sell their land, however, they received only a small portion of what the land was actually worth. Although the university promised to compensate owners, most of the residents were poor renters. It was hardly fair, argued community activists, to suggest that residents could be "fairly compensated" by such displacement.

After a number of legal battles and public denouncements, the university decided to only annex eight blocks in the Blackland neighborhood. "This has been a very emotional and painful period for everyone involved," said Edwin Sharpe, vice president for administration at the University of Texas at Austin. In December 1989, the university released an official position paper announcing the decision. The paper explained that the difficult situation was a conflict between what constitutes "the greater good to society" (Lueck A1). On one hand, concluded the paper, affordable housing clearly provides a much-needed source of shelter for poor Austin residents. On the other hand, university development can serve as "provision for the growth of a public institution that has a statewide and even national mission." The "pain" that Sharpe describes thus comes from a scaling back of plans to serve a national (rather than merely a local) body.

Since these early days of urban gentrification on the East Side, neighborhoods east of the interstate have continued to play a central role in Austin's development changes. The most recent chapter in east Austin's drama was initiated by a citywide plan to make significant changes to the entire area, with the help of a large series of grants. When the city council made plans to transform the character of east Austin, it affected the very historical structure of the East Side. As I learned on my visit to the old neighborhood a few years ago, and as many more longtime residents have come to realize, the East Side will never be the same again.

The ARA: Official Development on the East Side

In 1998, east Austin was again officially designated as a "slum and/or blighted area" in order to secure a large series of grants to redevelop the area. The evocatively named Austin Revitalization Authority (ARA) was now in charge of rezoning and reconstructing the heart of the East Side. According to the ARA's mission statement, the program intended to "restore the cultural and economic viability of our neighborhood" (Austin Revitalization Authority). The ARA launched its ambitious plans under the heading of three main goals: respect, revitalization, and restoration. Together, these three goals focused the ARA on "working to restore the cultural and economic viability of our neighborhoods" (Austin Revitalization Authority). Indeed, the mission of revitalization is woven throughout the ARA's business and community development plans.

One of the first projects spearheaded through the ARA and the city's development plans was the Dr. Charles E. Urdy Plaza. The plaza is a small area in the middle of a busy neighborhood. Its beautiful centerpiece is a fifty-foot-long mural picturing African-American historical images from the East Side. The mosaic, aptly titled "Rhapsody," shows colorful images of longstanding east Austin sites, like the Ebenezer Baptist Church, as well as everyday images of people living and playing in their East Side homes. When you stand in the middle of the plaza, you can look around and see examples of the change literally surrounding you. From the plaza's center, you can see the huge new mixed-use building that the ARA built. The architecture is sleek and new, though many of the offices sit vacant. Behind the new building sits the bright yellow and red exterior of Victory Grill, an old East Side standard that is known for its blues music and barbeque.

Ironically, another early component of the plan created a forty-thousand-square-foot office-retail building, the space for which was acquired through eminent domain and public seizures of homes. Some of these parcels were again listed by the city as "substandard structures" that were to be demolished after current tenants received "relocation assistance." The homes for the office building were reclaimed from the everyday streets depicted in

"Rhapsody," the mural that now serves as a showcase for east Austin's transformation. The office-retail building housed a few upscale restaurants and some private companies, though the main tenant was the ARA itself. Slick frosted glass lines the bottom row of the forty-thousand-square-foot space, and the modern design looks attractive. But the building, which is mostly devoid of thriving businesses, looks terribly out of place among the historical vernacular architecture around it. This incongruity is quickly becoming a mark of east Austin's latest development: the old juxtaposed with the new.

Perhaps the most ambitious project among the ARA's plans were the Eleventh and Twelfth Streets Community Redevelopment Projects. According to the city's own description, this project aimed to develop East Eleventh Street as a "visitor-oriented destination," while the Twelfth Street corridor would be a mixed-use area of live and work spaces. Since the ARA's earliest days of planning, changes within the Eleventh and Twelfth Street corridor have attracted a great deal of attention and praise from Austin city leaders and the local media. In 2004, revitalization efforts appeared to be emerging into physical realities. The abundant praise drew heavily from the language of resurrection, as if the East Side had been resurrected from the dead. One *Austin American-Statesman* article, titled "Renaissance on East 11th Street," is representative of the media rhetoric surrounding the East Side's renewal: "The street was once the bustling hub of Austin's African American community before it gave way to abandoned buildings, empty lots and crack bazaars in the 1980s. Now, after years of talk and plans, the area is ready for its coming-out party. Reality has hit the ground in the form of two stately buildings that the Austin Revitalization Authority hopes will anchor East 11th's new beginning and spark a wave of public and private investment" (Schwartz, "Renaissance"). Rhetorics of death and rebirth dominated news reports of the Eleventh and Twelfth Street corridor. One 2004 story from the *Daily Texan* even calls upon a rhetoric of magic in order to praise the corridor's transformation: "For one East Austin street, fairy tales do come true," begins the profile. "A few years ago, the cultural, racial and musical utopia of East 11th Street was almost lost to neglect, but due to recent development efforts funded by the Austin Revitalization Authority, it seems that the neighborhood may someday return to its glory days" (Hollett). The story goes on to praise the "cultural makeover" within the corridor, a magical transformation that claims to change one place into another through a new set of conditions. The ARA's founder, Byron Marshall, tells the reporter, "'We hope to fix up this whole area and maybe spur further development that will make the East End a safe, fun, popular place to be again'" (quoted in Hollett).

But the East Side's revitalization depended on fundamental changes to the area's structure and demographic makeup. In 2001, the Austin City Council issued the "Central East Austin Neighborhood Plan," which publicly outlined its vision for development on the East Side. The plan was careful to underscore the importance of preserving ethnic and cultural traditions, yet the city council's language also announced specific plans to attract "a diverse range of people" through new development. In sunny language, the report states, "The neighbors feel it's clear that this area has turned a corner, and welcome the many efforts by public and private entities to revitalize the area culturally, socially, and economically. . . . Neighbors aimed to create an environment where needed revitalization can proceed unhindered while still protecting the opportunities and assets enjoyed by the longtime and current residents of the neighborhoods" (City of Austin 3). In an area where the population had previously been 90 percent minority and significantly below the median income average, attracting "a diverse range of people" would inevitably mean targeting a whiter, wealthier population.

One of the most radical changes to the East Side has been the fast-paced construction of luxury lofts and condominiums. Construction of the first lofts was done in partnership with the ARA. Aimed at a young, professional, and wealthy audience, East Side loft developments could offer urban living for slightly cheaper (though well above average) prices than other downtown lofts. But they first had to battle east Austin's poor reputation. It's not surprising that the main marketing tool in much of the promotional literature was an emphasis on a "new" East Side. Even the name "east Austin" is erased and the area instead becomes the "East End District" or "Austin East." In one company's splashy online portfolio, we are told that "Austin East isn't a new concept or a dream for the future. . . . It is currently the home of incredible restaurants that are packed every night and some of the coolest and most unique coffee shops around" (Ragland Realty).

Another new development advertises the million-dollar units like this: "Panoramic views of downtown, East Austin and the hill. . . . Clean, green, modern design with smart, urban floor plans. Ideal location—the fringe of downtown, in vibrant East Austin." Not only is location to downtown emphasized, but also the "cleanness" and "greenness" of the lofts. These words may signal a break from the typical images of east Austin, which are usually described as dirty and uninviting. Likewise, advertisements for the ESTE loft development pose the telling question "Do you belong east?" with the following answer: "With trendy coffee houses, art studios in abundance, and easy access to the entertainment district, this is truly a dynamic neighborhood" (Constructive Ventures). The question "Do you belong east?" is not an idle one for some potential buyers. Wealthy white residents often felt as though they did not belong east. (Or, as in my case with the apartment hunter, they may have been told that they did not belong east.) Thanks to gentrification, however, now they did.

The Real Deal: Protesting Gentrification

Across the country, gentrification is one of the most powerful issues of urban development. It has become the subject of popular movies that tend to feature people down on their luck who are preyed upon by developers (as in John Sayles's 2002 film *Sunshine State* or the 2004 film *Barbershop 2*), or else well-meaning people who inadvertently gentrify (as in 2010's *Please Give*). The topic has also emerged on the stage, most notably in the wildly popular *Rent*. Likewise, in the one-woman play *Doña Rosita's Jalapeño Kitchen*, a Mexican restaurant owner named Rosita is offered a nice sum of money for her land, although developers have no intention of preserving her barrio restaurant. Instead, the space will be turned into a strip mall catering to the changing demographics on the East Side. Rosita is torn about this decision, since she is the last neighborhood holdout. Her friends and neighbors have all sold their tiny houses to developers in order to move into bigger (and whiter) spaces. Rosita's concerns about development manifest themselves as nightmares about the neighborhood's *chili cultura* turning into a bland existence filled with white picket fences, mayonnaise, and white bread. Though *Doña Rosita's Jalapeño Kitchen* was written by a California playwright, its connection to Austin's East Side gentrification is unavoidable. In 2006, the East Side playhouse Teatro Vivo staged *Doña Rosita's Jalapeño Kitchen* as a way of giving voice to the many different lives that were affected by development in the East Side barrio. If there is one lesson to be learned about gentrification from *Doña Rosita's Jalapeño Kitchen,* it is that the arrival of development means the displacement of many people.

In case Doña Rosita seems like a far-fetched character, one would only need to visit Austin's East Side to meet women and men who are living this story. Mary Lopez and her daughter tell the story of how developers began knocking on neighborhood doors to pressure them into selling after the city agreed to allow developers to construct a seventy-foot high-rise on Señora Lopez's block. Each month, developers returned with higher and higher offers to her. She stood firm, refusing to sell the house that she had been living in since 1953. Even after threatening letters were sent to her house multiple times, she still refused to sell. Yet, Señora Lopez's neighborhood would never look the same after the construction of lofts, shopping plazas, and parking spaces ("La Casa Lopez"). Another neighborhood resident, Laura Garnett, also sees through the promises of developers and city officials. "The illusion is getting better, but the real deal is getting worse," Garnett says while looking around the streets. "You can see it's getting prettier. But at the same time, what's happening to the elderly or the children?" ("3: An East Austin Narrative").

The reality is that many of the old residents are moving outside of Austin altogether, mostly to distant suburbs like Pflugerville (Copelin). Property prices in these suburbs are much lower than in the new East Side, where longtime residents are being offered unprecedented amounts of cash for their property. In fact, while the African-American population decreased in east Austin from 1990 to 2010, the small suburb of Pflugerville has experienced a significant increase in its minority population. The number of black residents in Pflugerville jumped from 4 percent in 1990 to 14 percent in 2008 (U.S. Census). So many African-Americans have relocated to the suburb that the biggest Juneteenth celebration (a long-standing holiday that honors the abolition of slavery in Texas) has moved from the East Side to Pflugerville. But Pflugerville is far from Austin's central core. A typical commute would take over thirty minutes by car, and it would be nearly impossible for someone who relied on public transportation.

Doña Rosita's nightmare of new people moving in while simultaneously pushing out her beloved chili cultura seems not to be completely fictional. East Austin is welcoming so many new residents that at least one local magazine jokingly announced, "You know someone isn't from Austin when they ... currently live on the eastside" ("Genties"). While this line spoofs the recent influx of new East Side residents who rent expensive lofts and flip old houses into updated residences, the situation is no laughing matter for longtime East Siders. In 2005, the Waterstreet Lofts sparked a great deal of anger from East Side residents. The lofts, which started at $180,000 for spaces that were barely over eight hundred square feet, appeared in the middle of a traditionally Latino neighborhood with small family houses that were worth nowhere near the average price of a small loft. In an interview with the *Austin Chronicle,* the developer admitted that property taxes would be a serious problem for local residents in the coming years. The Waterstreet Lofts would inevitably price families out of their homes (D. Welch). Due to higher property taxes, residents could not afford to live in family homes that were owned outright.

Similarly, when plans were announced for the Robertson Hill Apartments—three hundred luxury units with rents starting at $1,200 a month— neighborhood groups were outraged. These particular apartments not only promised increased traffic, but the fifty-foot-high construction would block East Side residents' view of the downtown skyline. Mark Rogers, secretary of the Guadalupe Association for an Improved Neighborhood, lamented the wall that would further remove east Austinites from the new Austin happening around them. According to Rogers, "It's a stunning view at night and our neighborhood has enjoyed that [for] over a century" (Morton C1). But the view would soon become a premium available only to the wealthy Robertson Hill tenants. In order to assuage any fears that these apartments might be anything short of real Austin, however, prospective tenants were reassured in advertisements that Robertson Hill was "Authentically Austin." As if to make this point a reality, the courtyard in front of the apartments was designed to look like a town square, complete with signposts pointing to such important East Side landmarks as the George Washington Carver Museum and Cultural Center, historically black Huston-Tillotson University, and the Texas State Cemetery.

Groups like People Organized in Defense of Earth and Her Resources (PODER) marched and protested these kinds of developments as a continuation of the racist policies that originally pushed minorities into the East Side in the first place. "As the city has grown, there's no place to grow but East Austin—as if people weren't already there," PODER founder Susana Almanza stated (quoted in Carlson 25). East Side residents regularly appeared before city council meetings in an attempt to voice their concerns. Residents like Frances Martinez spoke passionately against the changes that seemed directly to threaten the future of east Austin's longtime Latino population. During one heated meeting, Martinez stood before the city council and proclaimed, "Nuestro barrios, Nuesta gente, Nuestra tierra y nuestra libertad!" Soon after Martinez spoke, another local resident voiced his concern at the same meeting about the racism and ethnocentrism of newcomers in east Austin.[2] Almanza herself regularly appealed to city council during meetings, where her message consistently emphasized the destruction inevitably caused by development on the East Side. "Let the poor and the working poor communities of color live in the urban core," pleaded Almanza. "We don't need high priced condos and lofts for East Austin. We can't afford them and they are not compatible to our current housing."[3] The plot line of *Doña Rosita's Jalapeño Kitchen* plays out in a very serious way on Austin's East Side, where residents truly are faced with dramatic choices between holding out against aggressive development and finding another way of life.

The influx of middle- and upper-class white residents has also created an increased cultural clash, according to Almanza:

[The new residents] come in saying they really like East Austin because it's an open community. People gather in the front yards, their backyards. But then they come in, and they put these walls up. They put aluminum fencing in . . . all of this stuff is going to change it back to the same thing they were leaving because they wanted the openness." She also says that new residents immediately began to complain about noise disturbances coming from numerous cars and loud music. "They don't realize we have big families . . . this is how we've always played [our music]". (Keating)

Almanza's claims have been validated by some nonprofit agencies studying east Austin's changes. According to a report by the nonprofit group Basic Initiative, "While most of these newcomers rave about the open community and vibrant culture that is unique to East Austin, often times they were swift to demolish existing buildings on the property to make way for the installation of luxurious urban lofts and Mc-mansions without fully comprehending its impact on the existing place. This physical displacement of the original residents and buildings has left East Austin in a crippled state. A break in the community structure occurs and a new dynamic is formed. The flavor of the old neighborhood is essentially lost in the shuffle" (Basic Initiative). Almanza and other East Siders fear that the city's plan of targeting economically advantaged residents will inevitably drive out minorities and lower-income families who have lived in the neighborhood for years. At the very least, the way of life in east Austin will never be the same.

If you talk to people who live on the East Side, many are skeptical that this plan can ever help Latino and African-American residents. "The ARA was created to fulfill the initiative of transforming the 11th and 12th street corridor into a business zone with African American businesses supported by government funding," says Akwasi Evans, publisher and editor of the Austin's African-American newspaper, *Nokoa*. "Now 11th and 12th streets are being transformed into a business corridor for white-owned businesses" (Barrios A1). Andy Garrison, director of the *East Austin Stories* documentary project, also questions the ARA's strategy where value and property is concerned. His voice is almost pained as he considers the changes happening in the area. "East Austin will be an economically thriving community, but not because more jobs are created," he laments. "Austin is just pushing further out into the east, and everything shifts. Basically, central Austin is just increasing its square mileage by pushing into east Austin" (Garrison). The ARA's policies only encourage loss, he explains. They do not add value. "We only know how to make things more valuable, not how to work with the value that's already there." Many residents are passionate about opposing these changes, though the force is hard to stop.

Furthermore, as Almanza and other critics allege, the urban renewal effort is rife with cultural exploitation. Part of the selling point of the new East Side is the "charm" of east Austin culture. Yet, longtime residents often find a paradox in this attraction: middle-class residents want to retain the unique cultural feel of east Austin without actually preserving the black and Latino cultures that helped build the neighborhoods. This paradox was at the heart of a passionate protest in 2002 against the Heritage Society of Austin's plans for a tour of historic homes on the East Side. When the Heritage Society organized a tour of homes and buildings in east Austin, residents and local groups like PODER raised an alarm. The Heritage Society announced that it wanted to showcase turn-of-the-century homes by bringing in people who would not normally see this area of the city.

Demonstrator Joe Quintero led a march in spring 2002 against the Heritage Society's tour. Quintero argued that the tour was meant to encourage middle-class whites to buy and renovate the very homes for which blacks and Latinos could not get loans. The Association of Mexican-American Neighborhoods also protested the tour's historically inaccurate interpretation of east Austin history. Almanza, another protest leader, explained that the tour asked people to pay "homage to houses and their design and forget about the people who lived in these particular homes" (Herrera 5). The tour seemed to be just another instance of unavoidable encroachment and displacement among longtime East Side residents.

Antigentrification graffiti in east Austin. Photo by Jenny Rice, 2007.

THE GOOD AND THE BAD | 143

Equivalence Claims

While many people do vocalize opposition to gentrification, there is another common response that is worth investigating. This response is rooted in a rhetorical undecidability. Its speakers claim that gentrification has both good and bad effects, which makes any more definitive judgment nearly impossible. The problem is that rhetors often write themselves out of interventionist roles because the ethic of undecidability trumps the ethical call for action. This is not to say that a better alternative is to think in terms of binary—gentrification as all good or all bad. To be sure, gentrification in impoverished neighborhoods is complex, manifold, and difficult to dismiss as completely harmful. However, in the analysis that follows, I will make a distinction between complex claims of equivalence and simple claims of equivalence. Both kinds of claims are quite widespread in public debates and deliberations over gentrification. They are very common ways of talking about development's effects in general. The differences between these two types of claims relate to the way rhetors write themselves into or out of the rhetorical scene. Whereas complex claims of equivalence can help to place speakers or writers within a scene of rhetorical agency, simple claims of equivalence tend to cultivate a space of exception. By engaging in a rhetoric of simple equivalence claims, speakers and writers are thus excluded from the call to ethical and rhetorical intervention.

Complex Claims of Equivalence

During my visit back to the old neighborhood where my small house once sat, I stopped to talk to Mark Rogers, executive director of Guadalupe Neighborhood Development Corporation. Rogers works directly with the community by helping residents find affordable housing throughout the East Side. When someone needs to find a low-cost apartment or house, they usually call him first. I asked Rogers about the perceptions of these changes among residents. How do people talk about the lofts, the flipped houses, the half-million-dollar homes that sit next to houses formerly valued at fifty thousand dollars? Well, began Rogers with a broad smile, of course east Austinites complain about the influx of white people into a neighborhood of color. It's a common sentiment. "Younger folks are kind of pissed about it," he said. But he also hears older people talk about the positive changes. The houses are finally being fixed up. The neighborhoods are safer.

When I told Rogers my story about the apartment hunter who warned me away from the East Side, he interrupted my story: "What years were you here?" I thought for a second. "Early nineties." He nodded his head, "Yeah, it was really rough at that time. Not always a really safe place for young women." I stumbled for a while and then agreed with him. Things definitely did seem safer. There are more spots to hang out and socialize. There are shopping choices beyond the run-down convenience store that sold gallons of milk and loaves of bread. I followed up on Rogers's response. "The ARA defends its plans by saying that gentrification will help everybody in the neighborhood. Do you think they're right?" Rogers thought for a few seconds. "A lot of people recognize that positive things have happened because of gentrification. But it's screwed up, you know. Because now they can't afford to live here. They can't afford to buy a house in the very neighborhood where they grew up." I tried my best to put these responses into a coherent framework. It is screwed up, as Rogers put it. But there are also some undeniably nice changes. I left his office feeling a bit confused. I had not expected him to acknowledge the complications of gentrification. After all, the development and changes in the area were making life hard for many of the people he served. But he did not end there.

Plenty of other people feel that gentrification is an absolute injustice. Around the streets of east Austin, signs and graffiti reading "Yuppies off the East Side" began appearing with some frequency after the new lofts were built. Stop signs regularly featured this slogan painted with a stencil. In front of a new high-priced loft signs appeared overnight: "Stop gentrifying the East Side" and "Will U give jobs to longtime residents of this neighborhood?" (Hampson). It does not take long to uncover the tensions between these mysterious sign authors and residents who see gentrification as a more complex issue. One morning, I walked through East Side neighborhoods with the hopes of photographing just a few of these signs. During my walk, I discovered a not-so-hidden backlash against these anti-yuppie signs. Stickers reading "Stencilers off the East Side" appeared next to the many stencils splashed on the front and back of street signs. One *Austin Chronicle* article even took a jab at the ubiquitous stencils. Sure, said the author, "you feel cool" when stenciling that rebellious sounding phrase. But, "yuppies do not care what you think. Plus, that blocky font looks suspiciously like latté" ("Looking for Cheap Dirt"). Graffiti, stencils, stickers, and homemade signs pop up across neighborhoods like a loud textual conversation between invisible groups. While moving through the neighborhood, you cannot help but find yourself in the middle of the argument.

During my morning photography walk, I thought about the tensions between these voices. The complaint about "yuppies" seems obvious enough. East Austin is shifting demographics in radical ways. High-priced lofts and boutique coffee shops are not made for the existing East Side population. They are made for people with money and leisure time, for singles, young families, students, and professionals. In a word, they are made for yuppies—or at least one concept of what yuppies look like. Yet, my instinct told me that it was more complicated than yuppies versus anti-yuppies. After some additional digging, I discovered that the conversation is indeed much more complex.[4] Consider how one blogger ponders the "Yuppies off the East Side" slogan that appears all over his east Austin neighborhood: "Is it possible this message is talking to me? I'm certainly not Young anymore, having recently completed my 40th trip around the sun. And not really Professional. I do earn a decent wage from the university, but I wear shorts to work most days. I get my hair cut at least once a year, sometimes twice. . . . I did recently buy a home on the near-east side, site of the old Robert Mueller airport, in fact. So maybe they are talking to me" ("Yuppies Off the Eastside?"). However, continues the blogger, his new home is in the site of Austin's old airport that had been abandoned for years. His new development reserves 25 percent of its space for low-income residents (compared to the 10 percent reserved in the loft developments partnered with the ARA). He concludes by arguing that, instead of a black-and-white statement about who should or should not live on the East Side, we should all make a call for "responsible eastside development."

At the same time, even some antidevelopment critics have become more reflective about their own part in gentrification. For example, another local Austin blogger who calls himself "The Accidental Gentrifist" explains his name in terms that recognize the changing public experiences and encounters that are available to Austin citizens: "If you've grown weary of paying rent, you want to buy a house in central Austin, and your income is anything approximating average, chances are better than good that you'll end up with a fixer-upper on the East Side—not that this is an unfortunate situation. But if you improve your little lot, or do anything which might make your new neighborhood more conducive to development, you are, like it or not, a de facto element of gentrification. And I'll be honest: it sounds worse than it feels" (Reed). This blogger captures the complexity of lower-middle-class residents who also have been squeezed by citywide development. Displacement is happening at multiple levels across the city, and gentrifiers are not unified in their economic status. The Accidental Gentrifist frames the local issues in terms of a ripple effect, one that is related to a much larger process of development.

Michael Schliefke's popular local comic book series, *Tales of the Really White Vigilante*, also takes up many of these topics in graphic novel form. In

Schliefke's story, the superhero begins by fighting the yuppies who are moving into Austin's East Side, even building a wall around the area to keep out yuppies and carpetbaggers. But he ultimately realizes his own implication in the East Side's change by virtue of his own relocation. The Really White Vigilante is himself a relative newcomer to the East Side, though he now feels compelled to regulate who should or should not be living there. (Artists are okay, but yuppies driving brand-new VW Bugs are not.) Schliefke explains that his graphic novel is meant to provoke a deeper kind of reflective discussion about how gentrification happens, and what our own roles are in the process. "I'm not sure if the issue has really been dealt with by many people," he says, "particularly those who are taking part in it." This is not to say that gentrification is not problematic, or that gentrification itself should not be debated and critiqued. However, Schliefke's comic raises the complex problems in gentrification critique, which is sometimes quite unreflective.

Plenty of other East Side residents recognize the complexity of development. In 1990, East Side community leader Tommy Wyatt sounded dismal about the neighborhood's future. Wyatt, publisher of the East Side African-American newspaper, the *Villager*, lamented that "commercial vibrancy is gone from much of East Austin. While the rest of Austin has grown and prospered, while the country has passed through the War on Poverty to the age of high-finance and electronic banking, East Austin has—to a large extent—watched over the fence" (Stanush A1). Wyatt's outlook is easy to understand. In 1990, the East Side did not have a single bank branch or even an ATM. Finally, in 1991, First City Bank opened an ATM on the East Side. It was a feat marked by news stories and press coverage. After the ARA's push for development began in earnest, east Austin residents increasingly had access to supermarkets, increased bus service, and better convenience store selections.

I heard the complexity firsthand during my photography trek through the East Side. The "yuppies off the East Side" stickers seemed to be everywhere, so I decided to just photograph as many as possible in an hour. As I walked up to a stop sign and snapped my camera, I heard a man's voice behind me: "Now, what are you doing?" I turned to see an older African-American man walking down the sidewalk. He introduced himself as Wayne and said that he sometimes lived with his sister on the street. I explained my mission of photographing the stickers, and he laughed. "What do you think about these stickers?" I asked him. Wayne shook his head: "I don't like those stickers. You know why? Because yuppies have yards, and I have a lawn business. I need yards to mow if I want to stay in business." I agreed and told him that my own father had started a lawn mowing business on the side. To make extra money, he mowed lawns in the evenings and on weekends.

We talked lawn mowing for a few minutes and then returned to the stickers. "You know," he continued, "change is good and important. Now, it's not good for black folks, because of the taxes of the property. You can't afford the houses anymore. But the new people coming into town make it safer. The drugs are just in one part of town now, and that's good for the kids. I have two daughters, and I want them to be safe."

His reasoning seemed to make sense, though I nodded my head less enthusiastically. Shouldn't Wayne be upset? After all, he was the one who was being affected by these changes. The lofts and their residents meant that his own home might be unaffordable now, thanks to a jump in property taxes. But, as a kid from a working-class family, I also understood what it meant to have increased opportunities like a lawn mowing business. Displacement can happen in a number of ways. He looked at me with a smile and asked, "You ever read that book *Who Moved My Cheese?* It's all about change and flexibility, and how you need to stay flexible. It's 2008, you know? Time for change. You can't get set in your ways." We talked a little longer, and then I said goodbye to Wayne. As I walked down the streets of my old neighborhood, I considered Wayne's words. He reminded me that development is complicated. Change on the East Side has meant the displacement of so much, yet it has also meant a world of increased opportunity. People like Wayne and the local bloggers who reflected on their places within gentrification are able to talk about how they are implicated in the multiple effects of development.

These kinds of complex claims manage to consider how our bodies are located within and moving across larger networks. Writers like the Accidental Gentrifist consider how they are ethically implicated inside local, regional, and even global flows of history and capital. This recognition can also be heard in the words of Marcel, an Oakland resident who called NPR's live talk show *Talk of the Nation* during an episode about gentrification. Marcel describes watching his old neighborhood in Oakland experience massive gentrification. Although five years earlier he could not even qualify for a $79,000 home improvement loan, Marcel now sat on top of potential gold mine in his Oakland home. "So it does, in a sick way, create an opportunity for people to build equity and have opportunities for ownership," concluded Marcel (*Talk of the Nation*). Marcel articulates his own complex position within a system. He is part of a community that is being targeted for displacement, yet he is also a participant. Marcel seems to recognize that this situation is "sick" in the way it pushes residents to become the agents of their own displacement. Yet, as Marcel also acknowledges, the choice to participate in this process is a decision that each resident must make for himself or herself. The sickness of such a "choice" lies in the uneven effects of choosing to stay behind. Marcel,

Wayne, and others are thus able to frame gentrification across a series of networks, which allows them to think about their own agency in complex ways.

Simple Equivalence Claims

But there are other kinds of responses, too. While some equivalence claims allow the speaker to consider his or her own complex agency within gentrification's process, other equivalence claims simply articulate gentrification as "both good and bad." Rather than opening up reflection on how development implicates us in compound ways across networks (including local, transhistorical, class-based, and transspatial networks), simple equivalence claims close down any significant call to reflection. The articulation of "both good and bad" serves as a final judgment, since any additional inquiry would require rhetors to move past a feeling of undecidability. Because simple equivalence claims are quite prevalent in public discourse, I am especially interested in the rhetorical effects of their circulation. How often is such equivalence drawn upon as a topos for entering public discourse?

Compare the bloggers we read above to local bloggers who engage in these kinds of simplified claims. One blog devoted to discussions of east Austin life considers how gentrification cannot be completely vilified. Sure, writes the blogger, some people are being displaced as a result of these changes. But, "I don't think it's such a *bad* thing. . . . It seems to me a lot of longtime residents don't seem to mind, either. I don't see people picketing in the street. However, as far as these new digs go, if it's good for the local economy, and is maintaining the integrity of the 'culture' on this side of the highway, I don't see anything wrong with it" ("Eastsiders: Alex"). Of course, the blogger himself suffers from a visibility problem. He claims not to "see people picketing in the street," which serves as evidence that longtime residents are not feeling any injury. The bad effects of gentrification are certainly there, he admits. However, the bad effects seem not to outweigh the good effects that gentrification brings. In short, it is good and bad in equal measure. This ambivalence thus becomes a conclusion in its own right. Further inquiry is unnecessary.

Similar kinds of judgments commonly circulate throughout public discussions about gentrification. For example, a locally produced documentary on East Side gentrification interviewed several younger residents about their thoughts on the neighborhood's changes. One young Latino man gave a lengthy response to the question about gentrification in his neighborhood. "When the condominiums came up, it brought more business to the area and more people started coming in. . . . But [it used to be] all Chicano neighborhoods, and now it's all white neighborhoods. The old families aren't there anymore because . . . they gotta move around when tax time comes." He weighs his words for a moment, and then smiles. "But, you know, everything has its pros and its cons" ("East Austin Gentrification Documentary"). This last line—everything has its pros and cons—serves as an ending point for his reflection. Gentrification contains both injurious and beneficial effects, a fact that becomes a judgment in itself. The camera pans to another young Latino man standing beside the first man. He considers his friend's words and then adds his own thoughts: "I'm always gonna love east Austin, you know? Shit, our families all been here forever. . . . And so now other peoples coming, and they like it. But, at the same time, a lot of the culture is leaving." Once again, the acknowledgment of dual effects creates a site of equivalence ("everything has its pros and its cons") that operates as rhetorical judgment. It is a *krisis*

The specter of undecidability allows these rhetors to "weigh in" on a public issue without articulating an exigence for intervention. One can be simultaneously for and against gentrification without ever seeming to refuse a rhetorical stance. Consider how a young record store owner, who moved to the East Side only a year earlier, explains his take on gentrification: "I'm personally opposed to gentrification, but you can't stop a lot of change. It's inevitable. . . . So I'm not necessarily for it, but I don't see that there's a lot of things that can stop it" (Gabrielsolidarity). The logic of inevitability works alongside the logic of benefit in order to create undecidable equivalence claims. When Jason Carnes, the country's top-rated over-thirty professional BMX rider, moved into one of the East Side's expensive new lofts, he was asked a similar question about east Austin gentrification. Carnes admitted that local residents were surely upset by these changes, but the changes were also inevitable. "To see the city grow into their neighborhood, I don't know," Carnes said sadly. "But what do you do? No matter where you are, the city will catch you" (Schwarz, "East Austin"). His response seems to writes himself outside of a complex agency. Instead, he is also caught in a stream of inevitability that brings both good and bad effects. Or, in the words of one developer, "Gentrification is not good or bad. It's a market force" ("Gentrification").

In these instances, undecidability and equivalence are not starting points for conversation. They are conclusions. As such, they are more like deliberative dead ends. They shut down true public debate before any kind of critical inquiry can take place. One reason lies in the way that these claims frame gentrification as a binary. As one online comment about east Austin's gentrification puts it, "There's two ways to look at gentrification. One is that it has gotten out of hand, and I agree with that. The other is that it is cleaning up these ghetto areas and driving out the violence. How could anyone disagree with that? Especially the people that have to live among it" (Joyness333). If there are "two ways to look at gentrification," then a conclusion about the situation's undecidability embraces a complex view. Indeed, this view is able to "see both sides," an ability that is praised in vernacular discourse.[5]

But there is another reason to call equivalence claims deliberative dead ends. Insofar as they allow for critiques to be made and absorbed without any call for reconsidering the need for intervention at multiple levels—including personal, local, regional, and global—simple equivalence claims help to cultivate a space of exception. They allow people to orient themselves to the scene of crisis without being called upon to think about transformation. Maybe this is why simple equivalence claims are used so often in official development discourse. Gentrification is rarely denied by city planners and city governments working to transform areas like east Austin. Instead, gentrification is framed as an undecidable act that is neither purely harmful nor purely beneficial.

For example, when plans for east Austin's revitalization projects were first announced, the city promoted the plans as beneficial to everyone involved. True, leaders admitted, corporate developments would be receiving significant tax incentives to build lofts and office parks on the East Side. But even these developments would ultimately benefit low-income residents. All developers receiving the incentives were required to pay 10 percent of what their city taxes would have been into a Homeowners' Assistance Fund, which would provide low-income families with utility payment vouchers. This fund was touted as a way "to mitigate the possible unintended negative side effect of increases in taxes and other costs on long-time homeowners in the area."[6] In addition, any development with residential or commercial space was required to reserve 10 percent of all units for people who earned less than the average minimum family income. The Austin Revitalization Authority (ARA) did acknowledge that one consequence of development is gentrification. However, the ARA steadfastly refused to apologize for the gentrification, calling it an ultimately beneficial process: "It is our hope that . . . gentrification serves the entire community" (Austin Revitalization Authority). Dr. Charles Urdy, one of the most recognizable leaders in both the Austin black community and the Austin city government, likewise admitted that gentrification was an issue in the midst of East Side development. As a longtime chairman and passionate supporter of the ARA, Urdy's insistence on the positive aspects of gentrification is no surprise. "Yes," Urdy admits in a television interview, "anytime there's development in a low-income area, gentrification is a problem" ("East Austin Gentrification"). However, Urdy refuses to stop there. Gentrification is not only a problem. It will ultimately bring some benefit to everyone.

People like Terry Ortiz, both an east Austin native and a structural engineer of several East Side developments, likewise talks up the positive changes that are happening as a result of development. "Because of new developments, there is some kind of activity in East Austin. Infrastructure improvements have taken place with new libraries, sidewalks." He goes on to argue that lofts and mixed-use developments "secure the neighborhood. Gang activity and prostitution go away in the disadvantaged neighborhoods" (Keating). Mayor Kirk Watson also happily touted the economic growth in east Austin as a result of development. "It's becoming much easier to recruit business to East Austin," he says. "I get people contacting me all the time about this. It's not so much 'What can the city do for me?' as 'This looks like an area of exciting opportunity.' People are starting to realize that an area that appeared not to be a potential economic engine—well, now it is" (Higgins).

One of the less stellar moments of equivalence claims comes from a city-hired developer named Anton Nelessen. During a community meeting designed to hear public input about design plans for the East Riverside corridor, Nelessen told the crowd that gentrification was not exactly a problem. In the crowded cafeteria of a local elementary school, Nelessen took the microphone and announced, "Gentrification is good. You need a balanced community of 20 percent low and moderate [income] against 80 percent other. If that tips, studies say communities go to hell. Whoever is here who is poor, let's say 100 people; we should bring 500 more [high income] people to balance them. But we need those [poor] people, (because) who is going to do your dishes, or cut your grass or water your plants?" (Gonzalez). Nelessen's insensitive comments outraged many people who attended the meeting (some of whom would later circulate his statements online). But they also reflect a dark parallel to the rhetoric used by city officials themselves. Although city leaders never framed development as a boon for the wealthy, as Nelessen seems happy to do, both kinds of rhetorical gestures frame gentrification as a combination of benefits and drawbacks. By not denying the harmful effects, official discourse can absorb the critical blows while moving forward.

It would be a mistake to define these kinds of rhetorical gestures as a new phenomenon. Framing gentrification and development as both good and bad has a long rhetorical history. One 1970 article on earlier gentrification on the East Side is cheerily titled, "Family Now Happier, Thanks to Urban Renewal." Yes, admits the story, moving is difficult for longtime families. But the benefits are worth it. The profile tells a story of pain and reward, all rolled into one. In 1972, the *Austin American-Statesman* featured an even more extensive account on the city's urban renewal efforts. The special section gave several before-and-after reports of East Side properties that had been revitalized. Consider Jim Voggle's New Deal Tin Shop, which was part of the renewal project. Voggle "was not too happy about moving at first, but looking back he thinks it's one of the best things that ever happened to him" ("Urban Renewal Special"). While forced revitalization had its share of negative impacts, including the surrender of longtime property on the east side of town, the news story concludes that the positive impacts offset those negatives.

Simple equivalence claims circulate well beyond the debates in Austin's East Side, of course. A Chicago community organization decided to take the question about gentrification out into the streets. Local residents in the Lawndale neighborhood were asked what they thought about the gentrification happening in Lawndale. One man enthusiastically told the questioner that he supported it. "Anything new come to the area, I welcome it. . . . I've seen Lawndale come up and go down. It's time for it to come up" (DDCOC, "Gentrification, Lawndale"). Sure, continues the man, gentrification brings change. But that change can also bring progress, too. Dorothy, another longtime Lawndale resident, also responds to the question by concluding that it has good points and bad points. On the one hand, gentrification in the African American community "is a failure [on the part of] our politicians to keep our community growing" (DDCOC, "Gentrification, Part 2"). On the other hand, gentrification could create a better opportunities for future community members.

One high school project in Coral Gables, Florida, asked students to create a visual and textual response to the trends of gentrification in their city (Coral Gables Senior High). Many students responded by framing the event of gentrification as one that contained both good and bad effects. For example, Isabelo writes, "If someone told me that they wanted to tear down my home for a million dollars I would say yes, it would make me happy. But I would feel bad for the people who rent in my house." Juan's narrative also captures a kind of undecidability concerning the changes around him: "Gentrification does not affect me at all because I'm used to it. I'm not saying that I agree with it, but if I have to leave, I leave. I think if you've been living a long time in a place, it is going to be hard to move out, but if you're used to traveling, moving is okay." Similarly, Jorge writes,

> I think gentrification has good and bad affects. For example, if I arrive at my home and find that my house is going to be destroyed, I will feel very sad. . . . On the other hand, if I live in a place where there are a lot of ugly houses and bad people, I would be happy because with gentrification, all these houses and people will be gone and new people and beautiful houses will replace them. I think that gentrification will be taking place

always because technology and new things are being created every day. (Coral Gables Senior High)

The students' conclusions become a form of judgment that is difficult to move beyond. Isabelo and Jorge both read gentrification as a condition that is sad for some, happy for others. This observation is their own way of joining the public conversations about development in their own backyard.

The rhetorical gesture of "both good and bad" has become so familiar, in fact, that it has even appeared in an interview with the actor Steve Buscemi. When he was asked about his life in Brooklyn, Buscemi praised the thriving artist culture that now infuses the neighborhood. Brooklyn is a great place to be an actor, artist, or cultural critic. Yes, said the interviewer, but what about the fact that longtime residents are being priced out of the neighborhood? Is Brooklyn too gentrified? Buscemi seems undeterred. "Gentrification is something that happens and has been happening," he responds. "The city is always changing neighborhoods, always changing, and it's something that happens and I try not to look at it as necessarily a bad thing or a good thing, but as something that just happens and there's good and bad that goes along with it" (Del Signore). Buscemi's comment falls into the pattern of equivalence claims that we see popping up everywhere, from high school projects to official city statements. It is good and bad, harmful and helpful. And with that, the *krisis* is over.

Equivalence claims allow the speaker to be both inside and outside the scene of public crisis. This rhetorical gesture allows one to oppose the impacts while simultaneously being part of the process. News stories about gentrification frequently spark resentment among individuals who fail to see themselves as gentrifiers. In response to a *Washington Post* editorial criticizing gentrifiers in Washington, DC's Columbia Heights neighborhood, a resident writes, "Since I am not Latino or black and have lived in Columbia Heights for only six years, I'm guessing I would be one of [the] gentrifiers. But I hardly spend my time . . . 'jogging near sunset as though [I] don't have a care in the world'—and none of my gentrifier friends do either. They volunteer in the community, as do I, tutoring at the Latin American Youth Center in Columbia Heights" (Testa). By making herself (and her friends) into an example of how newcomers can provide a benefit, this writer straddles a very hazy line of publicness. She argues that the criticisms of gentrification cannot be about her because she does not experience unbounded pleasure ("jogging near sunset without a care in the world") and because she spends her time in some degree of sacrifice (tutoring in the "community"). Her argument serves to carve out an exceptional space, where she is neither an insider nor an outsider. She is an exceptional subject.[7]

The claims we see above certainly function as what we typically call clichés. Many of the simple equivalence claims respond to a complex problem with a very commonplace answer about pros and cons. Those of us who are teachers have undoubtedly faced such responses from student papers and presentations. The claim that a difficult situation is both good and bad is not too far removed from the ultimate cliché: everyone has a right to their own opinions. What bothers so many of us about these clichés is that they seem to avoid genuine engagement with the subject. If I respond to a crisis situation by claiming that both sides have legitimate arguments, thereby avoiding any judgment about the factual and ethical appropriateness of a certain argument, then I have probably not truly given the situation much consideration. In fact, I can write my essay's conclusion almost on the spot. Abortion? It has both positive and negative effects. Congressional term limits? There are pros and cons to this proposal. Global emissions regulation? Everyone has a right to their own opinion.

The rhetorical cliché can seem equally as uncritical. When faced with the question of how to respond to gentrification, with all of its complicated layers of history and politics, some respondents simply reply with the most comfortable commonplace available to them: it's good for some and bad for others. Although this response is frustratingly insipid, it is difficult to fight because we cannot easily deny it. Gentrification is indeed good for some and bad for others, just as it also has both positive and negative effects. Still, the veneer of truth offered by such rhetorical gestures does not equate to an ethical and critical judgment on the part of the rhetor. The cliché does serve a purpose, however. David Bartholomae deftly outlines how student writers rely upon clichés when they are unfamiliar with the more complex rhetorical moves of academic discourse. When students draw upon the cliché, they are relying upon "a culturally or institutionally authorized concept or statement that carries with it its own necessary elaboration" (406). To conclude an essay on controversial topics by writing that "Everyone has a right to their own opinion" is not an abdication of responsibility, therefore. Bartholomae suggests that this cliché is a culturally warranted commonplace that has significant depth. We may not like to read it, but we surely understand the various implications this particular cliché has. For starters, "everyone has a right to their own opinions" implies that the issue is not easily adjudicated by obvious rules (without denying at least one party's claims to their own legitimacy). It also implies that "facts" are open to multiple interpretations, insofar as we are all situated in our own historical, social, and personal locations. As Ruth Amossy points out in her discussion of the literary cliché, "A threadbare figure can help . . . shape the receiver's attitude toward the text it belongs to, as well as to the social discourse it exemplifies" (34). The cliché is overstuffed with meanings, assumptions, values, and presence.

The use of commonplaces and clichés in student writing may thus be attributed to a lack of familiarity with the university's discourse.[8] Once students learn what "critical engagement" actually means, and how one appropriately responds to previous conversations that are already in circulation, they can move past statements that discourage further elaboration. The same might be said about clichés in public discourse. When a writer concludes that gentrification has "both good and bad effects," she is able to contribute to public discourse without being steeped in prior conversations, complexes, and historical layers. This rhetorical claim is what Bartholomae describes as a culturally authorized statement that carries its own elaboration. This commonplace is an entry point into public discourse; however, it also allows the rhetor to avoid judgment of any kind. The equivalence claims seen above are both public entrances and exits.

Simple equivalence claims are troubling because, like most clichés, they are uncritical in the way they approach rhetorical crises. But I find them troubling for another reason as well. These patterns of discourse serve as technologies that produce and maintain certain kinds of public subjectivities. In previous chapters, I have called these public subjectivities "exceptional" insofar as they straddle a space that is both inside and outside the public sphere. The equivalence claims that circulate in development discourse produce subjects who mediate their own relation to the public through a feeling of equivalence or undecidability. That is, the feeling of undecidability becomes a de facto public rhetorical stance.

Ronald Walter Greene and Darrin Hicks demonstrate how cultural practices of debate have helped to produce certain kinds of subjectivities rather than others. In "Lost Convictions," Greene and Hicks contemplate the lengthy history of switch-side debate in U.S. colleges and high schools, where debaters are required to debate both sides of a controversial resolution. The practice of debating both sides is a cultural technology, according to Greene and Hicks, that "organizes forms of democratic subjectification available in the present" (101). The subject cultivated through debate was one that meshed with a liberal sense of citizenship. By valorizing the skill of debating both sides equally well, formal debate practices sought to reassign "the convictions of students to the process of debate as a democratic form of decision-making. In this way debate training was no longer simply a mechanism for developing critical thinking or advocacy skills, but instead, debate was now a performance technique that made possible the self-fashioning of a new form of liberal citizen. The citizen's commitments were to be redirected to the process of debate" (112). Being able to debate with equally empathetic skill was thus hailed as a true mark of democracy. Switch-side debating is capable of organizing such forms of liberal subjectification because the debating subject is (re)oriented to debate itself as a form of legitimating. The debater is not valorized for his own personal convictions or passion. He is valorized for his ability to engage the process of debate: arguing from both sides. Greene and Hicks imagine how this cultural technology, embedded in such institutional sites as the high school debate tournament or speech class, helps to shape the ways that subjects imagine themselves practicing citizenship in a global sense. The technology of debate helps to cultivate liberal subjects by valorizing process over conviction.

We might draw a rough parallel between this act of subjectification and the ways that equivalence claims also shape a certain kind of subject. However, what we find in the patterns of equivalence claims is not debate. It is more like an affective experience of undecidability. The speakers and writers arrive at a point of undecidability, not as a roadblock but as a destination. True enough, this arrival is drawn from a process of (quasi-)deliberation, wherein the rhetor considers the equivalent weight of all arguments. But the process of deliberation itself is not the point. Whereas debate legitimates subjects through the process of "debating both sides," vernacular commonplaces of equivalence legitimate subjects through the affective arrival of undecidability. We feel torn about the issue.

Such arrivals are organized and channeled through a number of cultural mechanisms. Consider the recent cultural valorization of bipartisanship and political moderation. Senator Barack Obama's 2004 speech to the Democratic National Convention became a hallmark of the new vision of citizenship beyond political party affiliation. His speech was memorable in the way it blurred together "red states" and "blue states" in their mutual commonality. "We coach Little League in the Blue States and yes, we've got some gay friends in the Red States. There are patriots who opposed the war in Iraq and there are patriots who supported the war in Iraq. We are one people" (Obama). Likewise, John McCain was repeatedly lauded in the 2008 presidential campaign for his ability to reach the "other side of the aisle," moving beyond a single focus on Republican ideals. Reports from the 2008 campaign spotlighted both Obama and McCain's claims to be the true bipartisan candidate who could move past their own party's platforms and see issues from "both sides" (Liasson).

Media during the 2008 election cycle also spotlighted "undecided voters," many of whom were painted as thoughtful and responsible citizens agonizing over their decision. In Rudy Giuliani's address to the 2008 Republican National Convention, he reached out to voters who "still feel torn in this election." Giuliani's speech guides undecided voters to one candidate (McCain), though he skillfully plays up the difficulty of such a decision. Nearly every major news outlet featured at least one moderated forum with undecided voters, in order to hear their perspective. The news channel CNN gave some of the most noteworthy attention to undecided voters during a presidential debate by tracking the real-time "feelings" of thirty undecided voters in Ohio. Thanks to a handheld device operated by the undecided voters, CNN viewers could visually chart the voters' feelings of approval and disapproval in response to the candidates. After the debates ended, a CNN moderator then interviewed the thirty voters in order to gain more perspective on their ups and downs. Rhetorical gestures like these serve to frame undecidability as an effect of contemplative citizenship. The experience of feeling torn is itself a mark of thoughtfulness that is worthy of attention, perhaps because it transcends mere partisanship. Mechanisms like these help to legitimate equivalence as a form of public orientation. Therefore, arriving at undecidability is not necessarily seen as a refusal of publicness. Quite the contrary: it can legitimate a public rhetorical stance.

Exceptional States and Undecidability

If equivalence claims are entry points into public discourse, as I have described them above, then what is the problem? Why link them to exceptional public subjects? Surely there is nothing wrong with encouraging people to move past myopic versions of their own truth. And isn't gentrification truly a process that contains both good and bad? Doesn't undecidability play an important role in public discourse? How can we rhetoricians begin (and end) anywhere except undecidability? What would Gorgias say?

My interest in equivalence claims does not emerge from any hope of ending undecidability. Gorgias and the sophists teach us that rhetoric is born from the midst of uncertainty and unknowability. Gorgias is one of the most beautiful commentators on the presence of undecidability, though his work has not often been read in this light. Gorgias's "On the Nonexistent; or, On Nature" offers us a complex understanding of this tension: "I say that nothing exists; then that if it exists it is unknowable; lastly, even if it exists and is knowable, nevertheless it cannot be directly communicated to anyone else" (quoted in Untersteiner 145). Mario Untersteiner untangles this puzzle by suggesting that Gorgias does not imagine nothing literally exists. Rather, Gorgias is observing the way that nothing exists without contradiction. This observation forms the kernel of what Untersteiner calls the sophist's tragic epistemology: "Truth cannot . . . be incarnated in logos. For when we seek to grasp the contents of thought by which thought is conditioned . . . we are bound to find that the logos . . . is opposed by another logos which cancels the possibility of what has happened and what was willed. . . . therefore logos, the sole vehicle of truth, is divided into contrasting *logoi:* hence pure truth is impossible" (141). The tragedy of knowledge is the contrasting doubleness of the logos: for every right answer, another right answer also exists.

Perhaps another way of stating this epistemological situation is by restating it in terms of foundational knowledge: there is no final standard or rule to decide the Truth of human situations. We are merely confronted by relative paths and knowledges. Nothing exists in a final, fixed, universal form. Gorgias's statement that nothing exists thus exposes "a universal horizon where every possible intellectual experience is doomed to shipwreck," as long as that intellectual experience counts on an ultimately decidable Truth (Untersteiner 143). According to Untersteiner, then, "Gorgias felt the infinite sorrow of man, who never finds himself confronted by a single way" (142). The tragedy of human beings is that we cannot help but begin from the nonexistent or the undecidable.

But Gorgias is not the careless relativist that he has been made out to be. Rather, he champions the need for rhetoric because Truth is undecidable. He knows that we must act in the face of uncertainty. Similarly, Isocrates also considers our call to act in spite of not-knowing. As Isocrates writes in *Antidosis*, "My view of this question is, as it happens, very simple. For since it is not in the nature of man to attain a science by the possession of which we can know positively what we should do or what we should say, in the next resort I hold that man to be wise who is able by his powers of conjecture to arrive generally at the best course, and I hold that man to be a philosopher who occupies himself with the studies from which he will most quickly gain that kind of insight." His sense of conjecture is a kind of making-present in the midst of unknowability. We must depend upon some kind of judgment in order to create something (a way, an action, an argument) where none literally exists. Though we are lodged in a permanent state of undecidability, we must make present an ethical, humane, and sound course of action.

Many people have read these classic sophistic statements across arguments about rhetoric and epistemology. And, indeed, they are weighty statements about the necessity of forming discourse in the face of epistemic undecidability. But I would also like to read these statements as a comment on how to respond rhetorically to complexity and an unknowable world. Eric Charles White reads Gorgias as making a statement about action: this tragic epistemology does not paralyze rhetorical action, but instead grounds it in the specificity of embodied, material, and situated contexts. In Gorgias's theory, says White, "the persuasive force of a speech does not derive from its correspondence to a preexistent reality or truth. Truth is relative to the speaker and the immediate context. . . . Or to put it another way, there is no meaning outside of a specific context of rhetorical persuasion" (14–15). Practically speaking, this means that rhetors must make a logos present, since none are available to us in a pure realm of certainty. Although neither Isocrates nor Gorgias present their theories as management techniques, we can read them as offering an early version of something like this. To act, to engage with others in a public deliberation about pressing matters, we must use powers of conjecture to reveal a logos that is the best, most ethical course of action.

The complexity of gentrification is indeed ambiguous. It would be just as shortsighted to call for an end to gentrification as it would be to praise or promote it. This ambiguity can create a kind of rhetorical paralysis, which is partly revealed in these simple equivalence claims. Thomas Farrell offers some insight into this paralysis in his meditation on magnitude and rhetoric. Farrell writes, "We live in an era when everything, anything, and nothing may be considered important. As any preliminary scan of the information highway will confirm, there is nothing remotely imaginable that does not hold someone's rapt attention" (470). We arrive at equivalence not through a diminishment of choices, therefore, but through an explosion of choice. Gorgias may have imagined a tragic figure facing competing logoi that both seem to have the truth on their sides, but he might as well have imagined another tragic aspect of humans who are faced with endless calls for attention and energy. Farrell points to the growing flood of information competing for attention. I would bracket this critique and extend it beyond the technological present. The event has always been wild in its multiplicity.[9] How we remember and frame the event involves radically unstable circulation among my own mood, public memory, and accumulated energies of circulation. The work of making an event present, therefore, is no simple or neutral matter. It is a public act that is constantly undergoing revision. Therefore, Farrell writes, we are always playing the role of presence-making rhetoricians: "Rhetoric is the art, the fine and useful art, of making things matter" (470). The magnitude of gentrification and development presents us with many ways, many logoi. The right position does not exist within the scene of gentrification itself. Responding to the public crisis of place change therefore demands something other than correct reasoning. And yet, as Gorgias shows us, we must act.

Can we "make things matter" by staying in the mode of undecidability? Perhaps. Kenneth Burke is an eloquent rhetorician who writes about the muddle of ambiguity. Burke exploits "the resources of ambiguity," or "the areas of ambiguity [wherein] transformations take place; in fact, without such areas, transformation would be impossible" (*Grammar* xix).[10] However, adopting a position of ambiguity or undecidability is also a way to step into a public space of exception. Giorgio Agamben (drawing on the work of Carl Schmitt) describes the political state of exception as a condition of being outside and yet belonging. The state of exception is an "extreme form of relation by which something is included solely through its exclusion" (*Homo Sacer* 18). The sovereign exception is one who stands outside of law's application, yet who also belongs to it insofar as he or she can suspend the law altogether. We might use this theory to guide our understanding of the subject produced from equivalence claims: those who write themselves outside the conditions to which they belong. More to the point, exceptional subjects draw upon equivalence claims in order to write themselves outside the conditions that call for their intervention. So, while undecidability can be a way into public deliberation, we should remember that it is also a way out.

How do claims of injury and of equivalence work together in response to urban development and collectively help to cultivate a public rhetorical stance? As the examples in this chapter reflect, some people are pulled toward the site of injury insofar as they feel injured. Groups such as PODER and east Austin neighborhood activists do not make equivalence claims because they feel the pull of personal investment into the situation. However, not everyone feels pulled toward the site of injury. When asked why some east Austinites do not fight the gentrification and development, East Side activist Juan Valadez explains, "If you throw a dog a bone, he won't bite you and you're safe from him." ("3: An East Austin Narrative"). Likewise, when a grassroots group unsuccessfully tried to prevent an American Apparel chain store from opening in San Francisco's Mission neighborhood, one protester complained that people often "don't care about gentrification unless it affects them" (de Brito). In these instances, the feeling of awayness from injury sites seem to warrant rhetorical shrugs like ambivalence, ambiguity, and equivalence. The feeling of relation becomes, either way, an alibi of publicness. Relating toward or away from the injury site are two equal options that the public subject may adopt.

What are we to do, then? Since equivalence and ambiguity are cultivated through public technologies, it is difficult to redirect people away from such affective states. We cannot instruct people to feel angry, outraged, or injured by processes like gentrification and displacement. As I discussed in chapter 3, people's libidinal investments to such discourse are difficult to simply disconnect. There are deeply held attachments to discourses of undecidability, as the recent valorization of postpartisan discourse reflects. Furthermore, by asking people to feel less ambivalent about issues like gentrification, we do not address the more serious problem of how exceptional subjects orient to the public through feelings of decidability—either a feeling toward or away from decidability. In other words, the process of subjectification remains grounded in feeling. Consequently, we do not remedy the shortcomings of the true public subject of feeling. Our solution must instead look to a practice that encourages subjects who are rooted in an alternative beginning point. One possible practice is to cultivate public discourse that is rooted in inquiry rather than feeling.

6

Inquiry as Social Action

> I shall purloin no valuables, appropriate no ingenious formulations. But the rags, the refuse—these I will not inventory but allow, in the only way possible, to come into their own: by making use of them.
> —Walter Benjamin, *Arcades Project*

> There will always be a tension between what rhetoric makes and what "makes" or produces rhetoric.
> —Thomas Farrell,
>   "The Weight of Rhetoric"

I mentioned in chapter 1 that we needed to cultivate public subjects who are capable of imagining themselves as situated within many complex networks. Not only are we all located within a specific home-work nexus, but we are also located within regional, national, and global networks. Furthermore, each of us is situated within transhistorical and transspatial networks of place. The choices we make for ourselves have effects on future times and places that do not only parallel our own lives. Thinking through these networks demands an ability to imagine the incongruent and asymmetrical networks within which our agency is lodged.

    I pointed to the BP oil spill and the call for boycotting stations as an example of thinking in terms of networks. People were understandably outraged by the events that unfolded around the Deepwater Horizon drilling rig explosion. Negligence by BP seemed to have contributed to the explosion and subsequent spill, and stopping the flow initially seemed to be out of anyone's power. We watched helplessly as oil spewed into the water while BP unsuccessfully tried endless tactics to stop the spill. Of course, none of us wanted to feel helpless; we wanted to act. Not surprisingly, one of the most visible and organized calls to action was the national boycott against BP gas stations. E-mails, Web sites, letters, and even flyers asked drivers to pass BP filling stations the next time they needed gas.

No matter how good it feels to drive past a BP station, truly sustainable thinking demands that we think about this crisis across incongruent and asymmetrical networks. The gas sold in BP gas stations is actually extracted and refined by a number of other companies, with only a small amount of BP additives mixed in near the end of the process (Lieber). But, more importantly, driving past a BP station and into another gas station does not solve the problem of petroleum mining, which led to the Deepwater Horizon tragedy. Choosing Exxon or Mobile gas still supports the same system that causes problems over time (Begley). Boycotting BP does not consider how drilling is spread asymmetrically across many networks, including across international networks that often remain invisible. Although the Deepwater Horizon spill gained much attention at home, even greater oil spills in the Niger Delta have been happening for decades without much awareness in the United States. The popular call for us to boycott BP gas stations fails to place the event within multiple networks, which ultimately would call for us to consider much more dramatic changes than where we fill up next time.

Sustainable futures demand that we think about ourselves as beings who exist in multiple and asymmetrical networks. Intervention must also happen within networks; public subjects are never single. Therefore, becoming oriented to the public sphere is never simply a matter of joining publics or counterpublics. Whether or not we know it, we are already part of multiple networks. We are already in a relation to others and to the world. Transformative rhetoric thus requires that we learn how to think of ourselves within these multiple networks, and also how they might be otherwise construed.

One of the questions motivating me is how we can encourage public subjects who are capable of using the communicative moment to critically address changing landscapes. How can we encourage subjects who can make ethical judgments (*krisis*) about those changes, and who can work to rebuild and reimagine spaces for public discourse? We must pursue inquiry as a mode of publicness. My publics approach to place crisis means that I recognize an advantage to interrogating public discourse in order to investigate how it produces more or less effective subjects who can intervene in sustainable futures. But it also means that I see public talk itself as our best hope of making a change. By transforming the kinds of subjects that public talk makes, we can transform the kinds of rhetorical actions those subjects make.

Rhetorical Pedagogies and Exceptional Subjects

I have argued that the exceptional public subject is cultivated through vernacular patterns of public talk. Though this mode of production is important, I do not want to lose sight of another way in which such a key subjectivity is encouraged today. Closer to home, we might also consider the technologies of production that exist in our own rhetorical pedagogies. Are we inadvertently reproducing discourses that cultivate exceptional public subjects? The first time I typed this question, I happened to be sitting in a coffee shop. Beside me sat a young woman and a young man. I could not help but overhear parts of their conversation, and I could tell that they were talking about writing. The woman had her laptop open on the table, and they were both surrounded by notebooks. They were talking about essay assignments that were due in a few days. The woman looked at the man and said, with total certitude, "It's always easier to write about something you feel passionately about." The man nodded and they both went back to their work. Only a week earlier, during my own individual conferences with students who were completing their drafts, one student told me that he found this assignment easy because he could write about what was interesting to him personally. These two different scenes suggest a kind of victory for rhetoric and composition pedagogy. Aren't students like these examples of public pedagogy gone right? After all, writing is usually posed as an engagement with something the writer is invested in. And a good rhetorical pedagogue's job is to help students become invested. This, at least, had been my mantra for many years. And I know I am not alone.

Rhetorical pedagogies have a deep commitment to helping students make connections with public issues, including helping them to understand how those issues affect them. Composition studies especially takes up this challenge in undergraduate writing courses. For example, in "Living Room: Teaching Public Writing in a Post-Publicity Era," Nancy Welch outlines her own public pedagogy as a kind of bridge-building among individual students and larger community issues that hold significant meanings for them. For her part, Welch assigns union literature and newspapers (such as *Strike!* and *Labor Pains*), since a "majority of my students are going on to jobs—as teachers, social workers, healthcare providers, engineers, service workers, and technicians—that are, or need to be, union jobs" (485). By engaging in critical reflection about labor issues, Welch hopes that these students will connect their own plights with the ongoing public debates about ethical labor practices. Welch is thus engaging in a pedagogy grounded in students' investment. She sees their (potential) futures as union workers and laborers as leading to an investment in the ongoing conversations about labor practices, both current and historical. This kind of pedagogy operates from the premise/promise that by seeing connections and relations, students will become public participants.

Many scholars see the job of rhetorical pedagogy as helping students to forge real relationships with publics and counterpublics. Susan Wells's article "Rogue Cops and Health Care: What Do We Want from Public Writing?" makes one of the best arguments for a public writing pedagogy that engages in this work. Wells explains, "If we want more for our students than the ability to defend themselves in bureaucratic settings, we are imagining them in a public role, imagining a public space they could enter. I argue that we need to build, or take part in building, such a public sphere" (326). Public writing in the composition classroom, then, is a process of students "speak[ing] in their own skins to a broad audience with some hope of effectiveness" (334). Students in a public writing classroom thus seek to compose an engaged audience—a public—that can negotiate (about) taking action on a given problem or issue. Similarly, Christian Weisser advocates a pedagogy that "help[s] students discover the various counterpublics where their public writing might have a receptive audience, and, consequently, might result in significant outcomes" (107). Weisser argues that one key to successful public pedagogy is allowing students to "discover and write about all of the issues that affect their lives—not just those that have been delegated 'of common concern'" (109). The practice advocated by Wells and Weisser reaffirms that our jobs are primarily one of connection building. Teachers help students find and build relations that have meaning in their lives. For rhetorical pedagogues, the answer to public disengagement seems to be in cultivating connections between the public's crises and a student's own private life.

Although the actual means of pursuing this connection is unique to each scholar, there is some tacit agreement about the importance of helping students see the relevance of public issues in their individual lives. As Jeff Smith recommends in his attempt to combat the political passivity of "illegeracy," people "naturally take an interest in things that affect their lives, particularly if they feel it's up to them how those things will be decided. So what's needed is a framing of the issues that shows people the systems they're enmeshed in and outlines the real choices available to them. People then will want to reassume their political role" (210). According to Smith, our challenge is to show people how they are already affected by political events and debates. Ideally, once you make this revelation, people will begin to feel an investment. They will care once again, and this care will lead to action.[1] Even our work as teachers is often framed as necessarily beginning in feelings of investment, care, and so forth. In *Doing Emotion,* Laura Micciche reads pedagogy as primarily rooted in particular kinds of feelings like hope and belief. Transformative teaching, writes Micciche, is a matter of our "investment in producing compassionate citizens . . . as a result of which people care for and about others" (106–7). Without investment in care, both teaching and learning are seen as partial and, perhaps, even tragically flawed. Consider how many assignments in our most common courses (lower-level and introductory writing and speaking classes) reflect a pedagogical assumption that students should feel something prior to writing, speaking, or producing a rhetorical text. In choosing a topic, how many times have we encouraged students to choose a topic in which they are invested? *Choose something you care about.*

As rhetorical critics, we must learn to see our pedagogies as apparatuses (themselves embedded in an institution) that are designed to produce certain modes of self-understanding. Pedagogies are technologies that are invested in certain kinds of productions. By the way we talk about forms of argument, we tell students essentially how to see the world. We teach a preferred way of rhetorically engaging with problems. As James Berlin writes, "in teaching writing, we are tacitly teaching a version of reality and the students' place and mode of operation in it" ("Contemporary" 766). What does it mean, then, that so much of our pedagogy underscores the premise that publicness is related to one's feeling: the feeling of impact (including injury and benefit), the feeling of memory (or sense of relatability), or one's feeling of equivalence (the experience of seeing both sides, beyond your own version). By making feeling a prerequisite to publicness and to public rhetorical action, we are endorsing what Lauren Berlant calls the "true subject of feeling." This feeling subject is one whose very humanity is registered through an experience of feeling. That is, this figure indexes his or her way-of-being through the kinds of feelings experienced.

By yoking students' feelings of investment or excitement to public crises and exigencies, we promote the notion that feeling is the proper means of engaging these topics. Our practices often begin from a mantra about feeling investment in your topic. We endorse the belief that rhetorical intervention begins from a relation of towardness, so we guide our students to write about their own towardnesses. (A goal perfectly reflected in the coffee shop conversation between the two students excitedly working on their essays.) But, at the same time, this endorsement tacitly—against our best intentions—promotes awayness as an alternative mode of public orientation. Distance itself becomes another form of relation to the site of publicness. If I do not feel pulled toward the site of crisis, then my distance marks a legitimate stance in the larger rhetorical situation. Therefore, by grounding our students' sense of publicness in the work of feeling, we help to maintain the exceptional spaces I discussed in previous chapters.

We might move away from discourses that root rhetorical deliberation in care, impact, memory, and decidability. Instead, I want to encourage a pedagogical practice of inquiry as its own telos. Inquiry can become a form of social action where place changes are concerned. This pedagogy of inquiry asks students to develop a different kind of relation to place, crisis, and discourse. Inquiry becomes a habit, not a precursor to anything else. It does not matter whether one feels injured by the changes or has authentic memory or feelings about the changes, or whether the changes have some kind of decidable value. In fact, it does not matter whether one cares or does not care about the issue at hand. What matters is the challenge of inquiry itself.

This is not to say that I imagine some way in which feeling is removed from the site of pedagogy or public rhetoric. Such a task is not possible, nor is it desirable. Education will continue to be what Lynn Worsham calls an education of sentiment ("Moving Beyond" 163). However, we can imagine a different kind of investment and care that is habituated in the work of inquiry, not in the work of feeling. In order to pursue this different kind of subjectivity and rhetorical habituation, I want to explore some examples of how people are actually pursuing inquiry as a social response to urban development's crises. I will look closely at several past and ongoing projects that pursue a telos of inquiry among its participants. Many of these examples reflect a kind of public subjectivity different from the ones I developed in previous chapters. I have attempted to implement this kind of rhetorical approach in my own classroom, although the project is ongoing and far from perfect.

What Is Inquiry?

Crises and controversies are networks, and they invite our investigation into them. Inquiry is an endless survey of these networks within which a crisis is embedded. But inquiry is different from the epistemic of controversy and crisis (Who is correct? What shall we call it? Is this good or bad?). Within epistemic discourse, our aim is to find a perspective whereby the question can be answered. Inquiry, however, is not a pretext to a greater telos; it is its own telos. In shifting away from an epistemic perspective, inquiry looks much more like what network theorists John Law and John Urry call a performative ontology, or the investigation of networked relations (How is it composed? What are the working relations? How can we change the relations to remake this process?). Both kinds of discourse involve judgment (*phronesis*), insofar as we are making ethical and political claims about how the world should be. But the performative ontology of inquiry asks investigators to occupy a different kind of subject position. Instead of seeking resolution, the inquiring subject seeks to uncover the composition of a given scene (What are the relations that give it shape and form?). The subject is implicated within the process, and that relational position is also revealed in the act of investigation. Most importantly, the goal of inquiry is not always resolution.

In the opening pages of this book, I stated that sustainable thinking must be capable of thinking across multiple and asymmetrical networks. I make this claim because being public is a matter of living and working in (and, hopefully, reconfiguring) the networks at various times. In order to better understand what I mean by multiple and asymmetrical networks, I draw briefly upon a body of literature that has radically changed the ways we think about ourselves as social beings. Actor-network theory provides a model for understanding all kinds of networks, including networks of social problems. Bruno Latour and others introduced the field of actor-network theory in order to challenge the too limited concept of "the social" within sociology. Latour defines the social as ongoing action within a network, or "a type of momentary association which is characterized by the way it gathers together into new shapes" (*Reassembling* 65). As Latour explains it, his notion of actor-network theory is a means to expand the social beyond a "local, face-to-face" dynamic that is paradigmatic within sociology (65). Actor-network theory helps sociologists to rethink sociality as a distributed network of connections rather than as a singular substance that coheres into a whole. Latour's emphasis is not about how we (as individual agents) are either affected or how we affect. Rather, actor-network theory is more about how we *are* within a process. While we may not be conscious of the networks we inhabit, we are aware of the networks through a kind of embodied knowledge that is reflected in our behavioral adjustments.

For instance, consider how human users adjust their practices according to the particular ways the nonhuman materials work. For example, the local cultural conditions of my department's building provide a clear illustration of that nexus. After a few paper jams, you would learn to avoid using the coin-operated copier for double-sided papers. Better to feed the machine small batches at a time, which means that rush jobs should probably be taken to the library copiers. You would also learn that the mailroom is too awkward to have a nice chat, and that the east-west wings of the hallways will inevitably slow you down if you are in a hurry. This is more than an observation about traditional senses of "the social," for all of these local practices involve connections among humans and materials. Rather than seeing nonhuman materials as secondary objects functioning as tools for humans, Latour suggests that our local conditions are comprised of the interactions between the two.

In describing how the tight springs of an automatic door work, for example, Latour (writing as Jim Johnson) observes that it is the human user who must adjust his behavior: he must either speed up to catch the door, or else clear the way to avoid being squashed. "An unskilled nonhuman [door spring] thus presupposes a skilled human user," he writes ("Mixing" 301). In this case, the tightly sprung door actually imposes certain behaviors on its human users. Latour suggests that nonhuman actants can redistribute competencies, generate the potential for certain narrative frames, and even shift their own delegation of necessary action (309). In my case, the coin-operated copier has made me more organized than ever before. I know that I cannot simply run downstairs at the last minute to copy a handout for my class because the machine almost always has some problem. This means that I must plan the classes at least a few days in advance, giving the administrative assistant time to copy the handout for me. However, the maladjusted coin-operated copier also means fewer colleagues offer to copy an article or chapter that might be relevant to you. My previous local environment consisted of a free, working copier that was tucked away in a private room, which made it simpler for friends to simply run off an article and leave it in your mailbox with a sticky note that read, "Thought you might be interested."

Networks are not about fixed indexes of meaning but about relations among elements. Furthermore, networks are not human—or at least they are not merely human. As actor-network theorists Annemarie Mol and John Law explain, "Network elements may be machines or gestures. And their relations include all sorts of co-constitutions" (649). In *Communities of Practice*, Etienne Wenger shows us another example of how material, social, and institutional activity networks change not only how something is produced but also what is produced. Wenger undertakes an ethnographic study of insurance claims adjusters and their work environment in one company's office. Wenger is less interested in the actual process of claims adjusting than in the ways this particular office works. He follows the moves of one office worker, Arial, to document how she works within a network of practices. According to Wenger's analysis, Arial's office involves what he calls "constellations" of interconnected practices. "The term constellation refers to a grouping of stellar objects that are seen as a configuration even though they may not be particularly close to one another, of the same kind, or of the same size," explains Wenger (127). For example, Arial works smoothly by knowing which pieces of red tape can (and should) be bypassed in order to be productive.

Attaining a goal sometimes requires help from another adjuster, which means that you cannot bring lunch to eat on your own. Lunch at the deli may involve thirty minutes of office gossip and personal stories, but its ritual signifies a kind of friendliness among its participants. Arial's lunch talk is crucial in solidifying certain relationships across the office. So when she needs to bypass an unnecessarily bureaucratic step, those networks are already in place to help create shortcuts with the help of another office colleague. A constellation indicates particular proximities, which "are not necessarily congruent with physical proximity, institutional affiliations, or even interactions" (130). Lunch is an activity that involves much more than an immediate goal (to satisfy rumbling stomachs). Instead, it is an activity related to office politics, current projects, and the sly elision of company policies.

My discussion here is not a thorough explanation of actor-network theory, but I offer it as a way to provide vocabulary for what actor-network theorists call "network tracing" (Latour, "On Actor Network Theory"). Tracing a network requires one to reflect on the relational processes and linkages that form a network. In an excellent example of network tracing, Mol and Law track the relational existence of anemia and its cross-regional diagnoses in their discussion of the porousness and fluidity of anemia's diagnosis in Africa. The authors interview a number of Dutch doctors who have worked in different African subregions, all of whom conclude that anemia levels are extremely high among Africans. On the face of it, this diagnosis seems to be a simple matter of fact. Doctors are able to determine that high numbers of African patients have low RHB Hb (red blood cell hemoglobin) in their blood. Yet, ask Mol and Law, exactly where is the anemia to be found? When the authors begin to trace the networked elements that go into the Western conclusion that Africa has "high" levels of anemia, we begin to see complex relations among different elements that are present within these so-called factual diagnoses.

When a patient comes to see a doctor, she encounters screening techniques that differ based on the doctor's background. Western doctors depend upon listening to a patient's complaints, while a non-Western doctor often relies upon the (dis)coloration of a patient's skin and eyes. Lab machines used in detecting hemoglobin also differ between standard labs in the Netherlands and in African countries. Whereas Dutch labs often use photo-electric meters, African labs primarily employ less accurate hemoglobinometers. Language differences are also working within the constellation of Africa's anemia diagnoses. Not only are lab manuals written in English, demanding that the lab technicians translate across multiple dialects in order to follow basic procedure, but Western doctors also spend less time with African patients in the hospital as a result of the time spent translating between doctor and patient. Other elements present within any diagnosis of high or low anemia rates include organizational standards for acceptable ranges of hemoglobin. For example, the World Health Organization has set one important scale that is sometimes (though not always) used to determine what should be considered high or low. Furthermore, the decision to condense regional differences into a single topographic signifier called "Africa" is also an important element within this network. In places where civil war violence is a constant threat to citizens, examinations for anemia (via the clinical gaze of one's skin discoloration) may not be a priority among medical workers.

By tracing out this complex network, Mol and Law are not attempting to dispute the ontological validity of anemia. Low hemoglobin levels do exist and do cause serious physical problems. However, the active diagnosis, conceptualization, and treatment of anemia are located in the mutable relations among all of these elements. "It may flow in people's skills, or as part of the attributes of devices, or in the form of written words—any or all of these may carry anemia" (664). In other words, the concept "anemia" is an effect of the network itself. When an element of this network is altered or removed, anemia will show up differently for us. Its meaning and consequences are also likely to change as well. This is one reason why the network as a source of meaning-making is so important to understand.

Tracing a network has been described as an "empirical" investigation (Mol and Law; Latour, "Reassembling"; Doolin and Lowe). It is empirical insofar as it investigates contingent relations among elements within a conceptual region: an insurance claims office, regional anemia rates, a marriage, or a city's light rail program. However, network inquiry itself is not apolitical. Its empiricism does not displace its potential to serve activist goals. John Law and John Urry argue that inquiry into networks can help us to enact the social, not merely to reveal its workings. As a method, write Law and Urry, network inquiry and tracing marks a turn away from epistemology (with an emphasis on what is known from a particular perspective) to ontology (with an emphasis on remaking the known differently). Their use of ontology here is not a facile sense of fixed reality. Reality is created through networks of rhetorical acts. By inquiring into these relations, Law and Urry argue that we are better equipped to ask an ontological question of enactment: "Is it possible to imagine developing particular methods that strengthen particular realities while eroding others?" (397). For some actor-network theorists, the answer is yes. Bill Doolin and Alan Lowe make a similar point in their argument that network inquiry not only reveals how things are, but also how things could be (or have been) otherwise (75). The political potential of network inquiry lies in its ability to imagine new relations, thus creating a new network of meanings.

Network tracing is quite similar to what I have been calling rhetorical inquiry. These activities are fundamentally interested in what Annemarie Mol and John Law call "co-constitutions" and what Doolin and Lowe call the "underlying relationships that pervade contemporary society" (76). Just as Law and Urry suggest that such inquiry is concerned with ontology—or a remaking of reality—discourses of inquiry can perform such remaking of meaning through an investigation of co-constitutions. Moreover, the telos of network tracing and rhetorical inquiry is located within the process itself. Inquiry is the rhetorical goal.

The Difference of Inquiry

What does it mean to adopt inquiry as one's rhetorical goal? How does this practice differ from more recognizable responses to crisis and exigence? Let me explore inquiry in terms that may be closer to home, depending on where your theoretical home happens to be. In the work of inquiry (or even in network tracing), we might see something like the *flaneur* ethic that Walter Benjamin so passionately adopts in his *Arcades Project*. More than almost any other theorist, Benjamin gives us a logic for reading and researching the streets in their seeming banal details and encounters they afford. Benjamin's fragmentary method offers one research method that acknowledges scenes as only a frozen moment within a larger process:

> Streets are the dwelling place of the collective. The collective is an eternally unquiet, eternally agitated being that—in the space between the building fronts—experiences, learns, understands, and invents as much as individuals do within the privacy of their own four walls. For this collective, glossy enameled shop signs are a wall decoration as good as, if not better than, an oil painting in the drawing room of a bourgeois; walls with their "Post No Bills" are its writing desk, newspaper stands its libraries, mailboxes its bronze busts, benches its bedroom furniture. . . . The street reveals itself . . . as the furnished and familiar interior of the masses. (423)

Researching the streets, according to Benjamin, is a form of analysis concerned with the constellations of networks that make up our social field. In Benjamin's case, these were the networks embedded within and across the Paris arcades. The arcades were more than a fixed space; they were linked to large historical epochs and the movements of capitalism. Benjamin leads us toward a method that embraces what he dubs "the collective" as our field of operation. The street serves as our space of engagement, and while we cannot arrest its development, we can make use of the flashes. Benjamin thus illuminates an original logic of generative research that is focused on inquiry.

Benjamin's telos is collection for its own sake. "I needn't say anything," he writes. "Merely show. I shall purloin no valuables, appropriate no ingenious formulations. But the rags, the refuse—these I will not inventory but allow, in the only way possible, to come into their own: by making use of them" (460). For some, this method may resemble a starting point of argument more than a rhetorical response in its own right. Yet, this is precisely what Benjamin is proposing. Instead of appropriating ingenious formulations, Benjamin aims to "merely show." In the face of crisis, in other words, we may imagine other possibilities of critical response.

Benjamin's *flaneur* is an interesting figure to pair up with actor-network researchers. One aims to "merely show" the refuse, and the other aims to trace networked relations. Although they seem to be worlds apart, both methods manage to show how inquiry can serve as a guiding principle for people facing a crisis. More importantly, neither act depends upon a relation to the site of feeling: towardness, awayness, memory, decidability. Indeed, there is no site of feeling. There is only a moment, an event, that sparks the inquirer's tracings and collections. What is created is like an archive or a collection. The archive is what the actor-network tracers and the *flaneur* have in common. And the archive that they share is special in that it has no end in sight.

Most importantly, both Benjamin and actor-network theorists offer some perspective on how to imagine oneself in a different kind of public relation to others and to the world. Where a question, exigence, or crisis exists, the inquirer's approach to this scene is not yoked with his or her own feelings. Instead, the inquirer invests in this scene as a moment for inquiry. The moment of crisis becomes a moment for practicing one's ability to trace, collect, uncover, and follow. Crisis is an archivist's moment. This relation takes no account of how I am related personally to the scene of crisis. It does not depend on my feeling of towardness or awayness for my response. Only insofar as I use the moment for inquiry do I step into this alternative kind of publicness. In short, this alternative public subjectivity defines my role as a public subject through the activity of inquiry.

Let me stop here and give a small example of how these different kinds of subjectivities played out inside my own classroom when I taught an intermediate writing course at the University of Missouri called "Writing Mizzou." In this class, students were assigned the task of writing argumentative documentaries about a place or event in the campus community. Our research was conducted primarily in the university archives, where we worked closely with the archivists. Together with the head archivist, I asked students to focus on the history and life of the Legion of Black Collegians (LBC), the oldest and largest black student group at the University of Missouri. The archives contained an abundance of information on the Black Collegians, including organizational materials dating back to the 1960s and 1970s. No histories had been written on the organization, and the archivist was excited to share the materials stored in the files. Not only were past LBC publications preserved, but the university archives also preserved racist flyers and letters that appeared on campus throughout the 1970s and 1980s. These were the materials to which the LBC often responded in their own publications, but the flyers themselves were important to help us understand a wider context of race on Missouri's campus.

When I announced the focus of the class on the first day, I immediately began receiving e-mails from students who wanted to know whether I would be willing to consider other topics. Students assured me that they were interested and passionate about other subjects that could also be studied in the archives: campus architecture, other student organizations, or even important historical figures who contributed to campus life. During the next class, I once again announced that this focus would be our group's only task. Nobody would be switching topics for any reason. Some students appeared excited about the prospect of digging deep into the archives about a topic they didn't know much about. Others, meanwhile, were visibly disappointed.

Toward the end of the semester, when our research was nearing its completion, several students approached me about their difficulty in writing their documentary. More than one student admitted that their block was coming from a lack of personal investment. As white students, they felt disconnected from the historical details contained in the archives. They knew very little about what the LBC stood for or what issues they addressed. The students agreed that the racism found in these archives was horrible. But what else was there to say? How could someone with no memory of campus racial tensions, or no feeling of personal injury, really have an opinion or a perspective?

In response to these anxieties, I repeatedly launched into a narrative about how everything contains an argument. I encouraged students to find the argument buried somewhere in all of their research. What kinds of conclusions could they discover? What could they help their readers discover? I spent hours in my office with students and their drafts. Together we would look for the interesting argument that could be made. In each case, I experienced the "aha" moment that writing teachers strive for. Students mostly left the conferences feeling like they could actually reach an argumentative conclusion after all.

But when I received the fifteen documentaries at the end of the semester, I quickly realized that something was deeply wrong. The papers themselves were well-written, creative, and visually masterful. They were also well documented and researched. The class consisted of a strong group of writers, and their writing deserved the high grades that they earned. However, the conclusions themselves were troubling in the ways they reflected my pedagogy. They suggested something was wrong with how I encouraged students to approach the archives.

The papers could roughly be divided into three kinds of conclusions. Almost all of the papers used the archival materials as a way to shed light on the state of racism on Missouri's campus today. Some of the documentaries concluded that the archival materials showed vast improvements in terms of race. Several concluded that racism was no longer a problem on campus. The proof was there in the documents themselves: old flyers with rebel flags, scrawled with angry words telling "white people" that they should "wake up." Nothing like that appears on campus today, concluded several documentaries. Therefore, we live in a postracial era where racism is a dead issue. Other documentaries tempered this claim just a bit. It is true that racism is getting better, but some people still experience ugly incidents of racial discrimination. Though racism is different today than in the 1970s, it has not been completely obliterated.

Finally, the third set of documentaries ran in the other direction. Some of the more interesting arguments used the writers' own lack of knowledge about the LBC as evidence that racism was still alive and well on campus. These papers were tied to an ugly incident that happened on campus at the same time that we were working in the archives. Sometime in the early morning hours of February 28, the final day of Black History Month, someone threw several bags of cotton balls directly in front of the Gaines/Oldham Black Culture Center on campus. The cotton balls were lined up to look like rows of cotton, a symbolic gesture that was not wasted on the campus community. Two students were arrested for the incident, which they later described as a late night prank. The entire campus community responded, as did the local community.

Students in my class especially reacted to the openly racist reader comments in the Columbia city newspapers. Readers claimed that the story was being blown out of proportion by the liberal media and by a campus staffed by liberals. The many online comments in the newspaper's web versions were especially offensive. One commenter remarked, "Not making excuses for the two idiots but we have a president of the country who went to an anti-white church for 20 years. How about some perspective?" (Equaloff). Another commenter responded in shockingly offensive language to an African-American writer who was protesting the crime:

> Number one, yes there is racism against blacks, whites, Jews, Muslims, Mexicans, Kahki [sic] colored people. deal with it. It is life. That is the

point of freedom, people can think whatever they want, you will never change that. You only make it worse by letting it get to you! So your ancestors were enslaved by people that didn't care.... The white people brought you from a horrible place where you all killed each other and lived in dung huts.... but your people over came the hardships became better people and are now a free race in a free country. You should be proud of that. (FreeSociety)

Other letters were subtler in their language, yet the racism across the newspaper letters and message boards was shocking to read. Students read these letters and the callous responses to the cotton ball incident as evidence that racism is no less real today than it was in the 1970s, when the LBC launched vigorous antiracist campaigns on campus.

This conclusion certainly seems to be warranted, and I was amazed at the skill these students used in tying together archival material with events that were literally taken from the newspaper's front page. However, I was also disappointed with the way that these arguments fell back upon culturally and institutionally authorized commonplaces about injury, memory, and feelings of decidability. They relied on the notion that proper rhetorical arguments were to be grounded in feeling itself. There is nothing wrong with the conclusion that racism is still alive on campus. I agree with my students that the cotton ball incident shows that racism is not a dead issue. However, it is a mistake to confuse this claim's accuracy with a rhetorical stance capable of making an intervention into the scene of crisis. To point out and decry racism (or any other social ill) is not the same as adopting a truly public subjectivity. Ironically enough, it may be a way to write oneself outside the scene of public rhetorical action. To simply call for an end to racism (or an end to any other public crisis) risks closing the line of intervention too soon. We leave no space to consider the multiple networks across which this crisis is embedded, and through which we may rework the relations of power.

My disappointment with the documentaries was not due to poorly made arguments on the part of students. The arguments, claims, and reasoning were quite strong. However, I could not help but see each conclusion as untimely closure sponsored by the true subject of feeling. Some projects concluded that racism on campus was a nonissue because the writers did not feel the pull of racism, nor did they remember encountering (or hearing about) racist incidents. Other projects made a passionate argument in the exact opposite direction. Not only is racism alive and well on campus, but we must do something about it. Proposals ranged from requiring multicultural classes of all university students to increasing recruitment among African-American high school students. Still other projects concluded that there is indeed racism on campus, but it is not as bad as it once was. In all of these instances, the arguments inadvertently closed down other ways of relating to the subject of race on campus and across local, regional, and national spaces.

After I reflected on these papers, I realized my goal could have been different that semester. We could have started working from the position of inquiry where the crisis of campus racism is concerned. Together, we could have pursued the telos of collecting, tracing, and creating our own kind of critical archive. I could have used the initial moment of awayness expressed by the students (a moment that I expected to come even before the first class meeting) as an opportunity to foreground a different kind of orientation to the public sphere. Instead of writing themselves in relation to this topic from a personal feeling, students might have been pushed to see themselves in the role of inquirer in relation to this topic. Rather than trying to show them how and why they should feel the closeness of relation, I might have vigorously challenged the notion that we must care about the subject in order to become public subjects. I could have challenged them to stop caring about care.

If we had acted as collectors or archivists, on the other hand, we might have traced the campus and town threads that cut across both the history of the LBC and the recent cotton ball incident. This nexus proved to be an important element in both situations. Racism on campus is not contained to the physical space on campus, nor can it be understood as an effect of campus activities. How racism circulates on campus, how it is received and how one responds to it is necessarily tied up with local and regional details. The fact that Columbia, Missouri, is a predominantly white area surrounded by rural communities impacts how minority students encounter the campus as a whole. Moreover, the relatively working-class community of Columbia has a complicated relationship to the campus and the faculty who seem to be different from local residents. Faculty can seem more liberal, elitist, and even foreign. Critiques of the local and regional environment, including any element of racism circulating in this place, are likely to be read across multiple contexts. Both the cotton ball incident and the much longer history of campus racism are embedded across complex campus-town and campus-region networks.

In the practice of inquiry, we might also have traced the threads of preservation and its effects. Though our work was conducted exclusively in the university archives, we did not discuss how this material space and its artifacts also help to embed the local and institutional memory of racism. By giving racist flyers and posters a proper index within an official space like the university archives, the university helped to frame these campus incidents in particular ways. They could now be read as part of a history, albeit a painful one. In class, we flipped through the yellowing pages of racist literature and the counterliterature that fought back. It did indeed make the incidents on campus seem very real to students, yet it was preserved as a finished archive. The cotton ball incident, however, is unlikely to be archived in quite the same way. Many of the racist comments in local newspapers (including the campus newspaper) were exchanged online. Evidence of the many community and campus forums that were held to discuss the incident is also unlikely to appear in archival form. How such memories are "stored" and "indexed" is apt to become more complicated in the digital age, which has interesting consequences for how we publicly remember and think about racism.

Of course, there are any number of other ways we could have traced the various threads of race and place. This is not to say that a better answer to the problem of racism would have been made possible through this process. If anything, we would have found answers out of range in our inquiry because the process of collecting and tracing would likely have exploded race and place across multiple and asymmetrical networks. This might be frustrating to teachers who want their students to propose solutions to crises (whether racism, environmental change, or any other major problem) within the span of one project. However, this process may also have helped expose students to a different mode of encountering public crises. Rather than closing down investigations, the work of rhetorical inquiry actually encourages a sustained and ongoing investigation through the work of tracing, collecting, archiving, and reading the networks.

Models of Public Inquiry

I thought about this class for a long while. I decided to try again by creating a course that would approach the issue of place and crisis through a practice of network inquiry. But I was not sure exactly what this would mean. What would a class look like if we took inquiry as our primary telos? What kinds of writing would we do? What would be our goal? Would this class truly help develop ethical subjects who are capable of making rhetorical interventions, or would it continue to cultivate exceptional public subjects? To help answer these questions for myself, I began to look for examples of public inquiry in action.

Writing Austin's Lives

One of the first models of public inquiry I turned to was a citywide documentary project in Austin. In 2003, Sylvia Gale and Evan Carton, co-directors of the Humanities Institute at the University of Texas, decided to take seriously their goal of creating a "public humanities" program across the Austin community. They embarked on a major project that would potentially reach every single person living in Austin. Gale and Carton called their plan a community writing project, and it invited all Austinites to write about their experiences in the city. Stories would come from young residents and older residents, from longtime Austin citizens and newcomers who were only in the city temporarily. The project, called *Writing Austin's Lives*, was a citywide documentary endeavor, and it was certainly a massive undertaking.

Calls for submissions were plastered across the city. Gale and Carton wanted to be sure that every resident was aware that they were being asked to write. They recall the intensity of the search in its initial stage: "We actively campaigned to sound that call in and far beyond the city's writing circles. We placed ads in newspapers and ran radio public service announcements, made contact with schools, libraries, bookstores, community and religious centers, social service agencies and senior centers, and we hired a high-school student whose sole job was distributing flyers anywhere it seemed like people would be gathering in the Texas heat" (41). Writing was sure to be intimidating to many potential contributors, so the Humanities Institute helped to sponsor a large number of writing workshops across the city. The workshops were held in public libraries, schools, local bookstores, churches, and community centers. Flyers across Austin announced that the workshops were free and open to everyone. No writing experience required, the flyers announced. Furthermore, the calls assured writers that they could write in any style they wanted; no formula or goal existed beyond describing a fragment about the city ("Austin, Meet Austin").

Writing Austin's Lives is different from many other communitywide documentaries. The object of documentation was not necessarily city history (some of the stories do tell historical events, yet there is no guarantee of their reliability or correctness), nor was the object strictly about personal memories of lost places or feelings about the city. Instead, the object was simply to encourage Austin citizens to relay "finds" across the city. Six topoi were used to jump-start investigation:

1. My family's history in Austin
2. Where I live
3. The best day of my life
4. What I really need
5. My family's most treasured possession
6. What I see when I look at Austin

These topoi were inventional categories used to start inquiry. The writing itself might be histories or memories, but it might also be a description of a writer's current neighborhood. The writing might also be simply a brief description of a place, an experience within the city, or even the sounds of a neighborhood street. The fragment might even be a list of questions posed without answers.

Over the span of six months, the *Writing Austin's Lives* project received 947 personal stories written in both English and Spanish. Gale and Carton recall that the stories arrived "in crayon, on thin, yellowed sheets of typing paper, in stacks from teachers and writing groups, in envelopes covered with fancy, old stamps and in envelopes stuffed with photographs" (xi). The institute chose 127 of the stories to be published in a large collection that was sold nearly everywhere across the city. A local news station ran several writers' stories as features on the nightly news.

The documentary is a remarkable work of collective inquiry. There are no real themes that hold the individual pieces together. The documentary as a whole does not make an argument about the good or bad changes across the city. Neither does it offer any final vision of what a future Austin might (or should) become. Instead, what holds them together is a shared process of exploration. For instance, Antelmo Vasquez's entry, written in Spanish and translated into English, tells about his neighborhood and the people living there: "My neighbors here are Hispanic; some have been living in Austin for more than three years. . . . Some feel like they are tourists, buying their cowboy hats and great big cars to identify themselves. The young guys wear brown-colored shirts with the logo of a bull. It is said that there is a bull that is everyone's director and even represents all the sports teams. People even get their pictures taken with him" (210). Rosalinda Stevenson's story describes her old segregated neighborhood on the East Side: "Rosewood Park was right behind our house. I went to that park every day. That was my park. I spent most of my free time there. . . . Later on Urban Renewal would buy Aunt Bee's house and put some low-income apartments there, and we would move farther east" (269). Jennifer Reyes, a tenth grader living in Austin, writes about her experience of being a "troubled" teen in the city: "What I really need is a miracle. . . . Right now I am in Juvenile. This has been happening to me since I was 13 years old" (158). Each of these entries documents a fragment from the ongoing networks of Austin. The stories are placed side-by-side without additional narrative framework, which helps to performatively expose a complexity within the city. No definitive answers or arguments are possible, because these voices do not meld together in a coherent way. Yet, at the same time, these fragments cohere together in the work of mutual exploration.

Gale and Carton are careful not to take credit for the project's wild success. They write, "The success of *Writing Austin's Lives*, we submit, lies in the fact that it asked participants to share in the incarnation of culture, not only its consumption" ("Toward" 41). This insight opens up questions about what kind of work inquiry actually accomplishes. Carton and Gale argue that the citywide documentary project was more than a collective memoir. They suggest that *Writing Austin's Lives* was also constitutive, rhetorically speaking. Participants shared in what Gale and Carton termed the "incarnation of culture," which means that the telos of inquiry was both creative and rhetorically constructive.

Inquiry across networks has long been used as a form of constitutive rhetoric. Even Isocrates sketches a version of how rhetorical inquiry can lend itself to the "incarnation of culture." For Isocrates, facing moments of crisis always involves surveying *doxa,* or our public memories, beliefs, desires, and vernacular talk. More than mere opinion, doxa is not unlike the multiple networks we have been discussing so far. In *Antidosis,* Isocrates tells us that we cannot ever hope to uncover the Truth in any given crisis, yet we can use our "powers of conjecture to arrive generally at the right course" (271). According to Takis Poulakos, this formulation goes beyond the use of public opinion in order to persuade people about the correct course of action. Poulakos shows that Isocrates posits doxa as one way of cultivating new relations among citizens. Poulakos argues that Isocrates' primary use of doxa lies not in its connection to persuasion, therefore, but rather in its ability to constitute the identities of public agents: "Less interested in rhetoric as an instrument of symbolic influence with the sole end of winning over auditors in particular situations, Isocrates explored rhetoric's . . . power to create a world of its own making and situate audiences as potential inhabitants of that world" (65). Maybe *Writing Austin's Lives* isn't exactly what Isocrates had in mind. But the citywide documentary project certainly shows one way in which tracing the threads of doxa can invite citizens to imagine themselves in a different relation to the world.

As geographer Dolores Hayden notes, inquiry constitutes something valuable beyond an initial step toward a final argumentative conclusion. "The process that transforms places demands analysis. . . . As a field of wildflowers becomes a shopping mall at the edge of a freeway, that paved-over meadow, restructured as freeway lanes, parking lots, and mall, must still be considered a place, if only to register the importance of loss" (*Power* 18). In short, archiving, tracing, collecting, and surveying can do important work by placing the inquiring subject in a new relation to the world. These acts are also the beginning points for reimagining a new reality for these spaces. *Writing*

Austin's Lives does this very kind of analysis. By tracing the threads of place through circulating doxa, Gale and Carton "appropriated no ingenious formulations," as Benjamin says, but attempted to "merely show." Yet, in this act of merely showing the threads, they simultaneously invited readers to inhabit a different kind of world. The world that is constitutively written in their project is a multiple, complex, and untotalizable one. These collected pieces of mutual inquiry also help to un-write a version of this space as fixed in its meanings, histories, and futures.

The Neighborhood Story Project

Another model of public inquiry in action is found in the Neighborhood Story Project, an ongoing community-writing project centered in New Orleans's public housing projects. The Neighborhood Story Project began in 2004 as part of a writing program for high school students in the Lower Ninth Ward. Two teachers, Abram Himelstein and Rachel Breunlin, saw the desperate need to help young people confront the crises of their home places. Himelstein and Breunlin began working with Lower Ninth Ward youth in order to create documentaries that investigated New Orleans across its multiple, complex networks. When Hurricane Katrina took its toll in these neighborhoods, the Neighborhood Story Project became even more devoted to helping student writers address the crisis as rhetoricians who were capable of intervening. The documentaries were eventually published as a series of visually stunning books that takes on many different subjects about life in New Orleans's public housing projects.

The Neighborhood Story Project responds to place and its crises, but the documentaries themselves do not seem to arrive at any definite answers. At some level, the young authors are practicing what I would call an ethic of inquiry over an ethic of argument. When I asked Breunlin if she would agree with my characterization, she answered that the goal is to get the writers to consider New Orleans as a space of complexity, rather than a space of simplicity whose meanings are obvious, fixed, and unchangeable. Consequently, the documentaries are not merely personal memoirs, although there is much personal writing to be found in the texts. But the personal is only one part of a more intricate network. "We encourage them to connect their personal experiences to the larger historical and cultural forces at play in the city," she explains. "Such inquiry is necessary because while people are proud of their place, they aren't necessarily critically examining what's going on there. There isn't a lot of conversation between young and old people about how the city has changed, or why we live where we do. So the books provide a good opportunity to go on these journeys to learn the histories, to investigate how race, class, gender, and sexuality are spacialized, how performance traditions weave through the main and backstreets" (Breunlin).

The books are what Breunlin calls "a journey" rather than any specific arrival. The process of investigation serves as a mean of habituating young writers into a new kind of relationship with the world around them. Instead of seeing their home places as already fixed with meanings—regardless of whether those meanings are positive or negative—the work of inquiry helps students to understand these places as embedded in multiple meanings and relations. Breunlin remarks, "What I think the books do is give them the confidence to have a complex narrative—not to be pigeonholed, to be able to speak multiple truths."

In practice, the young writers venture out into their own neighborhoods, serving as local documentarians for streets that have largely gone unnoticed and undocumented. They begin their work by literally collecting and archiving oral histories, images, descriptions, community memories, and stories. Their method almost perfectly mirrors Benjamin's method in the *Arcades Project,* which theorizes the streets as "the dwelling place of the collective," which is "an eternally unquiet, eternally agitated being." Himelstein admits that he was initially worried that this collection method would yield books that look too much like a yearbook, with young writers simply pasting random pictures and captions. However, he quickly saw their value as pieces of vernacular anthropology. They are investigative pieces that dig into the spaces of young writers' neighborhoods (Himelstein).

Around 2007, the Neighborhood Story Project teamed up with another organization, the Porch, in order to create a new project called "7th Ward Speaks." This project uses the same inquiry practices of asking residents to interview other residents about life in the Seventh Ward. The interviews and collected fragments are turned into posters that reprint parts of the interviews, and the posters are then placed around the city. People in the neighborhood begin by participating in an interview. They are then asked if they would like to conduct their own interviews of other residents. The process can potentially ripple across the Seventh Ward, reaching all residents who are willing to speak (*Neighborhood Story Project*). A poster from the 7th Ward Speaks project, much like the books published by the Neighborhood Story Project, do not necessarily end with argument; they are fragments that seem to be working collectively toward a mutual exploration.

This different kind of approach to place is not without its challenge, of course. I regularly assign one of the first books from the Neighborhood Story Project, *The Combination,* in my writing classes. This book, written by high school senior Ashley Nelson, is a *flaneur*'s walk through the Lafitte housing project. Nelson "appropriate(s) no ingenious formulations," but instead merely shows the neighborhood across its multiple networks and threads. Nelson's book is divided into five headings: family, businesses, violence, representing and celebrating Lafitte, friends and neighbors. Each section features fragments of interviews, images from the neighborhood, personal memories, and thick descriptions of particular sites. In the section on violence, for example, Nelson includes an interview with Poppee, a true O.G. (original gangsta), images of graffiti and memorials to dead friends, a copy of a prayer, and a list called "What gets you put in jail in da hood." When I assign this book in my classes, students often express confusion about what Nelson's point happens to be. Is she saying that the neighborhood is good? Bad? Is she saying that we should be fairer to inner-city neighborhoods, since we are relative outsiders? Is she indicting us for misjudging places like her neighborhood? We gradually push past these questions to see something else that Nelson is doing: She is creating an archive; she is surveying the doxa. She shows us the many different threads that comprise a single space like the Lower Ninth Ward. In the course of this "mere showing," Nelson also invites readers to inhabit a different kind of relationship to the world—not one that we can claim to know better (or to not know at all), but one whose networks reach across us in many different ways.

Another book produced by the Neighborhood Story Project, *Signed, the President,* shows another way in which inquiry can lead to a more complex understanding of place and the networks that embody or are embedded in it. Young author Kenneth Phillips explores life in the housing projects of New Orleans's Seventh Ward and organizes his investigation around interviews with six members of his family. After each interview, he follows up on particular threads that were uncovered in the course of his family's responses. In Phillips's interview with Grandma Irma, for example, he asks about her decision to have children. Irma discusses what it was like to raise her children after a divorce, and what it was like to raise one particularly hardheaded child named Irvin. Following his interview, Phillips picks up on the thread of his Uncle Irvin, who was a fun-loving man and a wild rebel. Uncle Irvin was shot and killed in 2001. He recounts Irvin's life as a DJ and his relationships with local rappers like Mia X. Phillips also includes images of Irvin's funeral cards and program, as well as a beautiful description of his own dreams and visions where Irvin appears. These threads lead to a broader discussion of tragedy, including the Katrina disaster and his family's experience with homelessness after the flood. At the conclusion of the section, he asks Grandma Irma about her feelings when the St. Bernard housing projects were torn down. He then asks whether she is worried about her grandchildren, a question that sparks Irma's reflection on the power of proximity and prayer.

Although Phillips organizes his inquiry around personal memories and family interviews, his fragments and collections actually manifest a much broader picture of the connections among housing, violence, and especially the image of manliness. As Phillips writes in his introduction, the book looks "at how young men have been loved and nurtured in my community, but also sometimes [how they are] boxed in by ideas about what men are supposed to be" (1). His unique exploration of manliness is made possible by drifting across topics like the experience of public housing, mass displacement, fighting, classroom tensions between students and teachers, and even the experience of writing itself. In ways that are not immediately obvious, ideas about "what men are supposed to be" are locally embedded within these sites in New Orleans's Seventh Ward. *Signed, the President* is like a multidimensional map that exposes the reader to these connections.

Experiments in Inquiry: "The Rhetoric of the Midwest"

Projects like *Writing Austin's Lives* and the Neighborhood Story Project illustrate how inquiry can serve as an active (and activist) rhetoric for addressing the crises of place. The methodology is more than a way to index previously unknown facts or information. It is also more than a preliminary step on the way to some more important epistemic perspective (Who is correct? What shall we call it? Is this good or bad?). Instead, the method of rhetorical inquiry creates what Law and Urry calls a "performative ontology," or a performative revelation of the many relations and threads across which a process is embedded. It asks questions about the parts of this space, crisis, site, or network (How is it composed? What are the working relations? What happens if the relations are changed?). The goal of such performative work is to constitute new kinds of subjects who imagine themselves differently as public beings. As Law and Urry state, conducting a performative ontology means "that the world—and the objects, the institutions, and the people that make it up—is no longer a single thing. Instead of a 'universe' we are instead caught up in, and help to produce, a 'pluriverse'" (399). We create a rhetoric that invites audiences to imagine themselves as inhabiting multiple networks (or a pluriverse) that stretch our agency across spatial and temporal scenes.

Shortly after my experience with the archives class, I began to think about how I could create a new class that would take inquiry as a primary telos. I borrowed from models like *Writing Austin's Lives* and the Neighborhood Story Project, and I also reflected on the goals of such a course. My hope was that this class would help students to think of themselves as different kinds of public subjects. Rather than being exceptional public subjects, or subjects who maintain a relation to the public without intervening in the scene of crisis, I wanted to push students into new kinds of roles. This role would not ground subjectivity in feeling, but rather in the process of inquiry. In other words, the measure of public subjectivity would be enacted through the process of tracing, archiving, collecting, and investigating. Whatever the class would ultimately look like, I knew from the beginning that it would not look like a traditional writing classroom.

I also continued to think about the challenge to teach toward sustainable futures. For me, this meant that I would need to focus the class around specific places and crises. We would directly address contemporary challenges to our biocultures, including the places where we actually live and work. For this reason, I decided to make the Midwest our primary focus. Without knowing who my students would be, I had no way of knowing what places and spaces they inhabited. But I did know that we were all located (temporarily) in this single space: Columbia, Missouri. Some of the students were likely born and raised in Missouri, while others would be relative newcomers to the region. Some of us would consider this region to be our home, and others of us could only see it as a rest stop. Regardless of personal relation or feeling, however, the Midwest was a single place of convergence for us. I named my class "The Rhetoric of the Midwest," and I listed it online with a detailed description about what we would be doing that semester. Then I waited.

On the first day of class, I stood up to announce that this class would not do what a class typically does. Usually you come into class with a cloudy, distant idea of what the course's subject matter is. At the end of the semester, you expect to leave with a much clearer idea of the subject. You have mastered the content in some degree of expertise. In this class, however, we are beginning from a point of expertise. We all live in the Midwest, and many of us have grown up in this area. And even if some students did not know the Midwest from personal experience, they were surely familiar with the cultural tropes and topoi concerning the American Midwest: flat, bland, heartland, conservative, and so forth. Our goal would not be to master an unfamiliar subject. The goal of this class would not be to teach students content that they were unfamiliar with. It was the inverse: to unlearn what we presumed to know already about the subject. "By the time you leave the class," I told the students, "I hope you no longer know what the Midwest is." Students looked nervous and a little confused.

Throughout the semester, we read essays written by midwesterners, essays written about the Midwest, and even some texts written for midwesterners. In their own way, all of the texts we read treated the Midwest as a space of change. Many writers were pessimistic about the changing region: it was becoming too politically conservative, too monocultural, too dependent upon personal automobiles, too Christian, too boring, too fat. The texts that immediately garnered the most attention were those that criticized and ridiculed the region. Students leapt on one side or the other of these critiques quite swiftly. One of the most divisive essays was David Foster Wallace's essay "Ticket to the Fair," which recounted Wallace's trip to the Illinois State Fair. Foster describes the midwesterners attending the fair as obese, slow-witted, and physiologically sick. They seem to live in a different culture from the more cosmopolitan regions on the West or East coasts. According to Foster, they do not seem to distinguish authenticity from the plastic replicas around them. The grass is fake, the food is fake, and even the so-called authentic midwestern exhibits are fake. Students spent an hour in heated debate with one another about whether or not Foster was dead right or dead wrong. Students tended to respond to the texts from their own feelings. They talked about how they could relate to the authors, as well as how the authors' arguments felt distant or unfamiliar.

Similarly, Richard Rhodes's essay "Cupcake Land: Requiem for the Midwest in the Key of Vanilla" laments the slow dissolve of Kansas City from a thriving space into a suburban nightmare. For some students, Rhodes articulated the very feelings that they had harbored for years. Other students felt disconnected from Rhodes and his memories of 1970s Kansas City. As one student remarked during class, "I can't really comment on the article one way or the other. I'm from St. Louis." Ironically, these kinds of feeling-full responses gave us an opportunity to talk about how to talk. For several weeks, we had been discussing these texts from the vantage of personal relation (not to mention the lack of relation). I challenged them to think about alternative ways of talking about these texts and their ideas. What other kinds of responses could we create?

In order to show a different way of talking, I introduced students to our class wiki during the second week of class. The wiki is an online space that can be collaboratively edited and written. Wiki users can create new pages through multiple links that are not hierarchically ordered like a blog or other Web page. Any user can create a brand-new page from a word or phrase on another user's page. I told students that this wiki would be like a living archive for us. Using Benjamin's *Arcades Project* as a model, I told students that their task was to collect and archive the various topoi, tropes, observations, quotes, images, and specific lines that jumped out from the reading. At this point, our aim was to "merely show," I told the students. I instructed them that when they encountered something that should be entered into the archive, they should create a new space for it. Likewise, if they saw connections among the fragments, they might link them together without any additional comment. They were becoming investigators in this rhetorical scene.

The challenge of becoming an investigator proved to be a bit tricky. Repeatedly, the matter of opinion emerged as a sore subject. Students admitted that they felt like they were not actively thinking since they were not regularly framing their writing with feeling. One student asked when they were going to be able to "be themselves" in these responses. As uncomfortable as these objections were, they exposed a deep connection between feeling and publicness. Students felt that I had limited their ability to be a public subject by erasing personal feeling (the sensation of relation, memory, opinion) from the act of response. Yet, this exposure also gave me an opportunity to discuss new ways of reading and responding. Rather than seeing ourselves as subjects who could only respond from feeling, could we not also be subjects who discover and uncover connections, linkages, and relations within and across these texts? Is it possible to respond by tracing the threads? And, more importantly, what will happen if we do it? I acknowledged the students' nervousness while also asking for their willingness to participate in an experiment. "It's a thinking experiment," I said. "All I ask is that you suspend your disbelief for twelve more weeks." With some hesitation, they seemed to oblige.

Shortly after introducing the wiki archive, we dove into one of our main texts of the semester, William Least Heat-Moon's *PrairyErth: A Deep Map*, which served as one of the most challenging and useful guides for thinking and writing about place through the method of inquiry. In *PrairyErth*, Heat-Moon seeks to create what he calls a "deep map" of Chase County, Kansas. The space he has chosen is relatively unremarkable. Heat-Moon did not come to a place typically seen as rich in history, culture, or complexity; just the opposite. He writes that Chase County, Kansas is a "sparse landscape, seemingly . . . thin and minimal in history and texture, a stark region recent American life had mostly gone past, a still point, a fastness an ascetic seeking a penitential corner might discover" (15). Yet, Heat-Moon's book is vastly deep. *PrairyErth* offers a history of place that surpasses what most people see in more complicated landscapes. This is because Heat-Moon is guided not by the topoi that are already familiar to him (this place's history or its well-worn descriptions that circulate freely). He instead is guided by inquiry, becoming a "digger of shards" (15).

His method for conducting a deep map, or a "vertical history," of Chase County is unusual, to say the least. Heat-Moon says that he is "in search of the land and what informs it" (10). In order to conduct such a search, he textually digs into the shards that are embedded in this space. He digs from the soil on up to the surface. Readers are led into long investigations of how the soil, rocks, and grass interact in ways that have shaped what Kansas has become over time. For example, he meditates on the particular kinds of grass that cover the county's vast plains. The native grasses in this prairie land are perfect for nourishing cattle, but their sugar content is low. This makes the grasses imperfect for activities like brewing malt, which native landscapes in other regions can support. "Were Kansas known for barley instead of beef and wheat," Heat-Moon amusingly remarks, "local notions would be different, and Carry Nation would likely not have chopped up her first saloon thirty-five miles from here" (196). Whether or not Carrie Nation's temperance movement was centered in the Midwest because of the local conditions, Least Heat-Moon is relentless in his juxtaposition of vertical shards from the landscape. He collects geological fragments, social histories of floods and displacement, linguistic and etymological details, personal portraits of current residents, the histories of workers who are rooted to the land, and even discourse about Kansas.

Students sometimes did not know what to make of Heat-Moon's six-hundred-page book. *PrairyErth* resembles Benjamin's *Arcades Project* in its fragmentary and wandering style. The book frustrated any attempt to get at the epistemic questions we wanted to ask: Is he saying that the Midwest is a good place? Is he saying that Kansas is not as flat as it may appear? The sprawling and fragmentary drift left us feeling as though we were witnessing a kind of unraveling. His method leaves no possible thread unraveled. Like a true archivist, he juxtaposes a number of materials together in a single space. These include images, letters, descriptions, interviews, facts, and quotes. Heat-Moon pulls apart threads in what seems like a unified (and plainly obvious) field. His search to discover what informs the land slowly uncovers a multitude of pieces. The result is a portrait of Chase County, Kansas, that reveals how place is constituted across networks.

Students were especially taken with the extensive collection of quotes at the beginning of each section. Their collection mimics Benjamin's quotes and sayings in his *Arcades Project*. The quotes in *PrairyErth* appear without further commentary, always under the ambiguous heading, "From the Commonplace Book." Some quotes are drawn from historical guidebooks to Kansas, some from more recent texts about place and the land, some from works by Victor Hugo and Walt Whitman, and some from newspaper debates and reference guides. The quotes do not seem to introduce the section themes that follow, nor do they all form a coherent whole in their own right. Yet, as students quickly discovered, Heat-Moon collected these quotes as a way to create a commonplace book between him and his readers. One particular quote by Peter Steinhart became a class favorite: "Maps are a way of organizing wonder" (Heat-Moon 4). The work of inquiry, or of digging deeply into the shards, resulted in a mutual wonderment that was as useful as it was informative.

Heat-Moon's work became a methodological guide for beginning our own inquiry into place. We also drew upon N. Scott Momaday's *Way to Rainy Mountain*, which also pursues a rhetorical investigation into place. Momaday writes about the Kiowa people, yet he does not offer a linear history or straightforward narrative of his journey back to the Kiowa origins. Instead, his book stylistically juxtaposes fragments from Kiowa mythology, actual Kiowa history, and personal memories of revisiting his family's own story. These three strands are not hierarchical. Momaday archives the places of Kiowa people (from Montana to Oklahoma) alongside his own memories of family. One fragment does not inform another, yet the collected fragments and shards perform a kind of unraveling similar to what we see in *PrairyErth*. Momaday describes this approach to inquiry as an ethical imperative for all of us, insofar as we must consider the land. He writes, "Once in his life a man ought to concentrate his mind upon the remembered earth, I believe. He ought to give himself up to a particular landscape in his experience, to look at it from as many angles as he can, to wonder about it, to dwell upon it" (83). We returned to this quote many times throughout the semester, adopting it as our own particular challenge for inquiry. Such experience did indeed seem to call for us to give ourselves up to the landscape. Looking at the land from as many angles as possible demands a different way of performing responses and performing writing.

Toward the end of the semester, students began to better understand this method of rhetorical inquiry as an alternative way of talking about (and responding to talk about) place. Our goal was to see the multiple networks in which the Midwest is lodged. We became peculiar kinds of archivists, ones who testified to the constellations that moved together and apart from one another as part of this process. Students also needed to learn how to inhabit a different kind of subjectivity. Rather than validating their own sense of publicness through the experience and expression of feeling—in terms of felt agreement, relation, care, memory, or investment—they were being asked to become subjects who engaged the public world through questions, investigation, and wonder.

The course's final project called for students to create a deep map, the kind that Heat-Moon illustrates in *PrairyErth*. My directions for the deep map assignment were as follows:

> For this project, you will follow William Least Heat-Moon's method of making a "deep map" by also writing a topographic map of words. Heat-Moon shows us a way of mapping that can potentially re-orient our vision of the landscape. Like the deep map we read in *PrairyErth,* you will also perform a vertical history. Your deep map will need to choose one particular place (nothing larger than a county or city) that has definite boundaries.
>
> Start by digging into the native soils, rocks, grass, trees, weather habits, animals, and so forth. You should try to give us a geological-rhetorical "slice" of this space, not a total and perfect representation of the history. Your deep map will cut across the social, historical, personal, political, and geological forces that inform this place. Remember Momaday's call to look at the land from as many angles as you can. This is your challenge.
>
> Your final text will probably not resemble a traditional essay. Think about how texts like *PrairyErth* and *Way to Rainy Mountain* use layout, font changes, images, and headings in order to perform their investigation for readers. You should think of this project like a textual archive. There are a number of ways to perform it for readers, but you must consider the various effects that such layouts will have for your own audience. Word minimum is 1,500 and word maximum is 2,500 words. You should include any images, maps, documents, or illustrations that may be relevant. You will be graded based on how well you create a thorough archive, using all the available resources you can find.
>
> Remember: this is an experiment and a challenge. Your deep map is an opportunity to practice giving yourself up to a particular landscape through the work of rhetorical inquiry. Leave no thread unpulled.

The projects that resulted from this assignment looked much different from the papers I received in my archives course on race. These texts lacked the kinds of argumentative conclusions found in the documentaries. They did not leave readers with calls to actions or specific proposals. However, they did not turn away from rhetorical gestures. Students' deep maps invited readers to imagine these spaces differently, as more complex and multiply composed. A kind of archival spirit informed these deep maps, inviting readers to use the writing beyond what was imagined by the current text. In other words, the results of inquiry could spark further invention. The text became a facilitator of mutual exploration rather than a final word on an issue.

One student took a small Missouri state park and lake as her space. Her project began with several quotes culled about the area, including poems written about fishing in Missouri's waters. She next recalls fishing in this park's lakes with her father, though her attempts at fly-fishing were half-hearted and dispassionate. Her memory about fly-fishing flows into a meditation on the waters gushing beneath their boots. The springs churn more than ninety-six million gallons a day, and they flow from a valley. The steady flow of the spring attracted settlers in the early nineteenth century because it was such a rich source for mill work. Missouri introduced various fish into the streams at the beginning of the twentieth century, a practice that continues to be questioned globally. Stocking lakes and streams with fish is not a neutral act. It has consequences beyond this state park, since the ecosystem is altered with every new introduction of nonnative farm fish. It all has to do with microorganisms that are too miniscule to see.

Above the waters, the topography is classified as "karst." This means that there are lots of natural caves in the area. Missouri's landscape is largely karst. Groundwater dissolves layers of limestone over time to make sinkholes, caves, and natural tunnels. This state park is a perfect example of karst topography, with its series of connecting tunnels and caves. Driving out of town from Columbia, you cannot miss the tourist signs advertising cave tours near the park. Cave exploration and canoe tours have become a commodity that the state depends upon for revenue. Ideally, you would take a cave tour and then buy one of the souvenirs embossed with the name of the cave on it. Perhaps a small plastic replica of the cave or maybe a T-shirt advertising the tour company's name.

The student then considered the relationship between karst topography and Missouri's tourist trade. Daytrips to lakes and caves are a valuable source of livelihood for many small towns. Another karst region, Lake of the Ozarks, is almost entirely a tourist town, much like Branson. This means that the land is never simply in relation to the local people. It is triangulated: local people maintain the land for the benefit of others who come as tourists. The student included images of advertisements for small shops and restaurants sitting just outside the state park. The restaurants were named after the park and the springs themselves. They boasted "world famous" pies and desserts, though the claims all seemed to betray a self-aware sense of kitsch.

The student's creation could be best described as a work of rhetorical inquiry. Using a vertical history method, she collected fragments from a given space. She did not give a complete history, nor did she make any particular arguments about her discoveries. Instead, her text archived fragments from the geological landscape, historical experiences, and contemporary social and political scenes. By tracing these fragments from as many angles as possible, her text cut across local reflection into national (even global) spaces. She created less of a representation than an inquiry into the multiple networks of this space.

This inquiry is then available to readers as a point of departure. When I read her text for the first time, I immediately thought about current stories detailing how state parks in Missouri were increasingly serving as ad hoc meth labs. Local residents in rural areas were using the land in alternative ways to make a living. The meth produced in state parks like this one would travel across the Midwest, circulating mainly among working-class users. When the entire class read her final texts, students picked up on another thread exposed by her inquiry. She had discussed the natural springs and her own family's visitations to the area as a seasonal event. The seasonality of state parks and the surrounding communities lent a certain rhythm to this landscape, a rhythm that may be different from a landscape supported by steadier sources of employment and revenue. When the snow begins and the fly fishermen stop visiting the springs, concession stands and souvenir shops are no longer viable. Work itself has a rhythm. This concept took some students by surprise, sparking further thoughts about seasonality and survival. By surveying the networks within which this site is embedded, the student writer helped to generate a point of departure for her readers.

Such a project is not without its limitations, of course. Not everyone will be satisfied with the results of such an experiment. Indeed, there are times when we must make definitive arguments that leave aside inquiry. I would never abdicate my obligation to teach students how to make strong arguments in the face of rhetorical exigencies. However, I also see projects like the deep map assignment as a way to teach another skill that we have neglected for too long in rhetoric classrooms: inquiry. By emphasizing inquiry as a legitimate mode of relating to the world, we can help to cultivate citizens who avoid writing themselves out of the public scene of crisis. Inquiry challenges and contests those spaces of exception that so many public subjects inhabit. Our pedagogical practice cannot ever hope to completely overcome the rise of exceptional subjects, but it can create conditions for reflecting on its assumptions. "The Rhetoric of the Midwest" was far from a perfect course, and I learned just as much as my students did. Yet, the course is an example of how the rhetoric and writing classroom can contribute necessary and ethical changes within the public sphere.

Inquiry and Sustainability

It goes without saying that we have special roles as teachers of rhetoric. Not only can we intervene in crisis by transcending our own comfort zones, but our classrooms can also help encourage students to relate differently to the world around them. In "Rhetoric of the Midwest," I pushed students to experiment with the work of inquiry because I saw this as an opportunity to reflect on other modes of relating to place. Rather than continuing to think of themselves only as subjects who relate through feeling, I hope that the class also gave them some opportunity to think of themselves as subjects who relate through question, investigation, and inquiry.

But is the act of inquiry necessarily a rhetorical act? Thomas Farrell reminds us, "Rhetoric is the art, the fine and useful art, of making things matter" (470). Does inquiry make things matter in the way that more traditional forms of argument do? Inquiry, as a performative ontology of relations and networks, looks quite different from traditional forms of argumentation. Yet it is also embedded in judgment. The rhetor who collects, archives, traces, or inquires does not give up any claims to judgment (*krisis*). In fact, Quintilian tells us that judgment is embedded in all five canons of rhetoric. He remarks that some rhetors regard judgment as a sixth canon of rhetoric, since we appear to invent first and then judge. However, continues Quintilian, "I do not consider that he who has not judged has invented" (*Institutes* 3.3.5). The act of invention entails judgment and cannot be separated out like a multistep process. He writes, "Cicero . . . has included judgment under invention, but to me, judgment appears to be so mingled with the first three parts (for there can neither be arrangement nor expression without it), that I think even delivery greatly indebted to it" (3.3.5). Quintilian supposes that rhetors must call upon critical thought at every step in the process of public engagement, even in the inventional stage. The work of inquiry as a process—even as a process that may seem overly stylistic to some—is thus embedded within judgment.

To better understand how judgment plays a role in the work of inquiry, consider how Quintilian discusses the various kinds of questions (indefinite and definite) that rhetoricians take up (*Institutes* 3.5). Quintilian lists the various questions that fall under our consideration, as well as the kinds of discourse that follow from these questions. In this way, he theorizes an important link between the kinds of questions we ponder and the rhetoric that follows. Indefinite or general questions ("Should a man marry?") spark a much different discourse than definite questions ("Should Cato marry?"). Our questions guide us into particular rhetorical channels, and away from others. Since inquiry is the endless survey of the networks within which a crisis is embedded, it is comprised of questions and (therefore) particular vectors of rhetorical movement. The threads we choose to pursue, the shards we choose to archive, are never without consequence. They collectively change the resulting text of inquiry, which then invites further mutual exploration. Because the student in my class decided to pursue threads of karst landscapes and tourism, the class as a whole found themselves extending this inquiry into a discussion of seasonality, rhythm, and work. Her decisions led to a particular discourse, which means that her inquiry is not free of judgment itself. Therefore, when we use this process, we must also be aware that our collection will have effects (even unforeseen) in terms of how we talk about place and its problems. We are still firmly within the realm of rhetoric.

But why is this inquiry process necessarily sustainable? In chapter 1, I argued that sustainable public subjects need to think across networks. What is sustainable about rhetorical inquiry is not merely the exposure of networks, though that is an important part. Exposing and tracking the networks is work that ecocomposition is especially adept at doing. But I am advocating something more: a change to public subjectivity. By encouraging subjects who relate to the world through questions, wonder, inquiry, investigation, archive, we are disallowing subjects who write themselves out of the scene of rhetoric. We are closing down those spaces of exception. True public subjects of feeling can write themselves out of scenes for intervention, perhaps because they feel an awayness from the site of injury or memory. Or perhaps they feel a legitimate undecidability. But the public subject of inquiry is never exceptional, never outside the realm of inquiry.

This brings me back to the crisis of development. How can our public discourse ethically address the problems of development? There are many valid answers to this question, and I am not alone in asking such questions. However, from the vantage point of a rhetoric teacher, my answer returns to the site where I can make the best contribution: the classroom. Sustainable futures and more thoughtful development will depend partly on our ability to become nondistant subjects. Teachers can encourage such subjects through pedagogies that tacitly endorse ways of relating to the world. By helping students to imagine themselves as inquirers to crisis, teachers of rhetoric have already changed how they write themselves into the rhetorical scene.

Epilogue
WORKING IN THE *EPI-LOGOS*

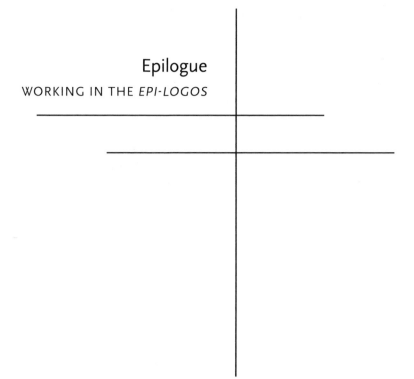

I struggled with what to call this short, concluding section. I could always call it a conclusion, but that designation may give the wrong impression that I will now tie up all the loose ends that have been unraveled in the last six chapters. Such a gesture would not only be artificial, it would be uninteresting. One of the claims driving this book is that we need to honor, cultivate, and revive a practice of inquiry. In exposing some of our common patterns of argumentation, as I have done here, I have not set myself up for *conclusions*. If anything, I have desperately sought for *inclusions:* an expanding archive of "vernacular voices" that helps us to understand the discourse we make and that makes us. I have included as many kinds of voices as I could find, yet there is always more to be said. When I asked friends what to call this section, Cara Finnegan suggested epilogue. *Epi-logos* has a strong rhetorical resonance, she remarked. I immediately agreed. This small chapter is very much an *epi-logos*, since it grows out of, or on top of (*epi*), the logoi that precede it. As I wrap up *Distant Publics*, I find myself asking what can or should emerge from the claims (the logoi) I made. If rhetoric is a process of knowing, doing, and making, then I now face the question of what can be made and done with the knowledge generated from such analyses.

Most obviously, a rhetorician can make and do discourses that cultivate stronger publics. David Zarefsky elegantly asserts that we rhetoricians have a duty to "engage in activities that respond to public issues and promote productive exchanges of ideas and participation in public discourse. These might include organizing and participating in town meetings, facilitating community-based deliberative groups such as the National Issues Forum, giving talks and writing essays on public issues, analyzing significant rhetorical texts or occasions for the benefit of public audiences" (37). In short, rhetoricians need to promote a culture of public discourse and exchanges. This is our charge.

Not a bad mission. In fact, it is one that I adopt when thinking about my goals. However, in *Distant Publics,* I have argued that we suffer not so much from a lack of public discourse as from public discourse (very much in circulation) that actually fosters distant, exceptional subjects. Promoting *more* public discourse is not necessarily our best means of making sustainable interventions. We need also to identify, analyze, question, and ultimately transform our most troubling patterns of public discourse. If we wish to change how people engage with crisis/*krisis,* it is this public subjectivity that must be transformed.

We cannot force a change in people's discourse habits, of course. That would be impossible. However, we can create alternative places for speaking and writing differently about problems. Instead of watching the ongoing cultivation of exceptional public roles, we can encourage ourselves and those around us to approach public problems through the guise of inquiry. These alternative spaces of writing and inquiry can help to promote a new way of being public, or of making and doing and knowing public *krisis* differently.

In Lexington, Kentucky, I have begun a community writing space called the Pop Up Writing Project. The pop ups bring together University of Kentucky students and community groups for a brief period of time in order to record, digitize, archive, and write. The writing space itself literally "pops up" in any space or time. A pop-up event identifies specific communities, populations, organizations, sites, or happenings ahead of time and sets up a particular location and time to hold the writing event. Posters, flyers, and local media then announce the date and location of the writing event.

Participants are invited to give their oral histories, tell stories, and bring artifacts (pictures, posters, and so forth) relating to this community or site. During the writing event, students set up media stations in order to record and interview the speakers, scan the artifacts, and collaboratively write descriptions with participants. At the conclusion of each pop-up writing project, the oral histories, stories, written descriptions, and scanned media will be housed in a unique archive on the University of Kentucky's digital humanities Web site. Each entry will be tagged and made searchable for both public reference and pedagogical purposes. The goal of this community writing project is to create a living archive of Lexington's public histories and its spaces of *krisis* (and crisis).

A community writing site would be the ideal place for projects that explore and inquire into community history, local spaces, and histories. It can also open up collaboration across university and community networks by serving as a site of exchange, a living archive opportunity that is too often absent in our public spaces. In spring 2010, for example, two students in my writing class conducted a semester-long inquiry into small urban gardening collectives in our town. Through initial research and interviews, the two students learned about a local collective called the Sick Porch that grows large amounts of food in neighborhood gardens. Although the Sick Porch has a number of members and volunteers, its activities are largely unfamiliar to Columbia residents and university students. The student writers, Christine and Andy, conducted many hours' worth of film footage in interviews with the collective's members. Through these interviews, Christine and Andy also learned about a local music group that was affiliated with the collective. Christine and Andy recorded the band playing live, and they used this music as a soundtrack to their documentary film.

The fifteen-minute documentary is an example of inquiry in action. Christine and Andy ask members how they got started in local gardening, what would lead a young person to devote so much time to organic community food issues, and what it actually means to have a collective. When we viewed the documentary on the final day of class, we asked Christine and Andy if the Sick Porch planned to use this film on their Web site. Christine laughed and said, "They don't have any Web site. Very low tech." Although the video was uploaded to YouTube, there is no central site where Columbia residents can discover texts like these. If a community writing site were available in our town, Christine and Andy could immediately post this inquiry-based text for other Columbia residents to view and explore.

The online Lexington community writing project uses all available means to create a long-term, sustainable, expandable, easily edited resource where everyone can archive their fragments, discoveries, questions. Rather than creating a space for argumentation or editorializing, I seek to create a space that adopts an ethic of mutual searching. It practices the work of a performative ontology, tracing the many threads of our community and histories in all spaces. Its spirit will be built around Thomas Farrell's notion that "Rhetoric is the art, the fine and useful art, of making things matter" (470). A space for archiving inquiry is valuable insofar as it makes all spaces, all queries, all investigations matter. Even more importantly, a space that values inquiry as a form of community discourse helps us to imagine ourselves as a different kind of public subject: one that relates to public space through mutual questioning rather than individual feeling.

The expandability of an online writing site is perfect for bridging our work in the university with a larger community beyond the campus. Online community writing sites can engage with semester-long projects, such as Christine and Andy's documentary. Yet, it can also link up with small fragments from anyone in the community. Thanks to the ease of mobile technologies, it is quite easy to upload an image, short video, or a brief update directly to social media sites. This community writing project imagines a more hopeful meaning of the phrase *distant publics*. We can imagine a horizon of publics in the (not too distant) future who write themselves into the rhetorical situation in more sustainable, ethical, and collaborative ways.

Troubling development will continue, of course. Sprawl will keep spreading, strip malls will continue to overtake green space, chain stores will endure. The same can almost certainly be said of other public ills. I am both wary and weary of conclusions that promise too much, so I am unwilling to pretend that my analysis promises to do away with crisis. What I have described in this book cannot wipe away the complex ideological, structural, and material problems that we currently face; however, as rhetoricians, we are capable of transforming the ways in which we talk to one another about crisis in public. More specifically, we can create spaces that encourage a different way of relating to our everyday rhetorical situations. The online community writing project is simply one way to activate different logoi in my local publics, but it is certainly not the only one. For that reason alone, I am comfortable ending this book with the epilogue, a small preview of *epi-logoi* to come.

NOTES

Introduction: Rhetorical Vistas

1. Although the conventions of language require that I describe a subject position as a pronoun (he, she, it), the subject is much more an act of rhetorical habitation. We are subject to positions, in other words.

2. Material on the Treaty Oak was found in the Austin History Center's Treaty Oak vertical file.

3. For examples of how rhetoric, composition, and communication scholars are using de Certeau's work on place, see Dobrin, "The Occupation of Composition"; Ackerman, "Teaching the Capital City"; Payne, "English Studies in Levittown"; and Wright, "Rhetorical Spaces in Memorial Places." See also Reynolds's excellent use of Lefebvre in *Geographies of Writing*.

4. See Syverson, *Wealth of Reality*, for an excellent study on the ecology of writing and the myth of the solitary writer.

5. Elsewhere Hauser offers a simpler definition of vernacular rhetoric as "a rhetoric of non-formal symbolic exchanges by which typical citizens, not just the marginalized, express opinions and seek agreement" ("On Reading" 217).

Chapter 1. Rhetoric's Development Crisis

1. For example, see www.deadmalls.com.

2. For a more specific definition of the built environment, see chapter 1 of McClure and Bartuska, *The Built Environment*.

3. Michiko Kakutani's *New York Times* review suggests that readers should

take Kunstler's book as "a kind of impassioned jeremiad" rather than "an objective assessment of our national landscape."

4. Humanist geography combines the study of place with a concern for how people get along in the world (see Adams et al.).

5. Jacobs and Appleyard partly blame the profession of urban planning and its tendency to make itself a rootless profession. "Too many professionals are more part of a universal professional culture than part of the local cultures for whom we produce our plans and products. We carry our 'bag of tricks' around the world and bring them out wherever we land" (115). This is not unlike our own academic problem of rootless professionalism. In fact, Jacobs and Appleyard echo Eric Zencey's argument that *our kind* in general is a *rootless* bunch: "As citizens of the *cosmo polis*, . . . professors are expected to owe no allegiance to geographical territory; we're supposed to belong to the boundless world of books and ideas, . . . not the infinitely particular world of watersheds, growing seasons, and ecological niches" (15). By and large, the nature of our scholarly work tends not to change even when our regional and local contexts change.

6. Resolution 20000518-033. May 18, 2000.

7. Thanks to Cara Finnegan for pointing me to Schudson's argument.

8. See Nussbaum, "Moral Expertise?" See also McCloskey 393–406.

9. See Soja; Sorkin; J. Smith; and Zukin.

Chapter 2. The Public Subject of Feeling (with Exceptions)

1. For another version of Bush as idiot, see Eberly, "Plato's Shibboleth."

2. For an extended explication of Hume's calm and violent passions, see Immerwahr 293–314.

3. This view of view of apathy and boredom challenges traditional and even popular views of emotions. Robert Solomon, one of the twentieth century's leading philosophers of the emotions, admits "indifference" as an emotion only insofar as it emerges as a sign of deliberate contempt for another person. In Solomon's formulation, indifference is experienced as an outerdirected feeling toward someone we deem "below whatever standard of evaluation" we choose (329). Additionally, Solomon calls something resembling true indifference—the experience of undecidability where another person or thing is concerned—"merely [a] lack of emotion" (328).

4. I am abbreviating a much longer and more complex conversation about the affective character of the subject. This conversation spans centuries, and it challenges the Enlightenment version of a subject that is either primarily rational (the traditional male subject) or primarily emotional (the traditional other). For various versions of this longer conversation, see Spinoza; Grassi; and Damasio.

5. This marks a refinement of the analysis I gave earlier on Kenneth Burke's butcher and shepherd, where I said that different feelings create different kinds of public subjects. Here I am arguing that a subject's publicness is often created through feeling in general: naked affect, even intensities of varying kinds.

6. Perhaps this is why Radiohead is so insistent in their hit "There There" that "Just 'cause you feel it, doesn't mean it's there."

7. See one such poll conducted by the California Voter Foundation, which found that "92 percent of infrequent voters say they like to vote. 62 percent strongly agree with the statement, 'I like to vote'" (California Voter Foundation).

8. A modern parallel might be found in those citizens who assert that living in a democracy means that we have a *right* not to vote, especially if all political candidates seem to be equally corrupt or somehow flawed.

9. This example comes from Antonio Ceraso, who posted the image on his Facebook page as a rather enjoyable illustration of Agamben's state of exception.

10. For more on the easement, see Agamben's *The Coming Community*.

11. See Mathieu's *Tactics of Hope* for an indication of the public focus that is growing within composition studies.

Chapter 3. Vultures and Kooks: The Rhetoric of Injury Claims

1. All testimony comes from the June 7, 1990, Austin City Council meeting video on file at the Austin History Center.

2. At least one resident openly embraced this charge in her written response to Dedman: "So Mr. Moffett thinks Austinites are 'Un-American' for not letting him pollute our beloved Barton Creek. And Mr. Dedman thinks it is devastating that Austinites are 'Kooks attracting kooks!' Then so be it. More power to the kooks who love Barton Springs" (Clark A8).

3. Material on the Circle C Ranch development is found in the files of the Austin History Center.

4. It was also named one of the eleven most endangered historic places due to the threat of development.

5. Translation by Christa Olson.

6. The Bodega Aurrera, as the Walmart Supercenter is called locally, ran a radio commercial that invited listeners to the store's grand opening. The excited announcer's voice concluded with the somewhat awkward slogan: "Bodega Aurrera, now as valuable as *you*." This slogan implies an interesting suggestion that opposing or shutting down the Bodega Aurrera would be an affront to *you*, the people.

7. In earlier versions of Facebook, Walmart's corporate page had well over one million "fans," though a number of anti-Walmart pages also feature large

numbers of detractors. As of December 2011, almost eleven million people "like" the Walmart corporate Facebook page. There are also sites like www.AmericansforWalmart.org and www.walmartwatch.com.

Chapter 4. Lost Places and Memory Claims

1. For an excellent overview of the ways epideictic has variously been described as didactic, see Sullivan 113–33. See also Hauser, "Aristotle on Epideictic" 17; Poulakos, "Isocrates's Use of Narrative" 317–28; Condit 284–98.

2. Austin Chamber of Commerce, "Population," 2008, www.austinchamber.com/DoBusiness/GreaterAustinProfile/population.html.

3. For an example, see the conversation thread in the *CityData* forum, "Kelso vs. Californian," Sept. 26, 2007, www.city-data.com/forum/austin/160561-kelso-vs-californian-3.html.

4. This distinction is intimately tied up with the city's own renaming of the area "The New Times Square" for promotional purposes. Yet the distinction between new and old Times Square does not seem entirely tied to this official renaming.

Chapter 5. The Good and the Bad: Gentrification and Equivalence Claims

1. Neighborhood Planning Demographics (1990, 2000) and Census Data (1990, 2000).

2. Austin City Council minutes, July 29, 2004.

3. Austin City Council minutes, Nov. 17, 2005.

4. The Austin anti-yuppie graffiti takes its cue from the "yuppie scum" graffiti that has been floating around cities for years. See curbed.com/archives/2008/06/16/comeback_story_yuppie_is_the_insult_du_jour.php).

5. Perhaps this is why equivalence claims are often accompanied by rhetorical gestures of tolerance and (racial) acceptance. When one East Side newcomer was asked about the backlash against gentrifiers, she defended her own presence with claims of racial equivalence among all East Side residents. "I know we look different on the outside and speak different languages," she remarked, "but people want the same things: to be respected, to be treated fairly" (Schwartz, "East Austin's Changing"). Gentrification is an extension of racial harmony, in other words.

6. Resolution no. 20050428-043.

7. In response to this double subject, Danny Hoch's one-man show, *Taking Over*, is meant to reinforce the argument that gentrifiers are creating harmful effects, even when they believe they are forces of good. The show is meant to performatively create the experience of *impact*. Hoch's show features a number of different characters who populate the Williamsburg neighborhood in Brooklyn.

There are the old-timers and the new-timers, like slick real estate agents and the young liberal newcomers who sing the praises of volunteerism. When asked why so many people in his audience respond negatively to his performance, Hoch replied, "a lot of young lefty people are pissed off because they feel implicated, particularly in my show. They feel like, Hey I'm not rich, I'm just struggling like everybody else. But, collectively, they're causing the problem. . . . Progressive-minded folks who gentrify neighborhoods may go in with good intentions, but they don't see that they're running over people" (Brekke-Miesner).

8. And, of course, it is not just students that fall back onto clichés. For an excellent discussion of clichéd teacher responses to student writing, see Skorczewski 220–39.

9. Here I am referencing Michel Foucault and Gilles Deleuze on "the event."

10. Or, as Bill Maher remarks in his documentary, *Religulous:* "I mostly preach the doctrine of 'I don't know.'"

Chapter 6. Inquiry as Social Action

1. Donald Lazere has a slightly different take on this pedagogical practice. Lazere is quite critical of the turn to "local publics" in order to make public debates relevant to students. Instead, he pursues attention to national politics as the place where critical thinking should be renewed. Lazere reads "publics" as a code term for somewhat infantilized attention to small issues of personal interest. The problem, he argues, is that this small turn is a move away from actual political debates (257–91).

WORKS CITED

Ackerman, John. "Teaching the Capital City." Keller and Weisser.
Adams, Paul C., Steven D. Hoelscher, and Karen E. Till. *Textures of Place: Exploring Humanist Geographies*. Minneapolis: University of Minnesota Press, 2001.
Agamben, Giorgio. *The Coming Community*. Minneapolis: University of Minnesota, 1993.
———. *Homo Sacer: Sovereign Power and Bare Life*. Stanford: Stanford University Press, 1998.
Ahmed, Sara. *The Cultural Politics of Emotion*. Edinburgh: Edinburgh University Press, 2004.
Albers, Jan. "The History and Future of the Vermont Landscape." Aiken Lecture, Vermont Land Trust. Feb. 15, 2006.
Alcorn, Marshall, Jr. *Changing the Subject in English Class: Discourse and the Constructions of Desires*. Carbondale: Southern Illinois University Press, 2002.
Allen, Lorraine. Letter. *The New London Day*, Nov. 17, 2009. www.theday.com/article/20091117/OP02/311179967.
"Americans Rank Climate Change as Top Environmental Problem." *LiveScience*, Nov. 3, 2006. www.livescience.com/4287-americans-rank-climate-change-top-environmental-problem.html.
Amossy, Ruth. "The Cliché in the Reading Process." *SubStance* 35 (1982): 34–45.
Appadurai, Arjun. *Modernity at Large: Cultural Dimensions of Globalization*. Minneapolis: University of Minnesota Press, 1996.
Arefi, Mahyar. "Non-Place and Placelessness as Narratives of Loss: Rethinking the Notion of Place." *Journal of Urban Design* 4.2 (1999): 179–94.

Aristotle. *Nicomachean Ethics.* Trans. Martin Ostwald. Indianapolis: Bobbs-Merrill, 1962.

———. *Rhetoric.* Trans. W. Rhys Roberts. New York: Modern Library, 1954.

Armstrong, E. *A Ciceronian Sunburn: A Tudor Dialogue on Humanistic Rhetoric and Civic Poetics.* Columbia: University of South Carolina Press, 2006.

Arnold, Mary. Oral History. *Texas Legacy Project,* Aug. 21, 1997. www.texaslegacy.org/m/transcripts/arnoldmarytxt.html.

Asen, Robert. "A Discourse Theory of Citizenship." *Quarterly Journal of Speech* 90.2 (2004): 189–211.

Augé, Marc. *Non-Places: Introduction to an Anthropology of Supermodernity.* Trans. John Howe. London: Verso, 1995.

Austin Chamber of Commerce. "Austin's Country Music Scene." Tour Fact Sheet Number 3. 1979.

Austin History Center. Various files, transcripts, and videos.

"Austin, Meet Austin" *Alcade* 51 (July/Aug. 2004): 50–55.

"Austin Office Vacancy Hits 19%." *Austin Business Journal,* Jan. 5, 2009. www.bizjournals.com/austin/stories/2009/01/05/daily22.html.

Austin Planning and Development Review Department. Comments. Aug. 21, 2010. www.ci.austin.tx.us/planning/cd_comments.cfm?CurrentPage=6.

Austin Revitalization Authority. Apr. 24, 2008. www.austinrev.org.

Ayensworth, Tim. Letter. *Austin American-Statesman,* June 19, 1990: A8.

Bachelard, Gaston. *The Poetics of Space.* Boston: Beacon Press, 1994.

"Bah Humbug." *Hartford Courant,* Dec. 21, 2006. blogs.courant.com/news_opinion_hunter/2006/12/bah-humbug.html.

Barrios, Jennifer. "New Life for East Austin." *Austin American-Statesman,* July 31, 2003: A1.

Barthes, Roland. *Empire of Signs.* New York: Hill & Wang, 1982.

Bartholomae, David. "Inventing the University." *When a Writer Can't Write: Studies in Writer's Block and Other Composing-Process Problems.* Ed. Mike Rose. New York: The Guilford Press, 1985. 134–65.

Basic Initiative. "East Austin: People, Architecture, Place." *BaSiC Initiative,* n.d. www.basicinitiative.org/images/historyofeastaustin.pdf.

Beach, Patrick. "Austin through the 'Weird' Looking Glass." *Austin 360,* Sept. 29, 2005. www.austin360.com/xl/content/arts/xl/2005/09/weirdaustin_09-29-05.html.

Beauregard, Robert A. *Voices of Decline: The Postwar Fate of U.S. Cities.* New York: Routledge, 2002.

Begley, Sharon. "Boycott BP!" *Newsweek,* June 7, 2010. www.newsweek.com/2010/06/07/boycott-bp.html.

Bell, John. "Disney's Times Square: The New American Community Theatre." *Drama Review* 42.1 (1998): 26–33.

Bellonci, Gioconda. Letter. *Austin American-Statesman,* June 4, 1990: A6.

Belluck, Pam. "Preservationists Call Vermont Endangered, by Wal-Mart." *New York Times,* May 25, 2004: A1.

Beniash, Jerry. Letter. *Austin American-Statesman,* Dec. 27, 2000.

Benjamin, Walter. *The Arcades Project.* Trans. Howard Eiland and Kevin McLaughlin. Cambridge, MA: Harvard University Press, 1999.

Berlant, Lauren. *Compassion: The Culture and Politics of an Emotion.* New York: Routledge, 2004.

———. *The Queen of America Goes to Washington City: Essays on Sex and Citizenship.* Durham, NC: Duke University Press, 1997.

———. "The Subject of True Feeling: Pain, Privacy and Politics." *Cultural Pluralism, Identity Politics, and the Law.* Ed. Austin Sarat and Thomas R. Kearns. Ann Arbor: University of Michigan Press, 1999. 58.

Berlin, James A. "Contemporary Composition: The Major Pedagogical Theories." *College English* 44 (1982): 765–77.

Berman, Marshall. *All That's Solid Melts into Air: The Experience of Modernity.* New York: Simon and Schuster, 1982.

Bernauer, James William, and David M. Rasmussen. *The Final Foucault.* Cambridge, MA: MIT Press, 1988.

Beyor, Leslie. Letter. *St. Albans Messenger,* Jan. 15, 2009. www.samessenger.com/Lettersview.asp?id=4821.

Bicknell, Sandra. Letter. *St. Albans Messenger,* July 24, 2009. www.samessenger.com/Lettersview.asp?id=4821.

Biesecker, Barbara. "Renovating the National Imaginary: A Prolegomenon on Contemporary Paregoric Rhetoric." Phillips et al. 212–24.

———, and John Louis Lucaites. *Rhetoric, Materiality, and Politics.* New York: Peter Lang, 2009.

Blair, Carol. "Contemporary U.S. Memorial Sites as Exemplars of Rhetoric's Materiality." *Rhetorical Bodies.* Ed. Jack Selzer and Sharon Crowley. Madison: University of Wisconsin Press, 1999. 16–57.

Boone, Lezlie. Letter. *Austin American-Statesman,* July 5, 1998: G2.

"Boycott BP? Don't Bother." *Newsweek,* July 21, 2010. www.newsweek.com/2010/06/07/boycott-bp.html.

Brekke-Miesner, Lukas. Interview with Danny Hoch. *WireTap,* Dec. 3, 2008. www.wiretapmag.org/race/43902/.

Breunlin, Rachel. Personal e-mail. March 5, 2010. Author's files.

Bright, Susan. "Crows, Vultures, Blacksuits." Pipkin 92.

Brown, Wendy. *States of Injury*. Princeton, NJ: Princeton University Press, 1995.

Brown, Zachary. "The Wal-Mart Epidemic." *Vermont Journal of Environmental Law,* Apr. 13 2005. www.vjel.org/editorials/ED10044.html.

Browne, Stephen H. "Reading, Rhetoric and the Texture of Public Memory." *Quarterly Journal of Speech* 81 (1995): 237–65.

Buchholz, Brad. "A Hole in the Wall, a Hole in the Heart." *Austin American-Statesman,* July 7, 2002: A1.

Burgess, Ernest. "The Growth of the City." Park and Burgess 47–62.

Burke, Kenneth. *A Grammar of Motives*. Berkeley: University of California Press, 1945.

———. *A Rhetoric of Motives*. Berkeley: University of California Press, 1969.

Cactus, The. 1970. Yearbook. The University of Texas, Austin. Texas Student Publications, Austin. 107.

Calhoun, Craig, ed. *Habermas and the Public Sphere*. Cambridge, MA: MIT Press, 1991.

California Voter Foundation. "California Voter Participation Survey." Jan. 27, 2006. www.calvoter.org/issues/votereng/votpart/keyfindings.html.

Carlson, Neil. "Urban Gentry." *The Housing Puzzle*. Ford Foundation Report. (Spring 2003): 22–25.

Carr, James H., and Lisa J. Servon. "Vernacular Culture and Urban Economic Development: Thinking Outside the (Big) Box." *Journal of the American Planning Association* 75.1 (Winter 2009): 28–40.

"Carta Abierta Al Presidente Fox." *Reforma,* Oct. 9, 2004: 17A.

"Casa Lopez, La." Dir. Andrew Cadelago, Lauren Hardy, and Isaac Simon. East Austin Stories, 2008.

Casey, Edward S. "Public Memory in Place and Time." Phillips et al. 17–44.

Charland, Maurice. "Constitutive Rhetoric: The Case of the *Peuple Québécois*." *Quarterly Journal of Speech* 73 (May 1987): 133–50.

Charles, David. *Aristotle's Philosophy of Action*. London: Duckworth, 1984.

Cicero. *De Oratore*. Trans. E. W. Sutton. Cambridge, MA: Harvard University Press, 1942.

City of Austin. *Central Austin Combined Neighborhood Plan*. August 2004. www.ci.austin.tx.us%2Fplanning%2Fneighborhood%2Fdownloads%2Fca%2Fvis_goals_10.pdf&ei=85vnToKJGaXWoQGN9bjFDQ&usg=AFQjCNFQYMA9HH3DE68ZsXR2SD8x65JzuQ.

———. *Central East Austin Neighborhood Plan*. Austin, 2001.

Clark, Jennifer. Letter. *Austin American-Statesman,* July 10, 1990: A8.

Clinchy, Don. "On Earth as It Is in Austin." Gale and Carton, *Writing Austin's Lives* 387–88.

Cloud, Dana. "The Materiality of Discourse as Oxymoron: A Challenge to Critical Rhetoric." *Western Journal of Communication* 58 (1994): 141–63.

Collier, Bill. "Barton Creek." *Austin American-Statesman*, July 1, 1990: A1.

———. "Council Considers Development Plan in Marathon Session." *Austin American-Statesman*, June 8, 1990: A1.

———. "Developers Consider Options after Loss in 13-Hour Session." *Austin American-Statesman*, June 9, 1990: A1.

———. "Point of Contention: Plan to Develop Scenic Area Sparks Barton Creek Fight." *Austin American-Statesman*, June 4, 1990: A1.

"Community Change in East Austin." LBJ School of Public Affairs. Policy Research Project Reports Series No. 160, 2007.

Condit, Celeste M. "The Function of Epideictic: The Boston Massacre Orations as Exemplar." *Communication Quarterly* 33 (1985): 284–98.

"Condomania Lives! Mobile Manor Next Trailer Park Casualty." *Austinist*, July 31, 2008. austinist.com/2008/07/31/condomania_lives_mobile_manor_next.php.

Constructive Ventures. "Este: The Newest Address on East 6th Street." www.docstoc.com/docs/37495231/ESTE-The-Newest-Address-on-East-6-Street-Do-You-Belong-East--Este.

Cooper, Marilyn. "The Ecology of Writing." *College English* 48.4 (1986): 364–75.

Copelin, Laylan. "Race Puts Spotlight on Old, New East Austin." *Austin American-Statesman*, Jan. 15, 2008. www.statesman.com/news/content/region/legislature/stories/01/15/0115txhouse46.html.

Coral Gables Senior High, District 7. "Narratives and Drawings by the Students of Troy Community Academy." www.artmurals.org/county/coralgables.htm.

Costas, Peter L. "Dispelling the Myths about the Fort Trumbull Project." *New London Day*, Nov. 6, 2005. www.theday.com/article/20051106/DAYARC/311069800.

Cox, J. Robert. "The Die Is Cast: Topical and Ontological Dimensions of the Locus of the Irreparable." *Quarterly Journal of Speech* 68.3 (1982): 227–39.

Cranston, Seana. "Supremes Take Liberty with Takings Clause." *Concerned Women for America*, n.d. www.cwfa.org/articles/8412/LEGAL/scourt/index.htm.

Cravey, Robin. "Treaty Oak." Austin: Tilted Planet Press, 1989.

"Creating a Great Downtown." Downtown Austin Alliance R/UDAT Review 2000. Dec. 2000. www.ci.austin.tx.us/downtown/docs/rudat_review_2000.pdf.

Crowley, Sharon. *Toward a Civil Discourse: Rhetoric and Fundamentalism*. Pittsburgh: University of Pittsburgh Press, 2006.

D'Agostino, Ryan. "Where the Streets Have No Name." *Money Magazine,* Dec. 1, 2005. money.cnn.com/magazines/moneymag/moneymag_archive/2005/12/01/8362028/index.htm.

Damasio, Antonio. *The Feeling of What Happens: Body and Emotion in the Making of Consciousness.* New York: Harcourt Brace, 1995.

Daniels, Charlie. Radio interview. KLBJ. Dec. 8, 1980.

Darr, Teighlor. Letter. *Austin Chronicle,* Dec. 17, 2007. www.austinchronicle.com/gyrobase/ReaderComments/?ContainerID=572849.

Davis, Mike. "Fortress L.A." *City of Quartz: Excavating the Future in Los Angeles.* New York: Vintage Books, 1992.

Davis, Rod. "Austin's Bizarre Bazarre." *Dallas Times Herald,* Sept. 18, 1983: A19.

DDCOC. "Gentrification, Good or Bad? Lawndale, Chicago." *YouTube,* June 17, 2008. www.youtube.com/watch?v=mSVlbKhw5P4.

———. "Gentrification, Good or Bad? Part 2." *YouTube,* June 1, 2008. www.youtube.com/user/DDCOC#p/u/27/DwoCwis_5F4.

de Brito, Andrea. "American Apparel Battle Heats Up." *San Francisco Bay Guardian,* Jan. 30, 2009. www.sfbg.com/blogs/politics/2009/01/american_apparel_battle_heats_1.html.

de Certeau, Michel. *The Practice of Everyday Life.* Trans. Steven Rendall. Berkeley: University of California Press, 1984.

Delany, Samuel R. *Times Square Red, Times Square Blue.* New York: New York University Press, 1999.

Del Signore, John. "Steve Buscemi." *Gothamist,* May 27, 2010. gothamist.com/2010/05/27/steve_buscemi_issue_project_room.php.

"Development Forces the Backyard to Close." *Austin Sound Check,* Apr. 24, 2008. www.austinsoundcheck.com/development-forces-the-backyard-to-close.

Dick, Philip K. *The Shifting Realities of Philip K. Dick: Selected Literary and Philosophical Writings.* New York: Vintage, 1996.

Dobrin, Sidney, and Christian Weisser. *Natural Discourse.* Albany: State University of New York Press, 2002.

———. "The Occupation of Composition." Keller and Weisser 15–36.

———, and Christopher J. Keller. *Writing Environments.* Albany: State University of New York Press, 2005.

———, and Christian Weisser. *Ecocomposition: Theoretical and Pedagogical Approaches.* Albany: State University of New York Press, 2001.

Doolin, Bill, and Alan Lowe. "To Reveal Is to Critique: Actor-Network Theory and Critical Information Systems Research." *Journal of Information Technology* 17.2 (2001): 69–78.

Draper, Robert. "Adios to Austin." *Literary Austin.* Ed. Don Graham. Fort Worth: Texas Christian University Press. 351–59.

Drew, Julie. "The Politics of Place: Student Travelers and Pedagogical Maps." Weisser and Dobrin 57–68.

Duany, Andres, Elizabeth Plater-Zyberk, and Jeff Speck. *Suburban Nation: The Rise of Sprawl and the Decline of the American Dream.* New York: North Point Press, 2000.

Dubose, Louis. "Where's Julia Butterfly?" *Austin Chronicle,* Oct. 6, 2000. www.austinchronicle.com/gyrobase/Issue/story?oid=oid%3A78867.

Dubose, Terry. Letter. *Austin American-Statesman,* June 13, 1990: A24.

Dunn, Laura. *The Unforeseen.* New Yorker Films Video / Cinema Guild, 2008.

"East Austin Gentrification." *Austin Now.* KLRU, Austin, Texas.

"East Austin Gentrification Documentary." PODER. *YouTube,* May 16, 2011. www.youtube.com/watch?v=abRqka8nuRQ.

East End Flats. www.eastendflats.com.

"Eastsiders: Alex." *East Austinite,* Jan. 5, 2009. eastaustinite.com/blog/?p=2358.

Eberly, Rosa A. *Citizen Critics: Literary Public Spheres.* Urbana: University of Illinois Press, 2000.

———. "Plato's Shibboleth Delineations; or, The Complete Idiot's Guide to Rhetoric." Hauser and Grim 45–52.

Ed Show, The. MSNBC. June 23, 2005. Television.

Eeckhout, Bart. "The 'Disneyfication' of Times Square: Back to the Future?" *Critical Perspectives on Urban Redevelopment.* Ed. Kevin Fox Gotham. New York: JAI, 2001. 379–428.

Eliasov, Monty. Video. *Save Our Springs Alliance,* n.d. www.sosalliance.org/?page=60.

Entertainment Weekly, Apr. 21, 2000: 72.

Equaloff. Online comments. *Columbia Tribune,* Mar. 12, 2010. www.columbiatribune.com/news/2010/mar/12/for-many-cotton-ball-incident-still-stings.

Ervin, Elizabeth. "Teaching Public Literacy: The Partisanship Problem." *College English* 68.4 (2006): 407–21.

"Fact Sheet: Compassionate Conservativism." White House Archives. Apr. 30, 2002. georgewbush-whitehouse.archives.gov/news/releases/2002/04/20020430.html.

"Family Now Happier, Thanks to Urban Renewal." *Austin American-Statesman,* Aug. 27, 1972: A1.

Farrell, Thomas. "The Weight of Rhetoric: Studies in Cultural Delirium." *Philosophy and Rhetoric* 41.4 (2008): 467–87.

Festa, Nicolo. Letter. *Austin American-Statesman,* July 11, 1990: A14.

Finley, M. I. *The Portable Greek Historians: The Essence of Herodotus, Thucydides, Xenophon, Polybius.* New York: Penguin, 1977.

Fish, Stanley. "Aim Low." *Chronicle of Higher Education,* May 16, 2003. chronicle.com/article/Aim-Low/45210.

———. "Save the World on Your Own Time." *Chronicle of Higher Education,* Jan. 23, 2003. chronicle.com/article/Save-the-World-on-Your-Own/45335.

Fleming, David. *City of Rhetoric: Revitalizing the Public Sphere in Metropolitan America.* New York: State University of New York Press, 2008.

———. "The Space of Argumentation: Urban Design, Civic Discourse, and the Dream of the Good City." *Argumentation* 12.2 (1998): 147–66.

Florida, Richard. *The Rise of the Creative Class.* New York: Basic Books, 2002.

Forrest, Hugh. Letter. *Austin Chronicle,* Aug. 11, 1989: 11.

Foucault, Michel. "The Ethic of Care for the Self as a Practice of Freedom." Trans. J. D. Gauthier, S.J. *The Final Foucault.* Ed. J. Bernauer and David Rasmussen. Cambridge, MA: MIT Press, 1988. 45–82.

Fox Business News. Rebecca Diamond interview of Andrew Rohn and Catherine Capellarro. Oct. 19, 2007. Television.

Fraser, Nancy. "Rethinking the Public Sphere: A Contribution to the Critique of Actually Existing Democracy." Calhoun 109–42.

FreeSociety. Online comments. *Columbia Tribune,* Mar. 12, 2010. www.columbiatribune.com/news/2010/mar/12/for-many-cotton-ball-incident-still-stings.

Fullerton, Kevin. "Council Watch." *Austin Chronicle,* May 26, 2000. www.austinchronicle.com/gyrobase/Issue/column?oid=oid:77382.

Gabrielsolidarity. "East Austin Gentrification Documentary PODER Part 3." *YouTube,* Jan. 9, 2010. www.youtube.com/watch?v=6OsrM7ZwR_k&feature=related.

Gadue, Ray. Letter. *St. Albans Messenger,* July 5, 2008. www.samessenger.com/Lettersview.asp?id=3424.

Gale, Sylvia, and Evan Carton, "Toward the Practice of the Humanities." *Good Society* 14.3 (2005): 38–44.

———. *Writing Austin's Lives: A Community Portrait.* Austin: University of Texas Humanities Institute, 2004.

Gallagher, Victoria, and Kenneth S. Zagacki. "Visibility and Rhetoric: The Power of Visual Images in Norman Rockwell's Depictions of Civil Rights." *Quarterly Journal of Speech* 91.2 (2005): 175–200.

Gans, Herbert J. "Political Participation and Apathy." *Phylon* 13.3 (1952): 185–91.

Garrison, Andy. Phone interview with author. Apr. 12, 2008.

Gaudiani, Claire. *The Greater Good: How Philanthropy Drives the American Economy and Can Save Capitalism.* New York: Henry Holt, 2003.

"Genties, The." *Misprint Magazine* 1.4 (2005). m.misprintmagazine.com/post/346912992/gentrificationissue.

"Gentrification." *Downtown Austin TV*. KLRU-TV, Austin. 2007. www.downtownaustintv.org/#/living/gentrification.

"Get It While You Can." *Austin Chronicle*, July 4, 2003. www.austinchronicle.com/gyrobase/Issue/story?oid=oid%3A166651.

Gieryn, Thomas. "A Space for Place in Sociology." *Annual Review of Sociology* 26 (2000): 463–96.

Goggin, Peter N. *Rhetorics, Literacies, and Narratives of Sustainability*. New York: Routledge, 2009.

Goldberg, Jeffrey. "Walmart Takes on the Girl Scouts." *Atlantic*, Aug. 5, 2009. jeffreygoldberg.theatlantic.com/archives/2009/08/walmart_vs_girl_scouts_of_amer.php.

Gonzalez, Eduardo. "Gentrification Sweeps through East Austin." *InCite* 1.1 (2008). incitealternative.com/the-difficulties-of-east-11th-s-development.

Goss, Jon. "The 'Magic of the Mall': An Analysis of Form, Function, and Meaning in the Contemporary Retail Built Environment." *Annals of the Association of American Geographers* 83.1 (1993): 18–47.

Grassi, Ernesto. *Rhetoric as Philosophy: The Humanist Tradition*. Carbondale: Southern Illinois University Press, 2001.

Green, Jeffrey E. "Apathy: The Democratic Disease." *Philosophy & Social Criticism* 30.5–6 (2004): 745–68.

Greene, Ronald Walter. "Rhetorical Materialism: The Rhetorical Subject and the General Intellect." Biesecker and Lucaites 44–65.

———, and Darrin Hicks. "Lost Convictions: Debating Both Sides and the Ethical Self-Fashioning of Liberal Citizens." *Cultural Studies* 19.1 (2005): 100–126.

Gregor, Katherine. "News." *Austin Chronicle*, Nov. 9, 2007. www.austinchronicle.com/gyrobase/Issue/column?oid=oid:559098.

Grimaldi, William. "Studies in the Philosophy of Aristotle's *Rhetoric*." *Landmark Essays on Aristotelian Rhetoric*. Ed. Richard Leo Enos and Lois Peters Agnew. Mahwah, NJ: Lawrence Erlbaum, 1998. 15–160.

Gross, Daniel M. *The Secret History of Emotion: From Aristotle's Rhetoric to Modern Brain Science*. Chicago: University of Chicago Press, 2007.

Gross, Joe. "Say Goodbye to Sound Exchange." *Austin American-Statesman*, Jan. 9, 2003: A11–12.

Gutiérrez-Jones, Carl. "Injury by Design." *Cultural Critique* 40 (1998): 73–102.

Habermas, Jürgen. "The Public Sphere: An Encyclopedia Article." Trans. S. Lennox and F. Lennox. *New German Critique* 3 (1974): 49–55.

Halloran, S. Michael. "Rhetoric in American College Curriculum." *Pre/Text* (1982): 245–69.

Hampson, Rick. "Gentrification a Boost for Everyone." *USA Today*, Apr. 19, 2005. www.usatoday.com/news/nation/2005-04-19-gentrification_x.htm.

Harper, Marques. "Look for Austin Sites in New Anthropologie Catalog." June 2, 2009. www.statesman.com/blogs/content/shared-gen/blogs/austin/shopping/entries/2009/06/02/look_for_austin_in_new_anthrop.html.

Harrigan, Stephen. "Vigil at Treaty Oak." *Texas Monthly*, Oct. 1989: 130–33.

Hartelius, Johanna. "The Rhetoric of Expertise." Diss. University of Texas, 2008.

Hattersley, Craig. "Armadillo World Headquarters." *Texas Observer*, Dec. 26, 1980.

Hauser, Gerard. "Aristotle on Epideictic: The Formation of Public Morality." *Rhetoric Society Quarterly* 29 (1999): 17.

———. "On Reading and Misreading the Rhetoric of Publics and Public Spheres." *Argumentation and Advocacy* 37 (2001): 217–20.

———. *Vernacular Voices*. Columbia: University of South Carolina Press, 2008.

———, and Amy Grim. *Rhetorical Democracy: Discursive Practices of Civic Engagement*. New York: Routledge, 2003.

Hayden, Dolores. *A Field Guide to Sprawl*. New York: W. W. Norton, 2004.

———. *Power of Place: Urban Landscapes as Public History*. Cambridge, MA: MIT Press, 1995.

Heat-Moon, William Least. *PrairyErth: (A Deep Map)*. Boston: Houghton Mifflin, 1991.

Heraclitus. *Heraclitus: Fragments*. Trans. and ed. T. M. Robinson. Toronto: University of Toronto Press, 1987.

Herrera, Leonard. "Charges of Gentrification." *La Presna,* May 22, 2002: 4–5.

Higgins, J. "A Look at Downtown Revitalization—Austin Style." *Tucson Choices,* Nov. 5, 2008. tucsongrowup.com/2008/11/05/a-look-at-downtown-revitalization-austin-style.

Hightower, Jim. "Declare Economic Independence." *Austin Chronicle,* Dec. 17, 2004. www.austinchronicle.com/news/2004-12-17/243206.

Hill, Rob. "An Austin Lifer." Gale and Carton 405–9.

Himelstein, Abram. Interview. "Community Gumbo." WTUL, New Orleans. Apr. 9, 2006.

Hollett, Jessica. "'Eleventh East' Receives Cultural Makeover Near U. Texas." *Daily Texan,* Sept. 13, 2004: A1.

Homer. *The Iliad*. Trans. A. T. Murray. Cambridge, MA: Harvard University Press, 1971.

Hume, David. *Letters of David Hume*. Facsimiles-Garl, 1983.

———. *A Treatise of Human Nature*. Charleston, SC: Nabu Press, 2010.

Hunter, Karen. "Bah Humbug." *Hartford Courant,* Dec. 27, 2006. blogs.courant.com/news_opinion_hunter/2006/12.

Immerwahr, John. "Hume on Tranquillizing the Passions." *Hume Studies* 18.2 (Nov. 1992): 293–314.

"Inner City Residents Plagued by Displacement." *Texas Tenants Union New* 2.2 (Spring 1980): 1–2.

Isocrates. "Antidosis." *Isocrates I*. Trans. David C. Mirhady. Austin: University of Texas Press, 2000. 201–64.

Jackson, Robena. "East Austin: A Socio-Historical View of a Segregated Community." Diss. University of Texas, 1979.

Jacobs, Allan B., and Donald Appleyard. "Toward an Urban Design Manifesto." *Journal of the American Planning Association* 53.1 (2007): 112–20.

Jacobs, Jane. *The Death and Life of Great American Cities*. New York: Vintage, 1992.

Jameson, Fredric. "Postmodernism, or the Cultural Logic of Late Capitalism." *New Left Review* 146 (1984): 52–92.

"Jim Bob Moffett Takes on Austin over Subdivision." *The Baton Rouge State Times*, Sept. 24, 1990: B2.

Johnson, Jim. "Mixing Humans and Nonhumans Together: The Sociology of a Door-Closer." *Social Problems* 35.3 (1988): 298–310.

Jones, Joseph Jay. *Life on Waller Creek: A Palaver about History as Pure and Applied Education*. Austin: AAR/Tantalus, 1982.

Joyness333. Online comments, "Texas: Obama and the Politics of Gentrification." *YouTube*. www.youtube.com/watch?v=MjQC_92NqMo.

Kakutani, Michiko. "Books of the Times—Decline of America's Landscape and the Blame." *New York Times*, June 15, 1993. www.nytimes.com/1993/06/15/books/books-of-the-times-decline-of-america-s-landscape-and-the-blame.html.

Katz, P. *The New Urbanism: Toward an Architecture of Community*. New York: McGraw-Hill. 1994.

Kearns, Thomas R. *Cultural Pluralism, Identity Politics, and the Law*. Ann Arbor: University of Michigan Press, 2001.

Keating, Caroline. "East Austin Growth Pushes Out Poor." *Daily Texan*, Aug. 10, 2005. www.dailytexanonline.com/2.4489/east-austin-growth-pushes-out-poor-1.976550.

Keller, Christopher J., and Christian R. Weisser, eds. *The Locations of Composition*. Albany: State University of New York Press, 2007.

Kelo, Susette. Speech to Cato Institute. *YouTube*, Jan. 26, 2009. www.youtube.com/watch?v=iFdn6BGVl1k.

Kelso, John. "Liberty Lunch Thrives as Laid-Back." *Austin American-Statesman*, May 7, 1983: A26.

———. "Savor the Gravy before Newbies Take It Away, Too." *Austin American-Statesman,* Apr. 20, 2008: B01.

King, Michael, and Lou Dubose. Oral history. *Texas Legacy Project.* Briscoe Center for American History, June 23, 1999. glifos.cah.utexas.edu/index.php/TexLegacyProj:Dubose_king_2023.

Koch and Fowler [Engineers for the City Planning Commission]. *A City Plan for Austin, Texas.* Jan. 14, 1928.

Kozmetsky, George, David V. Gibson, and Raymond Smilor. *Austin/San Antonio Corridor: The Dynamics of a Developing Technopolis.* Austin: IC² Institute, University of Texas at Austin, 1987.

Kunstler, James Howard. *The Geography of Nowhere: The Rise and Decline of America's Man-Made Landscape.* New York: Free Press, 1994.

"La Casa Lopez." Dir. Andrew Cadelago, Lauren Hardy, and Isaac Simon. East Austin Stories, 2008. Film.

Lagnado, Lucette. "Why New London, Conn., Still Waits for Its Ship to Come In." *Wall Street Journal,* Sept. 10, 2002: A1.

Lambert, Dave. Letter. *Austin American-Statesman,* March 26, 2001: A10.

Lambert, Pam. "Battling to Save Her House." *People,* Dec. 13, 2004. www.people.com/people/archive/article/0,,20146311,00.html.

Landreth, A. W. Letter. *Austin American-Statesman,* July 22, 1990: C2.

Langer, Andy. "Rent Party Blues." *Austin Chronicle,* Feb. 14, 2003. www.austinchronicle.com/gyrobase/Issue/story?oid=oid:145344.

Latour, Bruno. "On Actor Network Theory: A Few Clarifications." *Nettime,* 1997. www.nettime.org/Lists-Archives/nettime-l-9801/msg00019.html.

———. *Reassembling the Social: An Introduction to Actor-Network Theory.* Oxford: Oxford University Press, 2005.

Law, John, and John Urry. "Enacting the Social." *Economy and Society* 33.3 (2004): 390–410.

Lazere, Donald. "Postmodern Pluralism and the Retreat from Political Literacy." *Journal of Advanced Composition* 25.2 (2005): 257–92.

Lees, Loretta. "Urban Geography: Discourse Analysis and Urban Research." *Progress in Human Geography* 28.1 (2004): 101–7.

LeGates, Richard T., and Frederic Stout. *The City Reader.* New York: Routledge, 2003.

Lewis, Peter. "What's Doing in Austin." *New York Times,* Feb. 22, 2004. www.nytimes.com/2004/02/22/travel/what-s-doing-in-austin.html.

Liasson, Mara. "Measuring McCain and Obama's Bipartisan Efforts." *NPR,* July 2, 2008.

Lieber, Ron. "Punishing BP Is Harder Than Boycotting Stations." *New York Times,* June 11, 2010. www.nytimes.com/2010/06/12/your-money/12money.

html?scp=1&sq=punishing%20BP%20is%20harder%20than%20boycotting%20stations&st=cse.

Liggett, Helen. *Urban Encounters*. Minneapolis: University of Minnesota Press, 2003.

Long, Elenore. *Community Literacy and the Rhetoric of Local Publics*. Anderson, SC: Parlor Press, 2008.

Long, Joshua. "Sustaining Creativity in the Creative Archetype: The Case of Austin, Texas." *Cities: The International Journal of Urban Policy and Planning* 26.4 (2009): 175–232.

———. *Weird City: Sense of Place and Creative Resistance in Austin, Texas*. Austin: University of Texas Press, 2010.

"Long Live Liberty Lunch." *Austin Chronicle*, July 23, 1999. www.austinchronicle.com/music/1999-07-23/522427.

"Looking for Cheap Dirt." *Austin Chronicle*, May 12, 2006. www.austinchronicle.com/news/2006-05-12/364691.

Low, Setha. *Behind the Gates: Life, Security, and the Pursuit of Happiness in Fortress America*. New York: Routledge, 2003.

Lueck, Thomas. "Town and Gown Clash over Housing." *New York Times*, Apr. 9, 1989: A1.

Makagon, Daniel. *Where the Ball Drops: Days and Nights in Times Square*. Minneapolis: University of Minnesota Press, 2004.

Marback, Richard. "Speaking of the City and Literacies of Place in Composition Studies." McComiskey and Ryan 141–55.

Massumi, Brian. "Everywhere You Want to Be." *The Politics of Everyday Fear*. Ed. Brian Massumi. Minneapolis: University of Minnesota Press, 1993. 3–38.

———. *Parables for the Virtual: Movement, Affect, Sensation*. Durham, NC: Duke University Press, 2002.

———. *A User's Guide to Capitalism and Schizophrenia: Deviations from Deleuze and Guattari*. Cambridge, MA: MIT Press, 1992.

Mauk, Johnathon. "Location, Location, Location: The 'Real' (E)states of Being, Writing, and Thinking in Composition." *College English* 65.4 (2003): 368–88.

McCall, Nathan. *Them*. New York: Atria, 2007.

McCloskey, Donald N. "The Limits of Expertise." *American Scholar* 57 (1988): 393–406.

McClure, Wendy R., and Tom J. Bartuska. *The Built Environment: A Collaborative Inquiry into Design and Planning*. New York: Wiley, 2007.

McComiskey, Bruce, and Cynthia Ryan. *City Comp: Identities, Spaces, Practices*. Albany: State University of New York Press, 2003.

McKenzie, R. D. "The Ecological Approach to the Study of Human Community." Park and Burgess, 1925.

McKinley, James. "No, the Conquistadors Are Not Back. It's Just Wal-Mart." *New York Times,* Sept. 28, 2004. www.nytimes.com/2004/09/28/international/americas/28mexico.html.

McLemee, Scott. "Lazy Me." *Inside Higher Ed,* Apr. 5, 2006. www.insidehighered.com/views/mclemee/mclemee187.

Micciche, Laura R. *Doing Emotion: Rhetoric, Writing, Teaching.* Portsmouth, NH: Boynton/Cook, 2007.

Miller, Carolyn R. "The Aristotelian *Topos:* Hunting for Novelty." *Rereading Aristotle's Rhetoric.* Ed. Alan G. Gross and Arthur E. Walzer. Carbondale: Southern Illinois University Press, 2000. 130–46.

Mitchell, Don. *The Right to the City: Social Justice and the Fight for Public Space.* New York: The Guilford Press, 2003.

Modest Mouse. "Novocain Stain." *This Is a Long Drive for Someone with Nothing to Think About.* Up Records, 1996.

Mol, Annemarie, and John Law. "Regions, Networks and Fluids: Anaemia and Social Topology." *Social Studies of Science* 24 (1994): 641–71.

Momaday, N. Scott. *The Way to Rainy Mountain.* Albuquerque: University of New Mexico Press, 1976.

Moore, Steven A. *Alternative Routes to the Sustainable City: Austin, Curitiba, and Frankfurt.* Lanham, MD: Rowman & Littlefield, 2005.

Moran, Kate. "When Is a House Not a Home?" *New London Day,* July 23, 2005. www.theday.com/article/20050723/DAYARC/307239860.

Morris, Douglas E. *It's a Sprawl World after All: The Human Cost of Unplanned Growth—and Visions of a Better Future.* Gabriola, BC: New Society, 2005.

Morton, Kate Miller. "Luxury Apartments Rising in East Austin." *Austin American-Statesman,* Nov. 29, 2005: C1.

Moser, Gabriel. *People, Places and Sustainability.* Toronto: Hogrefe & Huber, 2003.

Neighborhood Story Project. "Creativity and Activism in the Seventh Ward: Collaborative Poster and Book-Making Project." www.neighborhoodstoryproject.org/seventh.html.

Nelson, Ashley. *The Combination.* Berkeley: Soft Skull Press, 2008.

"No One Home: 1 in 9 Housing Units Vacant." *USA Today,* Feb. 12, 2009. www.usatoday.com/money/economy/housing/2009-02-12-vacancy12_N.htm.

Nussbaum, Martha C. "Moral Expertise? Constitutional Narratives and Philosophical Argument." *Metaphilosophy* 33 (2002): 502–20.

———. *Upheavals of Thought: The Intelligence of Emotions.* Cambridge: Cambridge University Press, 2003.

Obama, Barack. Keynote Address. Democratic National Convention. Boston. July 27, 2004.

"Office Vacancy Rate Hits 16-year High." *Reuters*, Apr. 5, 2010. www.reuters.com/article/2010/04/05/us-usofficemarket-idUSTRE6340FH20100405.

"Office Vacancy Rates Vary Widely throughout United States." *Journal of Property Management*, Sept. 1, 2005. www.allbusiness.com/business-finance/leasing/841666-1.html.

Oliver, Bill. "Hard Times for the Oaks." Texas Deck Music, 1990. Live performance.

Olson, Kathryn M., and G. Thomas Goodnight. "Speaking in Community and Ingenium: The Case of the Prince William County Zoning Hearings on Disney's America." *New Approaches to Rhetoric*. Ed. Patricia Sullivan and Stephen R. Goldzwig. Thousand Oaks, CA: Sage, 2004. 31–59.

Orr, David W. *Ecological Literacy: Education and the Transition to a Postmodern World*. Albany: State University of New York Press, 1992.

Orum, Anthony M. Power. *The Making of Modern Austin: Power, Money, and the People*. Austin: Texas Monthly Press, 1987.

Owens, Derek. *Composition and Sustainability: Teaching for a Threatened Generation*. Urbana, IL: National Council of Teachers of English, 2001.

———. "Sustainable Composition." Dobrin and Weisser 27–38.

Park, Robert. "The City: Suggestions for the Investigation of Human Behavior in the Urban Environment." Park and Burgess 1–46.

———, and Ernest Burgess, eds. *The City*. Chicago: University of Chicago Press, 1925.

Payne, Darin. "English Studies in Levittown." *College English* 67.5 (2005): 483–507.

Perelman, Chaim, and Lucie Olbrechts-Tyteca. *The New Rhetoric: A Treatise on Argumentation*. Notre Dame, IN: University of Notre Dame Press, 1969.

Perry, Mike. "We're Just Like Austin When It Was Cool." *The Eagle*, Sept. 9, 2004. www.theeagle.com/brazossunday/faces/091204faces.php.

Peterson, Iver. "There Goes the Old Neighborhood." *New York Times*, Jan. 30, 2005. www.nytimes.com/2005/01/30/nyregion/30domain.html?scp=1&sq=there+go+the+old+neighbors&st=nyt.

Peterson, Tarla Rai. *Sharing the Earth: The Rhetoric of Sustainable Development*. Columbia: University of South Carolina Press, 1997.

———, and C. C. Horton. "Rooted in the Soil: How Understanding the Perspectives of Landowners Can Enhance the Management of Environmental Disputes." *Quarterly Journal of Speech* 81 (1995): 139–66.

Phillips, Kendall R., et al. *Framing Public Memory*. Tuscaloosa: University of Alabama Press, 2008.

Phillips, Kenneth. *Signed, the President*. New Orleans: Neighborhood Story Project, 2009.

Pipkin, Turk. *Barton Springs Eternal: The Soul of a City*. Austin: Softshoe, 1993.

"Police Nab 26 in Protest." *Austin American-Statesman*, Oct. 23, 1969: A1.

Poltergeist. Dir. Tobe Hooper. Metro-Goldwyn-Mayer, 1982.

Polycarpou, Lakis. "Interview with James Howard Kunstler." *Believer*, Nov. 2005. www.believermag.com/issues/200511/?read=interview_kunstler.

Pool, Katherine. "A Neighborhood Worth Fighting For." Gale and Carton 391–92.

Poulakos, Takis. "Isocrates' Use of Doxa." *Philosophy and Rhetoric* 34 (2001): 61–78.

———. "Isocrates' Use of Narrative in the Evagoras: Epideictic, Rhetoric and Moral Action." *Quarterly Journal of Speech* 73 (1987): 317–28.

"Pray You Now." *The Austin Wine Guy*, Apr. 16, 2009. Blog. www.austinwineguy.com/blog.html?pid=26.

Preston, David. Letter. *Wall Street Journal*, Nov. 27, 2009. online.wsj.com/article/SB10001424052748704402404574529661805368256.html.

"Public's Priorities for 2010: Economy, Jobs, Terrorism: Summary of Findings." *Pew Research Center for the People & the Press*, Jan. 25, 2010. people-press.org/2010/01/25/publics-priorities-for-2010-economy-jobs-terrorism.

Putnam, Robert D. *Bowling Alone: The Collapse and Revival of American Community*. New York: Simon & Schuster, 2001.

"Quack's, Coots and Watering Holes." *Austin American-Statesman*, June 7, 1999: A8.

Quintilian. *Institutes of Oratory*. Ed. Lee Honeycutt. Trans. John Selby Watson. Iowa State University, 2006. honeyl.public.iastate.edu/quintilian.

R. H. Johnson Company. *Metropolitan Kansas City: Year 2000 Shopping Center Report*. Kansas City, MO, 2000.

Ragland Realty and Management LLC. *East End Flats*, 2010. www.eastendflats.com.

Reed, Benjamin. "The Accidental Gentrifist Reviews *Tales of the Really White Vigilante*." *Austinist*, Dec. 17, 2007. austinist.com/2007/12/17/the_accidental_4.php.

Reese, Gary. "We Can't Go Home to the Armadillo Again." *Witchita Falls Record*, Jan. 2, 1981: A1.

Reinhold, Robert. "What's Doing in Austin." *New York Times*, May 5, 1985. www.nytimes.com/1985/05/05/travel/what-s-doing-in-austin.html?scp=6&sq=%22new%20austin%22&st=cse.

Relph, Edward. *Place and Placelessness*. London: Pion, 1976.

"Residents Battle Wal-Mart." WPTZ, Plattsburgh, NY. June 4, 2008.

Reyes, Jennifer. "Working for a Miracle." Gale and Carton 158–59.

Reynolds, Nedra. *Geographies of Writing: Inhabiting Places and Encountering Difference*. Carbondale: Southern Illinois University Press, 2004.

Rhodes, Richard. "Cupcake Land: Requiem for the Midwest in the Key of Vanilla." *Harper's* (Oct. 1987): 51–57.
Rivera, Dylan. "Austin Debates Incentives to Draw Intel Downtown." *Austin American-Statesman*, May 19, 2000: B10.
Roberts-Miller, Patricia. *Fanatical Schemes*. Tuscaloosa: University of Alabama Press, 2009.
Rodnitzky, Jerry. "Back to Branson: Normalcy and Nostalgia in the Ozarks." *Southern Cultures* 8.2 (2002): 97–105.
Rogers, Mark. Personal interview. Austin, Mar. 15, 2006.
Ross, Dana. Letter. *Austin American-Statesman*, June 19, 1990: A8.
Sante, Luc. "My Lost City." *New York Review of Books*, Nov. 6, 2003. www.nybooks.com/articles/archives/2003/nov/06/my-lost-city.
"Save Money, Live Better." Walmart Stores. Commercial. 2007. *YouTube*. www.youtube.com/watch?v=c2x5IAUqVSQ&feature=player_embedded.
Savlov, Mark. "Slacker, the Map." *Austin Chronicle*, Jan. 26, 2001. www.austinchronicle.com/issues/dispatch/2001-01-26/screens_feature2.html.
Scheick, William. "Gridlock." *Literary Austin*. Ed. Don Graham. Fort Worth: Texas Christian University Press, 2007. 443–46.
Schilb, John. *Rhetorical Refusals*. Carbondale: Southern Illinois University Press, 2007.
Schliefke, Michael. *Tales of the Really White Vigilante*. Self-published.
Schmitt, Carl. *Political Theology: Four Chapters on the Concept of Sovereignty*. Chicago: University of Chicago Press, 2006.
Schudson, Michael, "Changing Concepts of Democracy." *MIT Communications Forum*, n.d. web.mit.edu/comm-forum/papers/schudson.html.
Schwartz, Jeremy. "East Austin's Changing Landscape." *Austin American-Statesman*, May 5, 2005: A1.
———. "Renaissance on East 11th Street; Neighborhood Debuts Its New Look." *Austin American-Statesman*, Sept. 10, 2004: A1.
Scott, Lee. "The Company of the Future." Kansas City. Jan. 23, 2008. Speech.
"Sending Out an S.O.S." Save Our Springs Alliance, 2006. Video.
Shaviro, Steven. *Connected; or, What It Means to Live in the Network Society*. Minneapolis: University of Minnesota Press, 2003.
Shrake, Bud. "The Screwing Up of Austin." *Texas Observer*, Dec. 27, 1974: 27.
Simpson, Timothy. "Recycling Urban Spaces." *Western Journal of Communication* 63.3 (1999): 310–28.
Skorczewski, Dawn. "'Everybody Has Their Own Ideas': Responding to Cliché in Student Writing." *College Composition and Communication* 52.2 (Dec. 2000): 220–39.

Slosberg, Steven. "Kelo's Holiday Greeting to Foes." *New London Day,* Dec. 20, 2006. www.theday.com/article/20061220/DAYARC/312209903.

Sloterdijk, Peter. *Critique of Cynical Reason.* Translated by Michael Eldred. Minneapolis: University of Minnesota Press, 1988.

"Smart Growth." City of Austin. www.austintexas.gov/vision/community.htm.

Smith, Amy. "Smart Subsidies?" *Austin Chronicle,* Nov. 24, 2000. www.austinchronicle.com/news/2000-11-24/79553.

Smith, Jeff. "Against 'Illegracy': Toward a New Pedagogy of Civic Understanding." *College Composition and Communication* 45 (1994): 210–19.

Smithson, Cate. "Extreme Makeover: Gentrification Transforms East Austin." *ABC News.* Apr. 27, 2009. abcnews.go.com/OnCampus/Story?id=7399717&page=3.

Soja, Edward W. *Postmodern Geographies: The Reassertion of Space in Critical Social Theory.* New York: Verso, 1989.

Solomon, Robert. *The Passions: Emotions and the Meaning of Life.* Indianapolis: Hackett, 1993.

Spaulding, Nina. Letter. *St. Albans Messenger,* Mar. 21, 2008. www.samessenger.com/Lettersview.asp?id=2744.

Spinoza, Baruch. *The Ethics and Selected Letters.* Trans. Samuel Shirley. Indianapolis: Hackett, 1982.

Sprague, Rosamond Kent. *The Older Sophists: A Complete Translation by Several Hands of the Fragments in* Die Fragmente Der Vorsokratiker *Edited By Diels-Kranz with a New Edition of* Antiphon *and of* Euthydemus. Columbia: University of South Carolina Press, 1990.

St. Antoine, Thomas. "Making Heaven Out of Hell: New Urbanism and the Refutation of Suburban Spaces." *Southern Communication Journal* 27.2 (2007): 127–44.

Stanush, Michele. "East Austin: In the Shadow of Success." *Austin American-Statesman,* July 8, 1990: A1.

Stevenson, Rosalinda. "Heartaches." Gale and Carton 268–69.

Stewart, Kathleen. *Ordinary Affects.* Durham, NC: Duke University Press, 2007.

———. *A Space on the Side of the Road: Cultural Poetics in an "Other" America.* Princeton, NJ: Princeton University Press, 1996.

Sullivan, Dale. "The Ethos of Epideictic Encounter." *Philosophy and Rhetoric* 26 (1993): 113–33.

Swanner, Michael. "Austin Has Lost Something." *Austin Chronicle,* Jan. 21, 2005. www.austinchronicle.com/gyrobase/Issue/column?oid=oid:255073.

Syverson, Margaret. *Wealth of Reality: An Ecology of Composition.* Carbondale: Southern Illinois University Press, 1999.

Talk of the Nation. "Gentrification: Blessing or Blight?" NPR. Apr. 26, 2005.

Testa, Monica. Letter. *Washington Post,* Mar. 19, 2005: A23.

"Texas Showdown and the De-Austification of Austin, The." *Cultural Senescence,* Apr. 28, 2008. Blog. culturalsenescence.blogspot.com/2008/04/texas-showdown-and-de-austinification.html.

"This Old House . . . Was Her Home." *Ladies Home Journal,* Feb. 2009. www.lhj.com/volunteering/do-good-100/this-old-house-was-her-home.

Thomas, Mike. "Greed Is the Poison." *Austin Chronicle,* May 19, 2000. www.austinchronicle.com/gyrobase/Issue/column?oid=oid:77214.

Thorpe, Helen. "Austin, We Have a Problem." *New York Times,* Aug. 20, 2000. www.nytimes.com/2000/08/20/magazine/austin-we-have-a-problem.html?scp=18&sq.

"3: An East Austin Narrative." Dir. Jon Airhart, Mary Browning, and Drew Moses. *East Austin Stories.* 2009. Film.

Trainor, Jennifer Seibel. "'My Ancestors Didn't Own Slaves': Understanding White Talk about Race." *Research in the Teaching of English* 40.2 (2005): 140–67.

Trebay, Guy. "Hard Times Square." *Village Voice,* May 27, 1997: 34.

Tuan, Yi-Fu. *Topophilia.* New York: Columbia University Press, 1974.

Tynes, James. "I See Naked People." Gale and Carton 363–64.

U.S. Census Bureau. "ACS Demographic and Housing Estimates: 2006–2008. fastfacts.census.gov/servlet/ADPTable?_bm=y&-qr_name=ACS_2008_3YR_G00_DP3YR5&-geo_id=16000US4857176&-ds_name=ACS_2008_3YR_G00_&-_lang=en.

U.S. Dept. of Agriculture, Natural Resources Conservation Service. *National Resources Inventory, 2001 Annual NRI Introduction.* Washington, DC: Government Printing Office, 2003.

Untersteiner, Mario. *The Sophists.* Oxford: Blackwell, 1954.

"Urban Renewal Special." *Austin American-Statesman,* Aug. 27, 1972: 3.

"'Urban Sprawling' So Severe, Settlement's Cooking-Fires Can Be Seen from as Far as Greenwich Village." *The Onion,* Oct. 5, 2008. www.theonion.com/articles/historical-archives-urban-sprawling-so-severe-sett,2565.

Uteley, Steven. Letter. *Austin American-Statesman,* July 7, 1990: A14.

Vasquez, Antelmo. "El diario de un inmigrante." Gale and Carton 204–10.

Vidal, John. "Nigeria's Agony Dwarfs the Gulf Oil." *Observer,* May 30, 2010: 20.

Viva Les Amis. Dir. Nancy Higgens. Strike Productions, 2005. Video.

Vivian, Bradford. "Jefferson's Other." *Quarterly Journal of Speech* 88 (2002): 284–302.

———. "Neoliberal Epideictic: Rhetorical Form and Commemorative Politics on September 11, 2002." *Quarterly Journal of Speech* 92.1 (2006): 1–26.

Waddell, Craig. *Landmark Essays on Rhetoric and the Environment.* New York: Routledge, 1998.

Walker, Jerry Jeff. Pipkin 30.

Wallace, David Foster. "Ticket to the Fair." *Harper's* (July 1994): 35–54.

Wal-Mart: The High Cost of Low Price. Dir. Robert Greenwald. Brave New Films, 2005.

"Wal-Mart Controversy." WPTZ, Plattsburgh, NY. Oct. 5, 2009.

"Wal-Mart and Vermont." *Vermont Livable Wage Campaign,* Nov. 2005. www.vtlivablewage.org/walmart.htm.

Walters, Chris, and Jim Shahin. "Politics." *Austin Chronicle,* Sept. 7, 2001. www.austinchronicle.com/issues/dispatch/2001-09-07/xtra_feature4.html.

Warner, Michael. "The Mass Public and the Mass Subject." Calhoun 377–401.

———. *Publics and Counterpublics.* Cambridge, MA: Zone Books, 2005.

———. "Publics and Counterpublics." *Public Culture* 14.1 (2002): 49–90.

Wassenich, Red. *Keep Austin Weird: A Guide to the Odd Side of Town.* Atglen, PA: Schiffer, 2007.

Watson, Kirk. "Vote for Smart Growth." *Austin American-Statesman,* Apr. 30, 1998: A15.

WCAX, Burlington, VT. "True North Radio," Paul Beaudry. May 2, 2008.

Weisser, Christian R. *Moving beyond Academic Discourse: Composition Studies and the Public Sphere.* Carbondale: Southern Illinois University Press, 2002.

———, and Sidney I. Dobrin. *Ecocomposition: Theoretical and Pedagogical Approaches.* Albany: State University of New York Press, 2001.

Welch, Diana. "Protesters' Message: 'Stop Gentrifying East Austin.'" *Austin Chronicle,* Apr. 8, 2005. www.austinchronicle.com/news/2005-04-08/265699.

Welch, Nancy. "Living Room: Teaching Public Writing in a Post-Publicity Era." *College Composition and Communication* 56.3 (2005): 470–92.

Wells, Susan. "Rogue Cops and Health Care: What Do We Want from Public Writing?" *College Composition and Communication* 47.3 (1996): 325–41.

Wenger, Etienne. *Communities of Practice: Learning, Meaning, and Identity.* Cambridge: Cambridge University Press, 1998.

"What Local Businesses Do You Consider Icons?" *Austin American-Statesman,* Oct. 17, 2006. www.statesman.com/blogs/content/shared-gen/blogs/austin/talk/2006/10/17/what_local_businesses_do_you_c.html.

White, Eric Charles. *Kaironomia: On the Will-to-Invent.* Ithaca, NY: Cornell University Press, 1987.

Wilder, Michael. "Austin Is a Fading Beauty." Letter. *Austin Chronicle,* Aug. 23, 2002. www.austinchronicle.com/gyrobase/Issue/column?oid=oid:100649.

Will, George. "Despotism in New London." *Washington Post,* Sept. 19, 2004: B7.

Wilson, Nicole. "Talk Back." *Money* 35.2 (Feb. 2006): 22.

Wire, The. "Amsterdam." Prod. David Simon. Dir. Ernest Dickerson. HBO, 2004.

Woodward, Kathleen. "Calculating Compassion." Berlant, *Compassion* 59–86.

Worsham, Lynn. "Moving beyond a Sentimental Education." *A Way to Move: Rhetorics of Emotion and Composition Studies.* Ed. Dale Jacobs and Laura R. Micciche. Portsmouth: Boynton/Cook Heinemann, 2003. 161–63.

Worth, Reid. "CSC, Intel, & Smart Growth." *Austin Chronicle,* Aug. 23, 2002. www.austinchronicle.com/gyrobase/Issue/index?issue=2002-08-23.

Wright, Elizabethada A. "Rhetorical Spaces in Memorial Places: The Cemetery as a Rhetorical Memory Place/Space." *Rhetoric Society Quarterly* 35.4 (2005): 51–93.

"Yuppies Off the Eastside?" *Couple of Ideas,* Dec. 11, 2008. Blog. rattl.blogspot.com/2008/12/yuppies-off-eastside.html.

Zarefsky, David "Institutional and Social Goals for Rhetoric." *Rhetoric Society Quarterly* 34.3 (2003): 27–38.

Zencey, Eric. "The Rootless Professors." *Rooted in the Land: Essays on Community and Place.* Ed. William Vitek and Wes Jackson. New Haven: Yale University Press, 1996. 15–19.

Žižek, Slavoj. *The Sublime Object of Ideology.* Cambridge, MA: Verso, 1989.

Zukin, Sharon. "Politics and Aesthetics of Public Space: The 'American' Model." *Public Space,* 1988. www.publicspace.org/en/text-library/eng/a013-politics-and-aesthetics-of-public-space-the-american-model.

INDEX

Achilles, 64–65
actor-network theory, 168–73
affect. *See* feelings
Agamben, Giorgio, 66–67, 86, 161
agency, 15, 42, 62–64, 103–4, 120–22, 127, 144, 149–50, 163, 186
Ahmed, Sara, 55, 59–60, 81–82, 85
ambiguity, 160–61
apathy, 56–58, 61, 64–66, 95–96, 166
Aristotle, 32–33, 102
Armadillo World Headquarters, 99–102, 105, 107, 125–26
Asen, Robert, 17, 19, 45
Austin Revitalization Authority, 136–38, 151

Barton Springs, 34, 70–80, 84, 108–9
Benjamin, Walter, 173–74
Berlant, Lauren, 55, 62, 68, 81–82, 167
Burke, Kenneth, 14, 48–49, 83–84, 121, 160

Chicago School of urban studies, 28–29, 32
Circle C Ranch, 70–81
citizenship, 6, 17, 18, 37–38, 46–48, 55, 61–63, 67, 68, 82–84, 156–58, 194
clichés, 155–56
commonplaces, 20–21, 27, 47–48, 52, 72, 86, 96, 155–57, 177, 190–91
crisis, 6–7, 14–18, 28, 32, 37–38, 40, 61–62, 64, 66, 84–86, 95–96, 103, 125–26, 151, 154–55, 160, 167–68, 173–74, 177–79, 182, 194–96

debate. *See* deliberation
Deepwater Horizon, 42–43, 163–64
Delaney, Samuel, 126–27
deliberation, 6–7, 18, 32, 39, 43, 56, 48, 64–65, 95, 103–4, 114–15, 126, 157, 161, 168
democracy, 64–65, 76, 157
distance, as rhetorical stance, 44, 55, 61–63, 67, 86, 96, 103, 126, 167
Dobrin, Sidney, 10–12

East Austin, 129–43, 149–52, 161
Eberly, Rosa, 20, 47, 94
ecocomposition, 12–13, 196
emotions. *See* feelings
equivalence claims, 131–32, 144–59, 161–62, 167
Erwin, Frank, 2–4, 8, 9, 11, 13–15

feelings, 5–6, 44, 48–49, 51–62, 72, 95–98, 158, 162, 174; and students, 166–68, 188; subject of, 55–56, 61–63, 126, 162, 167, 177
Fleming, David, 25, 29, 39
Foucault, Michel, 45

gentrification, 4, 7, 27, 108, 112, 121, 130–31, 134–35, 138–55, 160–62
Gorgias, 158–60
Greene, Ronald Walter, 47, 72, 156–57

Habermas, Jürgen, 18, 47–48
Hauser, Gerard, 10, 19, 72

| 229

housing, 25, 28–29, 39, 107, 131–35, 141, 144–46, 183–86

idios, 47–48, 54, 67–69
injury claims, 81–86, 96, 161
inquiry, 164–96; as classroom practice, 178–96, 198–200
interests, common, 18, 47–48, 56, 68
Intel, 33–38, 119
investment, libidinal, 5, 65, 97, 161; and students 165–68, 175, 191
Isocrates, 47, 159–60, 182

"Keep Austin Weird," 22, 110–13
Kelo, Susette, 49–60
koine, 47–48, 54–55, 67–69, 96
koinos kosmos. See *koine*
krisis, 21, 32–33, 38, 132, 150, 164, 195, 198–99

Latour, Bruno, 169–72
Les Amis, 100–101, 108–9, 116–18, 126
Liberty Lunch, 100–101, 109, 113, 114
lofts, 123, 131, 138–42, 145, 150–52

memory. See public memory
Miller, Carolyn, 94

Neighborhood Story Project, 183–86
Nelson, Willie, 99, 105, 117
network theory. See actor-network theory
New London (Connecticut), 49–60

Owens, Derek, 41

pedagogy, 41, 165–68, 174–79
performative ontology, 168–69, 172–73, 186, 195, 199
Pericles, 46
phronesis, 32–33, 168
place, 7–18, 30–32, 40, 42, 46, 57, 103–4, 124, 168, 187–95
PrairyErth (Heat-Moon), 189–92
private and public, 18, 48, 54, 67–69, 83, 103, 166; spaces, 38–39, 113–18, 127
protests, 2, 4, 17, 43, 74, 87, 141–43, 146–47
public memory, 101–4, 113, 116, 122–28
public sphere, 16–19, 44, 48, 65–66, 68–69
public subjectivity, 6, 13–18, 20–21, 40–43, 44–49, 54–59, 61–62, 65–69, 72, 86, 98, 164–65, 168, 174, 177–79, 187; as exceptional, 5, 69, 72, 81, 86, 96, 103, 116, 126, 131, 156–62, 165, 194; as excluded, 66–67, 113, 116, 122, 128, 144

relationality, as rhetortical stance, 14, 18, 45–49, 55, 57, 59, 61–62, 66–69, 85–86, 96–97, 104, 126, 156, 161, 164, 167–68, 174, 178, 182, 188
rhetoric of place, 7–18
Roberts-Miller, Patricia, 121–22

Schudson, Michael, 37–38
Slacker (film), 122–23
Smart Growth (Austin), 34–35, 117
state of exception, 66–67, 81, 86, 101–4, 144, 151, 154, 161–62, 196
Stewart, Kathleen, 101–2
students, 39–41, 63, 96–97, 153–56, 165–68, 174–79, 183–99
subjectivity. See public subjectivity
sustainability, 5, 6, 14–15, 40–43, 62, 69, 85, 164, 169, 187, 194–96

talk, as public rhetoric, 15–21, 72, 84, 103, 164–67, 182, 200; limits of, 65
Times Square, 126–28
topos (topoi), 20, 78–79, 81, 84–85, 92, 94, 149, 180
Trainor, Jennifer Seibel, 63–64
trees, 2–15
Treaty Oak (Austin), 8–11, 13–15, 17, 19

University of Texas, 1–4, 135
urban renewal, 133–36, 142, 152–53, 181

vernacular rhetoric, 10, 16, 19–21, 72, 84–86, 96, 98, 127, 137, 151

Waller Creek (Austin), 1–4, 10–11, 13–14, 17, 19
Walmart, 87–94, 96, 97
Warner, Michael, 19, 44–45
Way to Rainy Mountain (Momaday), 191–92
wounds, 81–84
Writing Austin's Lives, 179–83

yuppies, 145–47

DISTANT PUBLICS

PITTSBURGH SERIES IN
COMPOSITION, LITERACY,
AND CULTURE
David Bartholomae and
Jean Ferguson Carr, Editors

Distant Publics

DEVELOPMENT
RHETORIC
AND
THE SUBJECT
OF CRISIS

Jenny Rice

University of Pittsburgh Press

Published by the University of Pittsburgh Press, Pittsburgh, Pa., 15260
Copyright © 2012, University of Pittsburgh Press
All rights reserved
Manufactured in the United States of America
Printed on acid-free paper
10 9 8 7 6 5 4 3 2 1

Library of Congress Cataloging-in-Publication Data
Rice, Jenny.
　Distant publics : development rhetoric and the subject of crisis / Jenny Rice.
　　p. cm. — (Pittsburgh series in composition, literacy, and culture)
　Includes bibliographical references and index.
　ISBN 978-0-8229-6204-5 (pbk. : alk. paper)
　　1. Rhetoric—Political aspects—United States. 2. Rhetoric—Social aspects—United States. 3. Persuasion (Rhetoric)—Political aspects—United States. 4. Persuasion (Rhetoric)—Social aspects—United States. 5. Discourse analysis—Political aspects—United States. 6. Discourse analysis—Social aspects—United States. 7. Community development—United States.　I. Title.
　P301.5.P67R53 2012
　　307.1'4014—dc23　　　　　　　　　　　　　　　　　　　　2012006939